AF540199

What Ails Indian Muslims

What Ails Indian Muslims

Edited by

Murzban Jal
Zaheer Ali

WHAT AILS INDIAN MUSLIMS
Edited by Murzban Jal and Zaheer Ali

First Published 2016

ISBN 978-93-5002-399-0

Published by
AAKAR BOOKS
28 E Pocket IV, Mayur Vihar Phase I, Delhi 110 091
Phone: 011 2279 5505 Telefax: 011 2279 5641
aakarbooks@gmail.com; www.aakarbooks.com

Typeset at
Arpit Printographers, Delhi 110 092

Printed at
Sapra Brothers, Delhi 110 092

Contents

Preface: Uncle and Nephews

Murzban Jal

We were fire O Hind, you've turned us into ashes.

Altaf Hussain Hali.

Now before our eyes lie dried tracks of blood, cut up human parts, charred faces, mangled necks, terrified people, looted houses, burned fields, mountains of rubble, and overflowing hospitals. We are free, Hindustan is free. Pakistan is free, and we are walking the desolate streets naked without any possessions in utter distress.

Sadat Hasan Manto.

Altaf Hussain Hali's verse on how fire was turned into ashes and Sadat Hasan Manto's idea of freedom in bloodied and charred distress is typical of the condition of not only the Muslims in South Asia with the retreat of the great Indo-Islamic culture, but also is typical of the tragic condition of the defeated revolutionary movement post-1857 when the British colonialists in tandem with the comprador upper caste elites constructed the imaginary Hindu-Muslim abyss. This colonial imaginary divide not only created what we call after Benedict Anderson "imaginary communities". It created the partition, a blow that would affect all subaltern people of the region. Muslims in India would be the most affected. They would not only be the ashes of Hali. They would be the nowhere people. They would become a people with and without a nation. In this sense, Muslims in India became a sign board of some sort of waste manufactured by British colonialism.

And with the departure of the Brits from South Asia, it

would be American imperialism that would enter South Asia creating this uncanny relation of Uncle Sam (USA) and nephew. First it was the Pakistani ruling elite who chose to be this ever willing nephew. With the collapse of the Soviet Union in 1991, the Indian elites who were also waiting ever so eagerly for this chosen role ran alongside the Pakistani elites. Uncle and nephew became Uncle and nephews.

Ayesha Jalal in her *The Pity of Partition* says that during partition "even the coolest of Indian minds had no time to think".[1] The first tragedy is that even after partition, the coolest of minds have ceased thinking, creating what we may call after Jürgen Habermas and Slavoj Žižek a *Denkverbot*, or simply a "prohibition against thinking". The second tragedy is that if partition happened in 1947, its ghost lives on. We are all possessed by this ghost of partition. We have thus become partitioned selves.

But partition and the makings of the fractured nations of India and Pakistan did not, as if, happen automatically. Jalal claims that Mohammed Ali Jinnah once said that the Indian nationalists "fathered this word on us".[2] The word is of course Pakistan. The father of Pakistan is in this rendering, the Indian national movement. The Indian nationalists would then father two illegitimate children—India and Pakistan. Now the Indian nationalists through the strange law of evolution as described by Darwin and the even stranger law of metamorphosis as outlined by Franz Kafka want to father the "Hindu Rashtra". In these very strange circumstances, we have to write a new novel *Uncle and Nephews* as a new rendition to Ivan Turgenev's *Fathers and Sons*. Uncle Sam is indeed watching over us.

In a certain way, one could say that the leitmotiv of this volume *What Ails Indian Muslims* could be found in the short stories of Sadat Hasan Manto (1912-1955), probably the greatest Urdu writer of the 20th century. And yet *What Ails Indian Muslims* while taking the Mantoesque formula of hard core proletarian realism is also based on a rigorous sociological analysis under the auspices of historical materialism.

While pointing the philosophical finger of suspicion onto colonialism and imperialism for the pathetic condition of

Muslims in India (as also entire South and West Asia), certain methodological remarks are necessary. The first methodological remark claims that we need to free ourselves from the Eurocentric imagery of abstract-universalist history for the largely forgotten problematic of the Asiatic mode of production, a problematic that Marx had opened in the early 1850s which remained at the margins of his *Grundrisse* and *Capital* and which would then move from the margins to the centre in his largely ignored *Ethnological Notebooks*. What we are saying is that we need to analyze the condition of Muslims in India in this genre of the Asiatic mode of production. The second methodological remark claims that caste is the essential socio-economic base of this mode. To paraphrase Marx, caste is the "solid foundation of Oriental despotism"[3]. But then there is a further epistemic development of the sociology of caste and the place of Muslims in this caste matrix from the Freudo-Marxist point of view that locates caste as:

1. Enclosed, deformed and clannish class system where social relations are based on domination and servitude grafted on the totem of pure upper castes and totem of polluted lower castes, thereby repressing the principles of liberty, equality and fraternity,
2. A form of Asian racism that propagates hatred and xenophobia (here hatred for Muslims), and,
3. As a new form of mental illness that we call "neurosis-psychosis" where all forms of critical thinking and the development of democratic idcology is totally destroyed.

What this volume asserts is that the analysis of the condition of Muslims in India has to be seen in this new repertoire. And since the Asiatic mode of production is now put on the epistemological map of critical historiography, the questions of "Indian feudalism" (to borrow the term from R.S. Sharma) combined with the question of the transition of feudalism to capitalism and the miraculous arrival of capitalism (and along with this arrival an equally miraculous arrival of the West European style of modernity and secularism) is irrelevant for the study of India. And this is because we follow Marx's critical reasoning of multilinear history, where all forms of Eurocentric reasoning that claims that modernity and secularism are only predicated on capitalism (rather the West European and North American liberal bourgeois trope) is radically critiqued.

What we have done is followed Samir Amin's theory of three waves of universal humanism and Kevin Anderson' philosophy of Marxist Humanism. Here what we have done is gone not merely beyond the unilinear theory of history where history is seen governed by abstract iron laws of history—a theory shared by Stalin and Francis Fukuyama—but also gone beyond the nativist and solipsist view of history. The history of Muslims and Islam is seen in this light.

And since bourgeois common sense is plagued by the manufactured differences between Judaism and Christianity (now aligned by Hinduism) on the one hand, and Islam on the other, just as Western Europe and the USA are seen battling with Islam, we need to put this humanist theory into limelight. We stress the three waves of universal humanism in terms of actual exchange of people and ideas beginning in the 5th century B.C.E. where the conflux of ideas is developed with the meeting of the Egyptians, Mesopotamians, Persians, Greeks, Indians and the Chinese which then mutated into Judaic, Christian and Islamic messianic theology. This first wave through Islam went to Florence which crystallized into the European Renaissance and Enlightenment that then was realized as the French Revolution, finally culminating into Marxism and the international communist movement. Our trajectory of historical reasoning follows the above stated methodology.

It is in this epistemic space that we place the very important issue of secularism in Asia, a secularism, as Asghar Ali Engineer so often pointed out, has its roots in the Indo-Persian narrative that reached its true flowering in the reign of Akbar. Secularism, in this sense, does not have to mime the West European bourgeois narrative of mere separation of politics and religion. Instead, we talk of the historicism and humanism (to borrow Antonio Gramsci's term) of both politics and religion. We do not mutter angry phrases against politics and religion. Instead, we try to see whether the humanistic and socialistic possibilities of politics and religion are possible.

But would imperialism and Uncle Sam allow this? Uncle Sam, we must note, is a WASP (White Anglo-Saxon Protestant), while the nephew is the savage-like native from Asia totally dependent on the so-called civilizing mission of Uncle Sam.

It is thus that we are saying that due to both colonialism and post-colonial imperialism that the question of Islam as the savage mind is placed central to the contemporary imagery of our present life-world. But this gesture of keeping Islam central to contemporary imagination is a disfigured and caricatured figure of Islam, Islam that is supposed to be inherently intolerant, violent and despotic. And it is this disfigured image of Islam that the global neo-cons have been parading as "authentic Islam". Like "the traditions of all the dead generations that weigh like a nightmare on the brains of the living", to borrow an excellent phrase of Marx,[4] Islam (courtesy the imperialist imagination) is made to weigh on our minds. Islam is something terrible and terrifying that has happened to our peaceful world.

This volume which comprises fourteen chapters is to settle accounts with this imperialist imagination that "conjures up the spirits of the past."[5] It is this imperialist "conjuring up of the dead of world history", this "awakening of the dead" and to attempt to make the ghost of the anti-Christ walk on earth, that this volume seeks to displace from the hegemonic position that imperialism has placed Islam.

It was Louis Althusser who had once said that philosophy is essentially political and that there can be no innocent philosophy. The stand that we have taken in this book is also essentially political, but political in an anti-imperialist sense. In this sense we are extending Ludwig Feuerbach's motto: the truth of theology is anthropology into the new dictum: the truth of theology is geo-politics. Besides being concerned with the burning issues of Muslims in India, we have also to deal with the issues of geo-politics.

It is thus to the question of geo-politics of imperialism and their voices sent by imperialism's Media Industry that we need also to excite our poetic imagination. Let us see what our poetic and political imagination is witness to. Once the elites of Western

Europe cried: "The king is dead! Long live the king!"; now they scream: "Communism is dead, let us now murder Islam!" It is in this tragic setting of high murder that we can recall the dialogue between Hamlet and the ghost of his murdered father. One should note in the quote below from Shakespeare's *Hamlet* that the ghost is that of communism and Hamlet is the modern Muslim:

Ghost (of communism): Revenge his foul and most unnatural murder.
Hamlet (as the contemporary Muslim): Murder!
Ghost (of communism). Murder most foul, as in the best it is,
But this most foul, strange, and unnatural.
Hamlet (as the contemporary Muslim): Haste me to know't,
that I, with wings as swift
As meditation or the thoughts of love,
May sweep to my revenge.
Ghost (of communism). I find thee apt;
And duller shouldst thou be than the fat weed
That roots itself in ease on Lethe wharf,
Wouldst thou not stir in this. Now, Hamlet, hear.
It's given out that, sleeping in mine orchard,
A serpent stung me; so the whole ear of Denmark
Is by a forged process of my death
Rankly abus'd; but know, thou noble youth,
The serpent that did sting thy father's life
Now wears his crown.[6]

It should now seem very simple: the serpent (imperialism) that stung Hamlet's father (communism), parades himself as the sole ruler of the earth. The struggle is thus for power, for imperial power. Besides this little dramaturgy, we are following Gramsci's methodology of historicism and humanism. Thus this volume that attempts to insert the methodology of historicism and humanism into the understanding of the condition of Muslims in India has the theme of imperialism and its local satraps, the Indian fascists—the Rashtriya Swayamsevak Sangh (RSS)—also etched at the background.

In contrast to a certain line of thinking that wants the dead to bury the dead, we evoke the spirits of the past. But this form of evoking the ghosts of the past is not to be confused with nostalgia, or a form of recalling a certain socialist utopia that somehow died. Instead, we evoke the ghost of the past to fight the ghosts evoked by imperialism. Thus in contrast to the ghosts of imperialism (we shall call this the "White Ghost") we recall the "Red Specter" and unleash it on imperial Europe and the even more imperial USA. But, one may ask: "What is this strange "White Specter" and the even more strange "Red Specter" and what do these two specters have to do with Islam and the Indian Muslims?" We then reply that the Red Specter is a humanist and an anthropologist, while the White Specter is an anti-humanist. This volume is about the Red Specter and the anthropological understanding of theology. We call this the anthropological reading of theology, from Feuerbach's dictum: *the secret of theology is anthropology*. The theologians seek to understand the nature of God; they seek spiritual answers to questions that can never be answered. For the theologians leave out the anthropological and political economical questions pertaining to religion. Thus: "What is the nature of God?", "Is God a capitalist or a socialist?", "Does the unequal distribution of wealth bother God?", "Is God a capitalist who loves exploiting the poor?", "Or is he a liberal democrat who asks humanity to be charitable and look after the poor?", "Or is God in fact a radical democrat, even a sort of a communist who made classless society, only to see that tyrannical class society evolved from this original classless society?"

Further questions emerge: "What is the place of money and capital accumulation in religion in general and the monotheistic religions in particular?" And most importantly: "What is the relation between interest-bearing capital (forbidden in Islam) and capital in general (forbidden by Marx, in fact taking the form of radical evil in Marxist philosophy)?" "Is Islam then not merely humanistic and revolutionary, but outrightly socialist itself?" And finally; "How would the socialist reading of religions be intelligible today to the public at large?"

To understand these important questions, let us look at a now rather forgotten religion called "Mazdakism" that emerged in imperial Iran at the end of the 5th century (C.E.). Known as a "communist religion" in the age of classical antiquity, this is how the rendering of the good religion went:

> Mazdak declared that God placed the means of subsistence (*arzaq*) on earth so that people divide them among themselves equally, in a manner that no one of them should have more than his share; but people wronged one another; the strong defeated the weak and took exclusive possession of livelihood and property. It is absolutely necessary that one takes from the rich for giving to the poor, so that all become equal in wealth. Whoever possesses an excess of property, women or goods, he has more right than the other.[7]

Another rendering of Mazdakism goes thus:

> Bread is the anti-dote for hungry men—
> An anti-dote not wanted by the full....
> Should not the corn in store be put to use?
> To hunger have a million succumbed,
> Whose deaths are due to idle granaries....
> The man of empty hand
> Is equal to the man possessed of wealth....
> To right the world all men must have sufficient;
> The rich man's plenty is abominable;
> The women, goods and houses are for all....[8]

It is in this context that we understand Kancha Ilaih's recent question: "Is God a democrat?", a question that forced the Vishva Hindu Parishad (VHP)—one of the wings of the fascist RSS—to file a case against Ilaih. To talk of religion is thus now dangerous.

To talk of Islam in the age of Islamophobia and fascism is even more dangerous. After all (as the imperialist culture industry claims), is not Islam violent, bent on creating jihad all over the world? Is jihad nothing (as the same votary of Islamophobia claims) but "Holy War" waged by the first converters to Islam to Sayiid Ahmad and Shah Ismail and the Islamic State (IS)? Or is it also like the "Holy War" that the Left Bolsheviks led by Nicolai Bukharin argued for in 1917? Should we thus not exorcise the specters of Islam and Marxism once and for all? So how does one rescue Islam from the imperialist? One does so by following the historicist and humanist method.

Yet this historicist and humanist historiography does not follow the path of what Dipesh Chakrabarty after Walter

Benjamin calls a "small history", small in terms of brevity, having also a "very particular end in focus".[9] Instead, we look at the larger side of history, where one argues after the philosophers G.W.F. Hegel and Georg Lukács for "dialectical totalities", thus freeing history from ethnocentrism and nativism. It is with this dialectical historicist and humanist light that we articulate the contours of this volume.

To conclude, we state that the best way to look at the realism of South Asian history with all its tragic overtures is to encounter the very first paragraph of Manto's 'Toba Tek Singh':

> A couple of years after the Partition of the country, it occurred to the respective governments of India and Pakistan that inmates of lunatic asylums, like prisoners, should also be exchanged. Muslim lunatics in India should be transferred to Pakistan and Hindu and Sikh lunatics in Pakistani asylums should be sent to India.[10]

Some of us find that we are transferred from Pakistan. And those who are not transferred from Pakistan are transferred from India. We are all transferred people housed in lunatic asylums. That is because we are all lunatics, fathers and sons, Uncle and nephews.

REFERENCES

1. Ayesha Jalal, *The Pity of Partition. Manot's Life, Times and Work Across the India-Pakistan Divide* (Noida: HarperCollins, 2013), p. 1.
2. Ibid., p. 7.
3. Karl Marx, 'The British Rule in India', in *Marx. Engels. On Colonialism* (Moscow: Progress Publishers, 1977), p. 40.
4. Karl Marx, 'Eighteenth Brumaire of Louis Bonaparte', *in Marx. Engels. Selected Works* (Moscow: Progress Publishers, 1975), p. 96
5. Ibid.
6. William Shakespeare, 'Hamlet', in *The Complete Works of William Shakespeare*, ed. V.J. Craig (London: Henry Pordes, 1983), Act. I, Sc. V, p. 949.
7. Quoted in Ehsan Yarshater, 'Mazdakism', in *The Cambridge History of Iran, Vol. 3, (2). The Selucids, Parthians and the Sasanian Periods* (Cambridge: Cambridge University Press, 1986), p. 998.
8. See Firdausi, *Sháhnáma*, Vol. VII, trans. Arthur George Warner and Edmund Warner (London: Kegan Paul, 1915), p. 204.
9. Dipesh Chakrabarty, *Habitations of Modernity: Essays in the Wake*

of Subaltern Studies (Chicago: The University of Chicago Press, 2002), pp. 3-4.

10. Sadat Hasan Manto, 'Toba Tek Singh', in *Kingdom's End and Other Stories* (London: Verso, 1987), p. 11.

Introduction

Zaheer Ali

Indian Muslims have been facing myriad problems and afflictions for long. It is usually assumed that their plight set in motion with the coming of the British and reached its nadir with the victory of the British forces in the ill-fated uprising of 1857. It is not that the majority of Muslims had a well-heeled and hassle-free existence before the colonial masters overthrew the Mughal rule. It was a small segment of the ruling class, nawabs and zamindars that had the power and privileges and in order to protect its interests, it ruthlessly oppressed and exploited the vast majority of underprivileged Muslims as much as it did the poor Hindus. Nevertheless, thanks to the propaganda of the theologians and sections of the Muslim elite, the ordinary Muslims had a psychosomatic and emotional satisfaction that they were the subjects of a Muslim rule that ensured the safety of their religion. So, a vast majority of them could bear appalling living conditions and brutal oppression for they had the mental contentment that Islam was secure. The loss of political power was devastating to the Muslim elite and to regain it they mobilized the Muslim masses to take up arms against the rule of the 'infidels'. The misadventures of Wahabi movement were the upshot of desperation of the Muslim elite who embroiled Muslim masses too to regain its lost glory. Later, many Wahabi activists had joined the rebel forces of 1857.

The colonial masters adopted an openly anti-Muslim policy after 1857 because in their estimation Muslims were the real culprits. Though the uprising of 1857 was confined to north and Central India, the Muslims in the entire subcontinent had to bear the brunt of the British policy. In those trying times Syed

Ahmed Khan launched a movement to help Muslims acquire modern and scientific education. His Aligarh Movement was opposed tooth and nail by the orthodox sections of the Muslims, but it ultimately achieved two things; firstly, it made a beginning to mobilize the Muslim *ashrafiya* (elite) to seek western education and two, it blunted the edge of government's anti-Muslim policies. The rising tide of Indian freedom struggle after the inception of the Indian National Congress alarmed the colonial masters and then they put into practice the deadliest weapon of their arsenal viz. the strategy of *divide and rule.* In the opening decade of the 20th century two events, purposely brought about by the British, goaded the Muslim elite to define the identity of their co-religionists in separate nationalistic terms. The partition of Bengal in 1905 and the establishment of the Muslim League the following year, laid down the foundation of Muslim separatism and ushered in the era of communal politics in the subcontinent. The colonial rulers played the communal card very deftly as subsequently they covertly promoted Hindu fascist forces such as the Rashtriya Swayamsevak Sangh (RSS) and the Hindu Mahasabha to enlarge the gulf between two major communities of the subcontinent. It vitiated the political atmosphere so much that even after more than a century, marked with bifurcation and trifurcation of the subcontinent into three independent countries, the fiend of communalism refuses to leave. In retrospect, one cannot help concluding up that the Muslims of the subcontinent, in particular, those of India suffered the most because of communal politics.

The partition of the country put the Muslims who chose to stay behind in India in a precarious condition and the genuinely secular Congress leaders such as Nehru and Azad on the defensive. During sixty-eight years of independent India's history only one phenomenon remained a constant, the plight of the Muslims. What's more, the scourge of Islamic terrorism, whether real or imaginary, has awfully spoiled the image of the Muslims all over the world particularly after the 9/11 attack on the World Trade Centre in USA. In India, the so-called Pakistan sponsored terrorist attacks, the worst being the carnage of 26/11 in Mumbai, have rendered the Muslims extremely vulnerable to the excesses of various security agencies. The situation is so bad that even if a Muslim religious place is the target of terrorist attack, the security agencies promptly round up young Muslims on flimsy grounds and often without any ground whatsoever. There are clear indications that some extreme Hindu organizations have adopted terrorism as a strategy to target Muslims. Some activists associated with such organizations have also been arrested. Nevertheless, the security agencies prefer to go after Muslims in the aftermath of every terrorist act.

Who is to blame for this perilous condition of Muslims? Is it the Congress that ruled for the major part of those sixty-eight years or the orthodox mullahs, invariably supported by the ruling elite, who never allowed the bulk of the Muslims to break free from the snare of religious-cultural identity and focus on real issues? Objectively speaking, it is the combination of both. The robust Hindu communal elements of the Congress never allowed its genuinely secular leaders to adopt and implement all-inclusive, judicious and equitable policies citing the possibility of a Hindu backlash whereas the self-seeking mullahs, actively sponsored by most political leaders, kept the Muslims masses endlessly embroiled in illusive issues such as 'Islam in danger', threat to Muslim Personal Law, *purdah,* Aligarh Muslim University, decline and imminent annihilation of Urdu, etc. Consequently, the combined energy of nearly twenty crore Muslims of India that should have been used to better the social, educational, political and economic conditions of the community was wasted, for last over sixt decades, promoting and defending non-issues.

In recent years, two reports have stirred the imagination of those who aspire to establish an all-inclusive, truly secular India. *The Sachar Committee Report* has officially authenticated the reality that was widely believed i.e. the Muslims, in terms of educational and economic indices constitute the most backward segment of Indian society while the Rangnath Mishra Commission Report recommended a policy of extending reservations to all the Dalits belonging to religious minorities, including Muslims and Christians in jobs and educational institutions to bring them on par with other Indians. Needless to add that the two reports generated a great deal of heat as their proponents and opponents refuse to de-communalize the debate and treat the whole issue merely as a question of uplift of a backward segment of society by means of affirmative action.

In order to bring into focus all the real problems of Muslims, Centre for Promotion of Democracy and Secularism (CPDS), a non-profit organization comprising intellectuals, academics, social activists and journalists had organized a two-day seminar in Aurangabad, a city whose history, cultural ethos and demographic makeup have a pronounced Muslim tinge. The present volume is a collection of some of the selected papers that were presented in the seminar. The two articles of late Dr. Asghar Ali Engineer have been included for their aptness and profundity. The editors express their thankfulness to Irfan Engineer for the permission for their inclusion.

The editors would like to thank quite a few people who helped us by various means in our venture. We express our deepest gratitude to Dr. Gautam Gawali who took keen interest not only in the organization of the seminar but also delivered the valedictory address of the seminar. Dr. Surendra Jondhale and Dr. Ramesh Kamble too merit our gratefulness for their unreserved support. In the same way, Dr. Bhalchandra Kango must be thanked for chairing the valedictory session.

Likewise, the trustees of the CPDS, Dr. Afaq Khan, Abdul Majeed and Sibtain Naqvi, Dr. Shuja Shakir and others deserve our sincere thanks for their stupendous contribution to organize an extremely valuable and memorable seminar. Dr. Mushirul Hasan who is currently recuperating from the serious injuries caused by a horrendous accident, was kind enough to accept our request for delivering the keynote address of the seminar, which is included in the present volume as Foreword. We express our good wishes for his speedy recovery. We must also acknowledge the significant part played by Dr. B. S. Waghmare, Professor and Head, Department of Political Science and Dr. Hameed Khan, Professor and Head, Department of English and Professer-in-Charge of Maulana Azad Chair of Dr. Babasaheb Ambedkar Marathwada University (BAMU), Aurangabad. The seminar would not have met with such a colossal success had they not collaborated with the CPDS for organizing it.

Foreword

Mushirul Hasan

As a professional historian, I don't comment on contemporary matters. But this theme on the contemporary state of Indian Muslims is one, which has been very close to my concerns as a citizen and as a student of contemporary affairs. As a matter of fact we recently did a report called 'Minorities at the Margin'. It has a substantial section that deals with the Muslim community and various problems associated with it. I don't like the title very much because behind its formulation, there are certain assumptions and prior assumptions, which I would like to question.

The term "discourse" on Muslims has undergone significant changes. There was a particular discourse after partition and people were fond of repeating that fact in relation to a large segment of Muslims migrating to Pakistan, that why the Muslims who did not migrate to Pakistan should live in India. That was in essence the right-wing Hindutva discourse, which was fairly significant, even though it may have not found expression earlier in terms of the members of Parliament or the members in the Constituent Assembly. But it was widely held belief, within Hindutva circles, which was of course, contested in the Constituent Assembly debates. What happened at the foundation of the Indian Republic was that these extremist ideologies went to the margins. As a result of this triumph of democratic values, India emerged as a secular country. But now with the victory of the BJP in the 2014 National Elections, and with Narendra Modi coming to power, the re-look at Muslims in particular and the changing discourse on secularism need to be taken very seriously.

But what followed was (especially, during much of Nehruvian period in 1964), a theory of "Indianization of Muslims" which was put forward by Balraj Madhok. This discourse of the "Indianization of Muslims" asked as to why Indian Muslims should not become part of what the right-wing imagined as the "national mainstream". *"Why shouldn't they be Indianized?"* was the question repeatedly asked. We know that this was the argument that was very close to the RSS's then political arm, the Jana Sangh's, point of view. And during much of the period of Indira Gandhi's government, the ideology of "Muslim appeasement" was systematically packaged and re-packaged. One heard of this illusory discourse of "Muslim appeasement" without any facts and without any systematic study, neither conducted by the Government of India, or any Muslim group in various parts of India for that matter. And everybody accepted that Muslims were appeased by the then ruling Congress party for election purposes.

And then came the Gopal Singh Report (1983). Gopal Singh, the Chairman, was asked by Indira Gandhi in 1983 to prepare a report on social, economic and educational conditions of the Muslim community. I have the privilege of reading that report. It is very important for it has highlighted those very aspects of Muslim community problems that the Sachar Commission has underlined. And if you look at the years from 1983 to 2010 when the Sachar Commission Report came out, you will see that there is no difference between the socio-economic and educational profile of Muslims. They are as backward in 2010 as they were in 1983. It is unfortunat that this comparison has been made. But if you look at the nemesis you will find how Muslims in India are extremely backward, economically and socially.

This report, done by us and which Oxford University Press has published, is the Evaluation Report of what has been done since we adopted Sachar Commission Report. Our finding is that there is no change in the condition of Muslims and that the plans and the projects that the Government of India put forth have not been implemented. In fact, you might have read very recently that Professor Kunnu, Chairman of Evaluation Committee has said that there is no money to hold meetings, no money to invite other members of the Committee to examine. This is the seriousness of the previous Government of India about the project —and that was the secular government led by the Congress Party. Clearly, on the basis of these years, starting from 1983, the question is not: "What Ails Indian Muslims", but *what ails the Indian Government*. That is really the problem. *The problem is governmental. It is a political problem.*

Communities, wherever they are and whatever their physical location, do have problems of employment, multiple problems of identity and problems of other kinds. All communities have problems. I as a student of history and as a student of the Muslim community do not see anything that is fundamentally wrong with the Muslim community. Yes, there is resistance to change; yes, Muslims girls and women do not have opportunities to education that they should have, as their counterparts in other communities; yes, drop-out rate of Muslim children in schools and colleges is very high; yes, there are other areas where their backwardness is fairly widespread. But these are the problems, which the community has to sort out in the process of change, prosperity and growth. When any society develops it also means that other sections also develop. So, the total progress, say the total progress of India brought about by, say, a growth rate of 8 per cent or 9 per cent will affect the Muslims. The growing urbanization of India will also affect the Muslims where it affects the OBCs, SCs, Brahmans and other castes of India. As a part of overall progress of society in general, certain changes will take place which will have to benefit even marginalized communities.

What we are saying is that nothing is fundamentally wrong with the Muslim community. It is not that the community is not willing to swim with the tide of development and change. There are a large number of Muslim youth who want to get into business, they want their children to go to good schools, and they want to go to the US to have successful and prosperous life. They certainly want all this. And if progress takes place and the benefits of that progress accrue to different sections of society, there is no reason, I repeat, there is no reason why the benefits of such progress will not affect the Muslim community.

I think, the fundamental problem is that, *the government is not committed to affirmative actions as far as the Muslim community is concerned.* There is nothing the Government of India has done, regardless of which party is in power to support the Muslim community in educational and economic terms. Whatever it has done, is merely symbolic, like throwing a few crumbs here and there, making a few concessions here and there, like providing Hajj subsidies. These are besides being merely symbolic, are in fact very small matters. The fundamental restructuring has not taken place. The development plan that should take the Muslim community as an important partner is almost totally absent. That is why Muslims are as backward as they were in the past.

One hears that they are backward because they want to remain backward! But who wants to remain backward? *Every body wants to progress.* But when the conditions are created in which there is overt and covert discrimination then it does raise the question about how secular is our commitment to the kind of participatory democracy that we have.

Since 1947, a large number of affirmative actions have taken place to uplift certain sections of Indian society. Reservations in some form or other have been provided. There are reservations in jobs, reservation in universities for other deprived social groups. One therefore asks: "Why not reservations with the Muslims that may not be on the basis of religion, but on some other social classification?" One is told that the USA is a secular country and a democracy. One also is told that the UK is a secular country and also a democracy. But it must be noted that both these societies provide affirmative action. You will see that all kinds of plans and projects for minorities and immigrants, whether they are Hindus, Muslims or Sikhs. The issue is that society is sensitive to the whole range of the problems of the immigrants as also to the problems of its minorities. The question that one needs to pose is that are we sensitive to our national minorities, especially to our religious minorities? Do we as a nation want the Muslim community to advance? I think there is a big question mark.

I am saying this, because of not only the apathy of the Congress party and the communal outlook of the RSS and the

BJP. One is saying this because political forces that cannot be on any count be classified as communal have also totally been neglectful of Muslims. Look at the West Bengal experience. There for 32 years the Left Front led by the Communist Party of India (Marxist)—CPI(M) was in power. Muslims are 25 per cent of the population of West Bengal, but their representation, according to Sachar Report is a pathetic 3 to 4 per cent. *What I said earlier applies all political parties in power*. There is a lack of commitment to the uplift of Muslim community. If the secular CPI(M) could not accommodate a large section of its population in its development plan, then what can we say about other parties and their policies?

So how do political parties negotiate with minority demands? "Setting up an Urdu University", one may answer. But how does it matter? It's purely symbolic that is not going to make a difference to the lives of Muslims, especially when Urdu, the language of Ghalib, is destroyed. In this case I am reminded of Ghalib's verse:

کی مرے قتل کے بعد اس نے جفا سے توبہ
ہائے اس زود پشیما ں کا پشیماں ہونا

The English rendering goes thus:

> He avowed penitence for cruelty after my slaying,
> Ah! The repentance of the one who is quick repentant!

The language is being emasculated. What is secure in having an Urdu University? But that is not the point. The point is that the political parties, I repeat, that the political parties are in no position to negotiate with the demands of Muslim community. That is why this minority is taken for a ride. Look at Lalu Prasad Yadav's rule in Bihar. He was a great supporter of Muslims. But look at the state: nothing has been done there for the uplift of the Muslim community. Also look at Mulayam Singh, the so-called great "Mullah-Mulayam" as he is called by the BJP. This so-called "Mullah" has done nothing for Muslims. In fact, during recent riots in Muzzafarnagar, his party followers have been found instigating riots, using the opportunity for election purposes. The tragedy is that in this process, the development programme that the current government is talking of can only be derailed. This is the great dilemma that we are confronted with. My point number two: no political party has sorted it out. As a minister if I offer Rs. 10 million for a project, I would be annoying ten people around me. Consequently if any political party does something for the Muslims, then it would be losing sum total of the vote of the non-Muslim population on the basis of the imagined "Muslim appeasement". That is the level of communal polarization that is taking place: Hindu vote to only Hindu leaders and Muslim votes only to Muslim leaders. This is bad for secular democracy, and certainly not good for any democracy.

But, on the other hand, there is a way out of this situation. The real problem today is to what extent the government is prepared to commit to minority's rights. That is the question. The government should under the Constitution of India, and not invoking any other principle, safeguard the rights of minorities. If the Government of India does that, no questions will be asked. Unfortunately, the government has not done that.

I think another important issue is of identity. In this respect, a lot of thinking needs to be done. We know that the late Asghar Ali Engineer was a great and remarkable fighter for different kinds of campaigns, who sought to change the mindset of the community, who sought to promote inter-faith reconciliation and dialogue. People who are in this social and political genre will now have to address the issue before the Muslim community. And these issues need to be addressed seriously.

For what ails the Muslim community—such issues are not sufficiently discussed and debated. I don't think we should leave it only to the parliament and other legislative assemblies, or civil rights groups to raise these issues. For example, the issue of empowerment of Muslim women has been very close to my heart. And I do believe that whatever may have been the reason for the backwardness of Muslim women, we (as the collective-democratic multitude) have to set things right. We have to provide correctives to our mindset and our attitudes on this subject. There is no getting away from the fact that Muslim women do require support, enormous support, so that they can play equal part in the life not only of family and community, but also in the life of the nation. This region of Maharashtra, for example, as we all know, has produced reformers, great reformers whose central plank was the emancipation of women. This region has made significant advances largely because it has protected the rights of women. Apart from education, they need support in other fields also, and I think that is what needs to be done. And in this respect I think the Ulemas and the theologians have to play important role in the life of the Muslim community. They really have to come forward and interpret Islam in a dynamic way in which the Prophet of Islam presented the religion, not just be *Muqqalid*, not just to revert to conformity or *Taqleed*, but to consider the realities of modern day life. Consider the empowerment of the community in the light of changes that are taking place.

Islam survived and flourishes because of its quality of adaptation, which is why it survived in Malaysia, North Africa, Europe and elsewhere. If Islam were stagnant it would not have spread as widely as it has. There is fundamentally a need to look at our own attitude, our own thinking and see how best we can modify our own attitude and change ourselves in the light of the *Quran* and the *Sunnat*.

I don't say that one has to to opt out from the Islamic faith to be true to secularism and the project of modernity. One has to remain true to one's faith. But one has also to see that one does not allow change, innovations and progress to be blocked by reactionary forces.

I also think that the search of nationalist and transcendental identity, especially "Muslim national identity", is something that I do not approve of. The days of Maulana Abdul Kalam Azad are gone. I am a great admirer of Azad. His thinking and his *Tarjuman-ul-Quran* is a fine example of how a syncretic idea can be extrapolated from the *Quran*. I also think Muslims will be better off retaining their regional loyalties. I am a great lover of Urdu and I feel very sad that the language of Ghalib and Meer is gone. But I do believe that Muslims of Maharashtra should speak Marathi and Muslims in Gujarat should speak Gujarati. They should identify with local cultures. And mind you, I should not be reminding that this has always been what the Muslims have stood by. The talk of bringing Muslims into the national mainstream is nonsense. They have always identified themselves with local cultures, local traditions; they speak local languages, eat the same food, wear same clothes. So, what is this "national mainstream" that the right-wing Hindutva forces are talking of? This "national mainstream" is the imagination of the RSS and BJP leaders. Muslims are very much a part of the national mainstream. It should be deepened and strengthened. This is because the struggle for survival is not exclusive to a Hindu or a Muslim or a Sikh. It is a struggle for all people in India. It is a struggle for Hindu workers as well as Muslim workers. It is struggle for Hindu weavers and the Muslims weavers as well.

And therefore if you are a part of collective national life, which we all are, we must identify ourselves with other people's struggles. If we are living in Maharashtra and there is an environment movement, which is as important to Hindus as to Muslims, then Muslims should whole-heartedly take part in it, because the degradation of environment is going to affect everybody. It will not discriminate between Hindus and Muslims or anybody else. It will kill me, if not me then certainly the next generation. While retaining your identity, it is important to be part of others' struggle in civil society. If you look at the problem from this perspective and identify with others' struggle, you will not be fighting a lonely battle. One should fight collectively.

The battle against Hindutva is not fought by Muslims alone. It is fought by thousands of other people belonging to different religions. Because followers of these religions also feel that if the battle of secularism is lost, it will be their loss too. Fascism does not discriminate between a Hindu and a Muslim. Hitler killed Jews as much as he killed other Germans and also communists. A lot is at stake. Therefore, it is very important to be part of future battles for the rights of tribals, Dalits and women. In such a diverse and a large country, and a complex society, there are no exclusive domains. I can't define that this is my territory; that these are my concerns. If you do that you would be in a trouble. We have to look at larger picture. We have to operate in a much wider domain. If we begin to do that, you will find more people joining our battle, many more coming forward for our cause.

I will take you back. The Khilafat Movement was exclusively a Muslim concern. But look at Gandhi who realized that sentiments of Muslims are hurt and came out to support it. He as a leader of the nation supported Muslims and the Congress came forward to support the cause. This is of great importance and a very good precedent to to be followed. One supports causes that affect particular communities as much as they affect the nation.

I also think that the youth of the nation have greater responsibilities and a very important role to play in this regard. Societies which question their assumptions are the societies which remain strong and forward-looking.

1

Problems of Indian Muslims: Real and Peripheral (An Overview)

Zaheer Ali

At the outset, it must be made clear that the usage of the term "Muslim" in this chapter does not stand for a monolith social category, because in India as well as all across the world, the Muslims like any other religious community, are divided not merely in terms of race, language, ethnicity and class, but also on the basis of caste and theology. The pan-Islamists and the proponents of the idea of a cohesive *ummah* would naturally demur to the observation ignoring the apparent ground realities of societies that Muslims inhabit. Most would also object to bracketing together caste and Muslims, insisting that caste is alien to Islam and it is essentially an Indian phenomenon. As we may see in the course of this chapter that caste has never been an unfamiliar institution to Islam and that it exists even among the Muslims outside South Asia. It is, therefore, obvious that the problems that confront Indian Muslims differ from group to group, class to class and caste to caste.

Two groups ironically poles apart in ideological terms, tend to treat Muslims, albeit for different reasons, as a monolithic social construct. The first one is, of course, the one that has already been referred to viz. comprising the pan-Islamists who derive a vicarious pleasure in projecting the Muslims of the world, the *ummah* as, to borrow a Quranic expression, a wall made of lead to withstand the onslaught of the *kafirs*. Besides Egypt's Ikhwan-ul-Muslimun and its South Asian incarnation, the Jamat-e-Islami, Jamaluddin Afghani, an arch enemy of Sir Syed was its most prominent exponent during the 19th century who had largely influenced the adventurist leaders of the Khilafat movement of the early 20th century. The second group is that of the Hindu Right which accuses Indian Muslims of thinking, acting, interacting and behaving socially and politically as a single bloc and it is this predilection of the community that helps the Congress party win elections and in return the successive Congress governments at the Centre have been pursuing the policy of Muslim appeasement. Both the claims are outrageously false as it will be made clear by the main thrust of this chapter.

The problems that Indian Muslims face get transformed in terms of their severity and consequences from region to region and group to group because of the heterogeneous character of the community. Additionally, these problems also differ in their magnitude; the real ones are those that gravely endanger the very existence of the vulnerable segments of Muslims and also destabilize the socio-economic and political interests of the entire community. The issues, the ones I prefer to call the peripheral problems, may be identified such as the erosion of the Muslim character of the Aligarh Muslim University, the detrimental policies of the Centre and some state governments towards Urdu and the controversy over the national song *"vande matram"*. I call these issues peripheral because they are promoted as the real issues of the Muslims by the most rabid leadership of the mullahs who, most probably as a part of the stratagem of their political bosses to keep the Muslims perpetually entangled in these peripheral issues, retain control over the gullible masses. It seems appropriate to first briefly comment on the peripheral issues to expose their triviality.

The ulema takes little interest in the real-world concerns of ordinary Muslims, focusing instead on religious, symbolic or identity-related issues, such as Urdu, the minority character of the Aligarh Muslim University, Muslim Personal Law and the Babri Masjid controversy. This must be seen, in part, as a means to promote their own interests and claims to authority, fearing that focusing on secular issues, including education, would result in the emergence of a leadership that would challenge their own position.

Aligarh Muslim University

There are a couple of incongruities that cannot be lost sight of when we make efforts to understand Muslim concerns about Aligarh Muslim University (AMU). The first one is that majority of Muslims who are usually drawn to register the protest against the so-called conspiracy on the part of the successive governments at the Centre to gradually erode the Muslim character of the institution, are themselves school dropouts. Their wretched circumstances do not provide them the luxury of completing school education let alone going to college or university. Secondly, the leaders of the agitation in most cases are the mullahs who have passed out from Madarssas and have nothing to do with the kind of education that is disseminated at the AMU. The third irony is that most mullahs in South Asia are trained by the conservative Deoband brand of theology. The founder of the Deoband seminary, Maulana Qasim Nanotavi was an arch enemy of Sir Syed and was violently opposed to the very establishment of Mohammedan Anglo-Oriental (MAO) College that ultimately became the AMU. Now, the question is why such people are extremely enthusiastic to retain the Muslim character of an institution, which had earlier declared by them as un-Islamic!

The Hindu Right too complicates the issue by labelling the AMU as a hub of pro-Pakistan elements and jihadists primarily because in the pre-partition days the university campus was dominated by the proponents of the two-nation theory. Though in the heydays of the Pakistan movement a section of the faculty and also of the students did promote Muslim separatism, the current scenario is altogether different. The tendency to perpetually accuse an educational institution of harbouring 'anti-national' elements primarily on the basis of its past is a malicious propaganda carried out mostly by the fascists of the Hindutva brigade. This does not, however, justify the fervent campaign of the Muslim orthodoxy to exploit the AMU for advancing communal politics. It must be emphatically underscored that the AMU is a Central University with a minority status since 1981 and for that reason 50 per cent reservation is provided to the Muslim students. Then, what exactly are orthodox Muslim leaders harping on?

Moreover, the issue of the AMU hardly concerns the overwhelming majority of the Indian Muslims because most Muslim students pass out from other universities, many of them have far better academic reputation than the AMU. The issue is on political agenda only of the communal Muslim leadership of UP and Bihar.

The Issue of Urdu

Similarly, the issue of Urdu is also exploited mostly by the North Indian communal leaders, an overwhelming majority of whom comprise the Muslim urban middle classes. There is no doubt that in North India, the traditional heartland of Urdu, the anti-Urdu policy was adopted and forcefully implemented immediately after the Independence. Such a policy continued to be in force even after the commencement of the Constitution, which recommends that the state should provide facilities to students to learn through mother tongues particularly at the lower levels of schooling. The anti-Urdu lobby of North India, especially in UP, had vehemently flouted the constitutional provision as a result of which Urdu was almost expelled from most of the educational institutions of North India.

A couple of facts about Urdu should be brought into focus here to have a balanced perspective on the issue. Firstly, Urdu is purely a South Asian language. Secondly, barring the propagandist literature that was created by the litterateurs to promote Muslim separatism in pre-partition days and recent trends to Islamize Urdu, the vast body of Urdu literature is absolutely secular. Thirdly, it is not only misleading, but downright outrageous to call it a language of the Muslims. For that matter, in the strict linguistic sense, associating any language to any particular faith is sheer nonsense. Specific languages originally belong to the specific geographical communities and practically a particular language also belongs to the people who speak, read and write it. A sizable body of Urdu literature was produced by those who were not Muslims. In the post-Independence era, Urdu has been one of the major casualties that severely damaged North Indian composite culture. Most of its non-Muslim patrons abandoned it after Pakistan (where it is the mother tongue of barely 3.5 per cent of the population) made it its national language. Consequently, in India Urdu is gasping for its survival.

Nevertheless, it must be emphasized in unambiguous terms that Urdu has never been the language of the majority of Indian Muslims. Prior to the partition when Urdu was widely in use, it was not the language of the Muslims who constituted the majority in their respective provinces viz. Bengal, Punjab, Sind and N.W.F.P. It was mostly confined to Delhi, UP, Bihar and parts of the ex-Hyderabad state. It is, therefore, misleading to project Urdu as the language of all the Muslims in India because the majority of them have no emotional or religious attachment with it. In this sense I call the issue of Urdu language as peripheral.

The Vande Mataram Controversy

Muslim reluctance to sing *Vande Mataram* is not without justification if we take into account the history associated with the song. Moreover, not only Muslims but the Sikhs[1] and Christians[2] also refuse to sing the song citing religious reasons. The song first appeared in Bankim Chandra Chattopadhya's novel *Anand Math* that was published in 1882. According to R.C. Majumdar, a historian who is held in high esteem by the Hindu Right, the novel's "central theme moves round a band of *sanyasis* called *santanas* or children, who left their hearth and home and dedicated their lives to the cause of their motherland. They worshipped the motherland as Goddess Kali...This aspect of the *Anand Math* and the imagery of Goddess Kali leave no doubt that *Bankimchandra's nationalism was Hindu rather than Indian.*"[3]

Additionally, Nirad C. Chaudhary in his *Autobiography of an Unknown Indian*, gives an idea of the political atmosphere in which the song was composed. According to him: "The historical romances of Bankim Chandra Chatterjee and Ramesh Chandra Dutt glorified Hindu rebellion against Muslim rule and showed Muslims in a correspondingly poor light. Chatterjee was positively and fiercely anti-Muslim. We were eager readers of these romances and we readily absorbed their spirit."[4] Most importantly, we must also consider what Rabindernath Tagore has to say about the song. In a letter to Subhash Chandra Bose written in 1937, Tagore writes: "The core of *Vande Mataram* is a hymn to goddess Durga: this is so plain that there can be no debate about it. Of course Bankim Chandra does show Durga to be inseparably united with Bengal in the end, but no Mussulman [Muslim] can be expected patriotically to worship the ten-handed deity as 'Swadesh' [the nation]... The novel *Anandamath* is a work of literature, and so the song is appropriate in it. But Parliament is a place of union for all religious groups, and there the song cannot be appropriate."[5]

In 1937, the Indian National Congress discussed the controversy surrounding the song in a meeting in which Maulana Azad was also present. Having discussed all aspects of the issue, it was decided that though in the song, the motherland was equated with the Hindu goddess Durga, the first two stanzas were purely in praise of the beauty of the motherland without referring to any deity. The Indian National Congress, therefore, decided that the first two stanzas of the song must be adopted as the national song. The decision was later endorsed by the Constituent Assembly on January 24, 1950. Thus, the official version of Vande Matram comprising only the first two stanzas, in fact, does not hurt anyone's religious sentiments. Most Muslims just get carried away by the propaganda of the communal leaders and show reluctance to sing the song. It must also be pointed out that on September 6, 2006, the All India Sunni Ulema Board issued a *fatwa* that stated in unambiguous terms that "the Muslims can sing first two stanzas of the song." The President of the Board, Syed Shah Badruddin Qadri Al-jeelani further added: "If you bow at the feet of your mother with respect, it is not *shirk* but only respect."[6]

The need, therefore, is to dispel the unfounded consternation among the common Muslims about the song by informing them that a religious scholar like Maulana Azad and in the recent past all the Islamic scholars on the Sunni Ulema Board have approved of singing the official version of the national song. The more valid argument should be that the first two stanzas of Vande Matram deserve to be revered for the simple reason that they were adopted by the Constituent Assembly as the national song. We cannot be selective about accepting the decisions of the Constituent Assembly because such an attitude could put the Constitution itself into peril.

Muslim Personal Law

There is another issue which I would not like to categorize as a peripheral one; nor would I like to treat it as a real problem. In fact I do not regard it as an exclusively Muslim issue because almost all religious communities, thanks to the colonial legacy, are governed by the community-specific laws in matters such as marriage, divorce, inheritance and adoption. It must also be underlined that almost all the so-called personal laws have misogynic origin that, in practical terms, results in asymmetrical standing of man and woman. Despite this the Muslim baiters harp on only about Muslim Personal Law. If the issue is to be viewed from the standpoint of human rights then the solution lies in adopting a common civil code for all Indians. This is not something that concerns only Muslims or a matter the Muslims alone can do something about.

The Constitution makers made the original mistake by allowing the continuation of community-specific civil laws by situating the issue of a common civil code in the Directive Principles of State policy. The Constituent Assembly should have adopted a common civil code right from the beginning. Since it did not, the Parliament should have done it in the mid-nineteen-fifties while passing the Hindu Code Bill. It is strange that liberal and secular leaders showed acute concern about the plight of Hindu women and therefore, adopted a purportedly egalitarian law for the Hindus. However, the same liberal and secular leaders did not think about the plight of the non-Hindu women! What held them down? The oft-repeated argument is that the so-called leaders did not intend to injure the religious sentiments of the minorities, in particular, Muslims. This is a phony line of reasoning on three counts. Firstly, was it all right to hurt the religious sentiments of the Hindus by passing the Hindu Code Bill? Secondly, if the so-called liberal and secular leaders were exceptionally careful about religious sentiments especially of the Muslims, then why they did not feel any qualms about making secularism and democracy based on the principle of universal adult franchise, the operational precept of Indian polity? The orthodox mullahs who are believed to have tremendous control over the Muslim masses call both the concepts un-Islamic. Thirdly, if the criterion for deferring the issue of a common civil code was to respect the religious sentiments of the religious minorities then why was the matter enshrined in Article 44 of the Constitution? It is plain to see for anyone who cares that the issue has been extremely politicized. Most political parties support or oppose the issue of common civil code purely on the political gains they can make out of it and not on commitment.

Real Problems of the Muslims

Muslims in India have been blatantly discriminated against since independence because in the popular perception they were responsible for the partition of the country. Nothing could be farther from the truth because in the Communal Award of 1932, it was explicitly enjoined that no major political decision concerning India would be taken without the consent of both the Congress and the Muslim League. In consequence, the country would have never been partitioned had the Congress not agreed to the plan Secondly, the movement for Pakistan was essentially an elitist one, which was initiated and sustained by the *ashraf* of UP and the Muslim business class of the Bombay Province. It was not the preferred political alternative in the provinces where Muslims constituted the majority. The common Muslims, therefore, had nothing to do with the separatist movement that was carried on by a political organization of nawabs, zamindars and businessmen, which the Muslim League was in reality. It must also be underscored that on accomplishment of their political purpose, a large number of Muslim *ashraf* migrated to Pakistan for they had the means and the motive. The overwhelming majority of the Muslims consisting mostly of *ajlaf* and *arzal* stayed back in India. It is extremely regrettable, therefore, that the lower caste Muslims who had always been the victims of intra-community social exclusion at the hands of *ashraf* and who had no role to play in the movement for Pakistan have to bear the brunt of Hindu communalism and state repression.

Security of Life and Property

Nehru has always been trumpeted as an absolutely secular person and a friend of the Muslims by the drum beaters of the Congress. Nevertheless, the reality seems to be the opposite of what has been propagated until now. In a recent exposure of a classified report on the Hyderabad massacre of 1948 that has not been declassified by the Government even after the lapse of 65 years, the most gruesome slaughter of the Muslims in independent India occurred under the premiership of Nehru. After the military takeover of Hyderabad state, which is strangely referred to as "police action", there were reports that the local Hindu fanatics in connivance with the Indian army unleashed a reign of killings and rapes of the Muslims to avenge the atrocities committed by the *Razakars*. In response the Nehru Government commissioned Pandit Sunderlal to submit a report after proper investigation. The report was submitted but was never made public because its findings were unpalatable for the Government.

A few unauthenticated versions have always been in circulation outside India which quoted conservative figures of the Muslims killed in the revenge massacre. For instance, a much lower but still shocking estimate was reported by Perry Anderson. He writes: "When the Indian Army took over Hyderabad, massive Hindu pogroms against the Muslim population broke out, aided and abetted by its regulars. On learning something of them the figurehead Muslim Congressman in Delhi, Maulana Azad, then Minister of Education, prevailed on Nehru to let a team investigate. It reported that a conservative estimate between 27,000 and 40,000 Muslims had been slaughtered in the space of a few weeks after the Indian takeover."[7] The Nehru Government, of course, never admitted the occurrence of massacre. What was scandalous that Nehru brazenly announced that Indian victory in Hyderabad was achieved without a single communal incident! The famous historian William Dalrymple in his book, *The Age of Kali,* informs that the Sunderlal Report has been leaked and published abroad, and "estimates that as many as 200,000 Hyderabadi Muslims were slaughtered."[8] It was the largest and the most gruesome pogrom against the Muslims in independent India.

Thereafter, the second mass murder of the Muslims took place during the spell of Meerut riots of 1987. On 22nd May 1987, 29 personnel of the Provincial Armed Constabulary (PAC), picked 42 young Muslim men from Hashimpura, a locality of Meerut, took them to a secluded place near Murad Nagar in Ghaziabad district and killed them in cold blood. Their dead bodies were thrown in the canals. The case was registered when the dead bodies were seen floating in the canals. Thereafter, only 16 PAC personnel surrendered and were immediately released on bail. The case was transferred to the Supreme Court in 2002 where it is still pending, which makes it one of the oldest cases before the apex court. As per the information sought through an RTI application on 24th May 2007, none of the accused was ever suspended and their complicity in the heinous pogrom was not even mentioned in the annual confidential reports.

The third pogrom is by now a much talked about issue which is usually seen as a well orchestrated stratagem of ethnic cleansing. The horrifying details of the 2002 Gujarat pogrom are universally well-known and, therefore, there is no need to repeat those agonizing incidents here. It would suffice to say that almost all the credible information points out various Hindutva organizations that are collectively known as the *Sangh Parivar* had meticulously planned and carried the anti-Muslim pogrom with the active support of the state agencies. A Concerned Citizens' Tribunal with the highly respected former judge of the Supreme Court, Krishna Iyer, as its chief came out with a 600-page report about the pogrom that stated in explicit terms that the post-Godhra massacres in Gujarat was "an organized crime perpetrated by the Chief Minister, Narendra Modi, and his Government." The report further emphasized that the"post-Godhra violence was pre-planned and executed with 'military precision' by the Sangh Parivar with the State's complicity."[9]

The pogrom not only stunned the secular and civilized sections of Indian society but also distressed the foreign India-watchers, most of whom had a desire to see the secular-democratic polity of India emerge successful. For instance, Martha Nussbaum commented: "There is by now a broad consensus that the Gujarat violence was a form of ethnic cleansing, that in many ways was premeditated, and that it was carried out with the complicity of the state government and officers of the law"[10] An inquiry conducted by the British High Commission arrived at the conclusion that the post-Godhra Gujarat killings had been pre-planned and the state government had actively backed the marauding hordes of rioters that were openly engaged in ethnic cleansing. The most valuable observation of the report was that so long as Narendra Modi remained in power, "the reconciliation between the Hindu and Muslim communities would not be possible."[11] Ironically, the man who has been indicted in such damaging terms by an independent investigative agency was named as the Prime Ministerial candidate by the BJP, and now has become the Prime Minister of India, and the media, most of which is controlled by the Hindutva Right, enthusiastically promote his candidature for the premiership of this plural country! On the issue it is appropriate to cite the observation of the Amnesty International in 2007 that expressed quite a few unsettling observations about India while noting that "justice and rehabilitation continued to evade most victims of the 2002 Gujarat communal violence."

Alongside the three pogroms mentioned above, there have been innumerable Hindu-Muslim communal riots in independent India. The most devastating among them in terms of loss of life and property especially of the Muslims have been the Ahmedabad riots of 1969, Moradabad riots of 1980, Nellie

(Assam) massacre of 1983, Bhiwandi riots of 1984, Meerut riots of 1987, Bhagalpur riots of 1989, Mumbai riots of 1992-93 and Assam riots of 2012. When these lines are being written, the Muslims are being killed in Muzaffarnagar, Meerut and the surrounding villages of Western Uttar Pradesh. However, the major riots that have been listed here had caused extensive damages to the lives and properties of the Muslims.

A close analysis of these riots may reveal the fact that most riots break out at places where Muslims do reasonably well in business and trade. Thus, the primary purpose of the Hindu Right is to dispossess the Muslims of whatever little economic sources they still hold onto. The second objective of anti-Muslim violence is political. A close study of the major Hindu-Muslim riots can also reveal the fact that the anti-Muslim riots break out in areas where the Muslim presence is sizable. This demographic feature of a city or town poses serious problems for the anti-Muslim political parties to get their candidates elected from such constituencies. Anti-Muslim propaganda supported by rumours and false stories, therefore, helps vitiate the social scenario which ultimately results in the outbreak of a riot. It is obvious that anti-Muslim propaganda and the subsequent violence consolidate the Hindu votes in favour of the Hindu Right. The Hindu Right may camouflage these two core objectives by accusing Muslims of all kinds of anti-national and anti-Hindu crimes to build up an atmosphere of hatred against the largest minority of the country.

Since 9/11, Muslims all over the world have become target of hatred and everywhere they face discrimination of various kinds as they are looked on as potential terrorists. The Indian Muslims too are facing the brunt of the current anti-Muslim wave. The situation, in India, at present is so bad that in the eyes of every policeman, a Muslim is a potential terrorist. It must be underscored in unambiguous terms that terrorism should not be tolerated by anyone under any circumstances. The irony, however, is that if there is a blast even in a mosque causing deaths of Muslims alone, the so-called intelligence agencies and the police get into action to arrest humble, innocent Muslims! The latest trend adopted by the police and other security agencies is to implicate Muslim youths in false cases of terrorism. As a result the hapless young Muslims arrested on trumped up terrorism charges usually spend years in jails and ultimately many of them are acquitted by the courts. However, in the course of this sinister process they end up as social and psychological wrecks. They also become unemployable because of the stigma of spending years behind bars albeit as part of conspiracy of communal minded security officers.

It is in this context that the recent directive of the previous Central Home Minister belonging to the Congress party, Sushil Kumar Shinde, to the states not to implicate and arrest innocent Muslim youths on trumped up charges of terrorism should be comprehended. Though, in view of the timing, the statement cannot be taken on its face value, the aggressive manner in which the BJP had condemned the statement has inadvertently revealed its real agenda about the Muslims. What exactly the BJP sees as objectionable in the statement? Should Shinde have advised the state to continue falsely implicating and arresting innocent Muslim youths in terrorism-related cases? If the previous Home Minister's directive was indeed issued with genuine concern and sincerity it is a just and proper, even though belated, step in the direction of restoring people's confidence in law-enforcing agencies.

The most urgent need is to pass the Communal Violence Prevention Bill, which has been languishing in Parliament for last 8 years. On this issue even the UPA II did not seem to be totally committed. Otherwise, how come Manmohan Singh's government thought it pressing to save the unscrupulous and convicted members of the legislatures through an ordinance but did not bother to protect the lives of innocent victims of communal violence by making an ordinance? Though the ordinance meant for protecting the convicted political leaders did not become a reality after Rahul Gandhi's vociferous condemnation of it, the prince in the khadi armour never felt the obligation to throw his weight behind the Communal Violence Prevention Bill. In a long and continuous series of communal riots, the Muzaffarnagar carnage was the latest one and like all previous riots it too was a well-planned anti-Muslim mass murder carried out by the Hindu Right with the active connivance of the local administration. In order to put an end to this diabolical continuing strategy against the largest minority of the country, the need for an anti-communal violence law can hardly be exaggerated.

Economic Exclusion

In addition to the physical decimation, Muslims are subjected to the worst kind of economic exclusion. The loyalty of Indian Muslims is always questioned by the Hindu Right, the ruling political class and the bureaucracy. The bias started immediately after independence. The most prominent leader who gave expression to prejudice against the Muslims publicly was not a leader of Hindu Mahasabha or a member of the RSS but Vallabhbhai Patel, the then Home Minister of India and a stalwart of the so-called secular Congress. "In a speech at Lucknow, in early January 1948 he (Patel) reminded his audience that it was in that town that 'the formation of two-nation theory was laid.' For it was the UP intellectuals who had claimed that 'Muslims were a separate nation.' Now, for those who had chosen not to go to Pakistan, it was not enough to give 'mere declarations of loyalty to the Indian Union', they 'must give *practical proof* of their declarations'."[12] So, here was the first Home Minister of free India demanding a *"practical proof"* of loyalty to the nation from the Muslims who decided not to leave the land of their ancestors.

Patel did not stop at giving a vicious warning to the Muslims, but embarked on a well-planned exclusion of Muslims from state institutions. Shortly after his Lucknow speech the secretary of the Home Ministry wrote to all the secretaries to be vigilant about the few Muslims who might still be working under them, because they could be potential spies of Pakistan. The letter clearly stated that the potential fifth-columnists, as the Muslim employees were being treated by Patel, posed a serious threat to national security because they might pass on secret information to Pakistan. The letter further cautioned: "It is obvious that they (Muslim employees) constitute a dangerous element in the fabric of administration; and it is essential that they should not be entrusted with any confidential or secret work or allowed to hold key posts."[13] So, the Indian state officially adopted an anti-Muslim policy right from the word go. It was ironical that such an obnoxious policy came into force when Nehru, supposed to be a truly secular man, was at the helms of affairs. What's more that this confidential circular was never rescinded by Nehru and continued to be in force until 1969.[14]

The policy of excluding Muslims from public services started by Patel and willingly continued by Nehru, and successive governments is firmly in place. Besides, government services, other economic opportunities have also been denied to Muslims because even the nationalized banks callously reject loan applications of the business-inclined sections of the community. The cruel joke, however, is that the Congress never loses any opportunity to project itself as the defender of Muslim interests and the Hindu Right, in particular, the BJP accuses the Congress of pursuing a policy of Muslim appeasement!

The reality is that Muslim representation in government services is abysmally low. Though the socially committed members of the community have launched various projects during the last two decades to prepare the educated youths for the competitive examinations, the average percentage of successful Muslim candidates was never allowed to go beyond 3.5 per cent. The people engaged in helping young Muslims prepare for the civil services allege that the blanket policy of the Union Government and also of many state governments is not to recruit more than 3 per cent Muslims in government services. Their allegation seems to be correct if we consider the following table[15] that gives a picture of Muslim representation in civil services during the last ten years:

Results Declared	*No. of Successful Candidates*	*Muslim Candidates*	*Percentage of Total No.*
May 2003	284	9	3.1
May 2004	413	13	3.2
May 2005	422	13	3.1
May 2006	425	12	2.8
May 2007	448	17	3.8

May 2008	734	27	3.67
May 2009	791	32	4.04
May 2010	875	21	2.4
May 2011	920	31	3.36
May 2012	910	30	3.29

The situation is even worse in the armed forces. It is obvious that the reason for under-representation of the Muslims lies in the partition of the country. However, the purportedly secular state of India has done nothing to correct the wrong of history; on the contrary it fervently follows a policy to keep Muslims out of Services. Mahavir Tyagi who was the Minister of State in Nehru's Council of Minister, "admitted that at the time of partition the percentage of Muslims in the services was 32 and now it had gone down to two."[16] It must also be pointed out that when the previous Prime Minister, Manmohan Singh, instituted the Sachar Committee to investigate the social, economic and educational conditions of Muslims and when the Committee members sought to know the percentage of Muslims in the military there was a hue and cry from the senior army officers who thought that it would communalize the 'secular' Services. Thereafter, in February 2007, surprisingly, a lieutenant-general supplied the exact figure of Muslims in the army that stood at 29, 093.[17] It means even after 60 years of independence the percentage of Muslims could not rise more than 2. The prejudice against Muslims by the Defence Establishment may be determined "by a press release issued by a defence office in Jammu in 2002. Seeking recruits for the Indian army, the press release said: 'No vacancies for Muslims and tradesmen'."[18]

Muslim representation in other elite services is also abysmally low. In the Indian Foreign Service they are 1.8 per cent while in the Indian Police Service the Muslim representation is 4 per cent. It goes without saying that there is almost a blanket exclusion of Muslims from the top and supposed to be highly 'sensitive' posts in intelligence agencies such as CBI, IB and RAW. Muslims are also barred from holding significant positions in Space Research Organisation and National Security Guard. Muslim representation in state government jobs is even worse in almost all the states. These facts have always been known to those who ever bothered to probe the issue. However, the official legitimacy to Muslim exclusion from all social, economic and educational spheres was made known when the findings of the Sachar Commitee were placed in the public domain in 2006.

It must be pointed out, however, that Sachar Committee was not the first of its kind to probe Muslim socio-economic and educational exclusion. Its precursor was the high level Gopal Singh Commission that was appointed on May 10, 1980 with almost similar brief that was assigned to the Sachar Committee. Gopal Singh Commission submitted its report to the Prime Minister on June 14, 1983. It was neither placed before Parliament nor its findings were officially made public. In order to estimate the callousness of the political elite it is appropriate to mention what Asghar Ali Engineer experienced. "When Shri V.P. Singh became the Prime Minister and convened a meeting of Muslim leaders and intellectuals," writes Engineer, "I asked him about implementation of Gopal Singh High Powered Commission Report. He, to my shock, was not even aware of any such report."[19] Though the findings of the Gopal Singh Commission were not officially made public, the data filtered through unofficially. As per the findings of the Commission, Muslim representation in the IAS had come down to 3.2 per cent while the SCs representation then (1980) was 9.9 per cent. In the IPS the Muslims percentage was reportedly 2.7 while that of the SCs was 9.8. Similarly, in IFS, the Muslim representation was much lesser i.e. 3.37 per cent in comparison with SCs percentage of 16.48.[20] Almost a quarter of a century later, when the findings of the Sachar Committee came to light, the condition of Muslims in many spheres got deteriorated even further. Despite the government's claim that it is committed to implement the recommendations of the Sachar Committee, the popular perception among Muslims is that just like the Gopal Singh Report or the Rangnath Mishra Commission[21] Report, nothing concrete would come out of it.

Nevertheless, the findings of the Sachar Committee are very significant as they provide us the severity of exclusion of Muslims in socio-economic and educational fields. In the field of employment the Committee findings revealed that almost 50 per cent Muslim men in the age-group of 25-45 were self employed and only 18 per cent were in regular employment as compared to 25 per cent Hindus. As regards government jobs, Muslim representation in all states was much lower in comparison to their percentage in population. Consider the following table[22] to have an idea about Muslim representation in State Government employment in the twelve States where there proportion in population is considerable.

Sr. No.	*Name of the State*	*Percentage Muslims in Population*	*Percentage of Muslims in Employment*
1	Andhra Pradesh	9.2	8.8
2	Assam	30.2	11.2
3	Bihar	16.5	7.6
4	Delhi	11.7	3.2
5	Gujarat	9.1	5.6
6	Jharkhand	13.8	6.7
7	Karnataka	12.2	8.5
8	Kerala	24.7	10..4
9	Maharashtra	10.6	4.4
10	Uttar Pradesh	18.5	5.1
11	Tamil Nadu	5.6	3.2
12	West Bengal	25	4.2

The notable figures are from Andhra Pradesh where Muslim representation in state employment is closer to their percentage in population. Conversely, the worst figures are from West Bengal where Muslims constitute one-fourth of the state population but their representation in state employment is merely 4.2 per cent. This is especially reprehensible because the CPI (M), the 'flag-bearer' of secularism was in power in the state for more than three decades. Though the figures for Jammu and Kashmir are not shown in the table, it must be added that the Muslim percentage of population in the only Muslim majority State is 67 while there representation in state employment is less than 50 per cent.

In the elite All-India Services, the figures reported by the Committee are not very different from those that were revealed by the Gopal Singh Commission. The Muslim percentages in the IAS is 3.1, in the IFS it is 1.8 and in the IPS 4. As a rule the Muslim representation in intelligence agencies and Space Research Organisation continues to be abysmally low. In the Railways, which is the largest single state employer the Muslim representation is merely 4.5 per cent. In judiciary the overall Muslim presence of 7.8 per cent in 12 states with high Muslim concentration is almost half of their percentage in country's population. Surprisingly in this category too, Muslim representation in Jammu and Kashmir is 48.3 per cent.

Economic exclusion of Muslims in the banking sector and other financial institutions is extremely pronounced. The findings of the Sachar Committee reveal the share of Muslims in "amounts outstanding" is only 4.7 per cent, which is lower than the figure of other minorities that is pegged at 6.5 per cent. The most loathsome aspect of the banking system that has been reported by the Committee is that many banks have adopted a policy to mark the areas with Muslim concentration as "negative" or "red" regions which means bank loans are not given to the residents of the areas who are overwhelmingly Muslims. Almost all the banks, public or private, victimize Muslims as a rule. Their loan applications are vehemently rejected not for any technical or procedural reason but only because the applicants are Muslims. As a result of it, a sizable section of the community that is business-inclined does not get the necessary support to become self-employed. In pursuance of the Prime Minister 15-Point Programme for the uplift of minorities, the Reserve Bank of India launched the banking and credit facilities for the targeted groups. However, as per the findings of the Committee these efforts benefited other religious minorities more than the Muslims. The other statistics are similarly appalling. For instance 94.9 per cent of the Muslims living below poverty line don't get the food-grains. In rural India, 60.2 per cent of Muslims don't own land and only 1 per cent own hand pumps or tube-wells.

Educational Backwardness

Muslims, as per the 2001 census constitute 13.4 per cent of India's population. However, in the field of education, they lag behind other communities. According to the Sachar Committee's findings the literacy rate for Muslims in 2001 was 59 per cent as against the national average of 65 per cent. Muslim literacy was also lower than that of the SCs and STs. At the school level 25 per cent of Muslim children in the age group of 6-14 either were not enrolled in the schools or dropped out at various stages of school education. At the undergraduate level only 1 out of 25 and at post-graduate level 1 out of 50 happen to be Muslim students. It must be underlined that according to the Committee's findings the major cause of low percentage of Muslims in education particularly at the primary level is the non-availability of Urdu medium schools in most states. Muslim women, in particular, awfully suffer from educational backwardness. According to the statistics made available by the National Family Health Survey, on the national level 66 per cent Muslim women are illiterate whereas in the state of Haryana almost all the Muslim women are illiterate.

Though, these appalling figures can partly be explained on account of the lapse of the state to uphold a constitutional commitment to make educational institutions available all across the country imparting elementary education in the mother tongue, other factors are equally responsible. The foremost is obviously poverty. The argument that after the guarantee of right to education as a fundamental right since 2010, poverty of Muslim parents should no more be an impediment to send their children to schools is not tenable. Firstly, it is too early to judge the impact of the Right to Eduction (RTE) on Muslims on all India level. Secondly, the real problem of the poor Muslim parents is not merely the payment of school fees and allied expenses. The real problem is how to augment the family income. For that reason most parents instead of enrolling their young children in schools force them to become lowly paid weavers, particularly carpet-weavers, zari-workers, tannery workers, bearers, hawkers, vendors, shop assistants, kiln workers, domestic workers, apprentices in tailoring, automobile repairing, masonry and even in some hazardous fields like quarrying. The meager wages that the young boys and girls bring home help the family carry on by some means. Thus, poverty and educational backwardness for most Muslims form a vicious circle and unfortunately they are hardly in a position to break it.

Another reason for Muslims to be backward in the educational field is the hold of the orthodox mullahs over the Muslim masses and the regressive ideas they preach almost daily in the neighbourhood mosques. Most of these mullahs do not have a background of modern-liberal-scientific education and for that reason they goad the poor Muslims not to enroll their children in schools but to send them to Madarssas. Mushirul Hasan writing on problems of Muslim education quotes the observation of Mohammed Ibrahim, the former chairman of the Minorities Commission of Madhya Pradesh, that many *ulema* have developed a vested interest in promoting and safeguarding Madarssas as their strongholds. Most importantly, Ibrahim says that most ulama are good only in dabbling into sectarian controversies and ignorant about the demands and needs of the contemporary world. Accordingly, they see "everyone else as ignorant, irreligious and atheistic."[23]

I also have reservations about the views of many activists and scholars who argue in favour of modernization of Madarssas by providing them state funding and recognition of their degrees. Taking a cue from this line of thinking the previous Government of Maharashtra had announced a grant of Rs. 10 crore for the modernization project of Madarssas in the state. This is an ominous development. Leave aside the pittance that is allocated for all the Madarssas in Maharashtra, the timing of the announcement is noteworthy, as it came just before the 2014 elections. Overwhelming majority of the Muslims of the state are hardly enthused to vote for the alliance of the Congress and the Nationalist Congress Party (NCP). So, obviously it is a political snare to entice Muslim voters. However, the more sinister design seems to be keeping most Muslims away from modern education that has always been one of the points on the agenda of anti-Muslim political and bureaucratic elite. In this sense, like the mullahs, the politicians and civil servants hostile to the Muslims, also have a vested interest in promoting and preserving the Madarssas!

Besides weakening the secular moorings of the Constitution, the state funding of Madarssas helps reinforce the propaganda of the Hindu Right about the policy of Muslim 'appeasement'. It may also result in consolidation of the Hindu votes in favour of the parties like the BJP and Shiv Sena, which is just fine with the anti-Muslim elements in the government. Today, it is Madarssas that are earmarked for state funding; tomorrow, the religious institutions of all communities would demand such financial assistance from the state. Now, imagine the enormous expenditure the state would have to incur on the antiquated education that has no relevance in the present-day world. It is also important to note that a very small section of Muslims send their children to Madarssas. The "politics of the Madarssas" is not beneficial to the Muslim community, Instead it benifits only the Hindi Right.

Madarssa education is out of sync with the realities of contemporary life. In the last resort, they teach a supremacist and radical version of Islam which is absolutely inimical to the ethos of a plural society like India. In addition to deriding the Sufi brand of Islam, most Madarssas encourage sectarian prejudices and detestation. For them a humane and liberal interpretation of Islam is sacrilegious. The question is in what way one can modernize such institutions? By teaching them IT, Computer education, science and technology? The result will be a mullah who along with having a supremacist and orthodox view of Islam will also have competence to deal with computers. How does it change the dominant worldview of the community which emphasises only on the life of the hereafter rather than meeting the challenges of the everyday living? Is there any guarantee that a nuclear physicist cannot be a supremacist, regressive and communal?

If Muslims have to really get rid of their educational backwardness, the need is they should wean themselves away from the Madarssas and join institutions of modern education. To accomplish this task not only the Muslim elite but all the responsible sections of civil society who believe in secularism and an all-inclusive development of a social order in India should come together. On their part, the Muslim elite can help loosen the grasp of the mullahs by monitoring the goings on in the neighbourhood mosques. The orthodox mullahs get unfair advantage of disseminating regressive ideas to the captive and gullible audiences from the pulpit almost daily. This practice should be done away with. Mosque is a place of worship and it should remain so. It should not provide a platform to ill-informed mullahs to indoctrinate the vulnerable Muslim masses about the 'sinful and un-Islamic' modern education. On its, part the state should abandon the policy of supporting Madarssas and honestly perform its constitutional obligation of spreading modern education and scientific temper among the people of India.

Political Exclusion

Muslim exclusion from the field of politics is equally glaring. In this context we must refer to a thorough study by Iqbal A. Ansari[14] that provides valuable data about the exclusion of Muslims from the institutions of political power. According to the study, the percentage of elected Muslim Members of Parliament never reached even 100. While the Muslims constitute 13.4 per cent of the population of the country, the number of Muslim members in the 16th Lok Sabha is merely 22, which is incidentally the lowest in the history of the Indian Parliament. The previous lowest representation of the Muslim was in the second Lok Sabha when only 23 Muslims got elected. The highest Muslim representation was in 1980 when 49 Muslims got elected to the Lower House of Parliament.

With regard to the State Legislatures, in the 12 Legislative Assemblies with considerable Muslim population, the number of Muslim members fluctuated between 21 and 49. In terms of percentage of the total membership of the state legislatures it can be translated between 4.3 and 6.6. The reasons for such an abysmally low political representation of the Muslims are mainly two. First, the so-called secular parties have never given tickets to Muslims in proportion to their population. Secondly, the post-electoral system is innately anti-minority, because a political party in such a system can afford to completely exclude an ethnic or religious minority and still win elections as

Narendra Modi has proved first in Gujarat and later in the Paliamentary elections of 2014. This is one area where Muslims are rendered absolutely powerless. It is alarming for a democracy that seeks pride as "largest representative form of government" and it is equally true that immediate corrective measures are badly needed. A switch-over to the list system based on proportional representation to political parties, *not to religions*, may grant the Indian Parliament a truly representative characteristic.

Affirmative Action

It is usually observed that any suggestion for affirmative action to uplift the socio-economic, educational and political status of Muslims in India invariably leads to the issue of making reservations available for the community in government jobs and educational institutions on the lines that have been provided to the SCs and STs. I, personally, have reservation about providing religion-based reservations. It would gravely erode the secular character of our polity that is already under attack by the Hindu Right. Secondly, the Constitution does not permit such a measure. In view of the current political scenario a constitutional amendment to make provision for religion-based reservation is highly unlikely and even if such an amendment is carried out, it would certainly invite a Hindu backlash and would politically strengthen the Hindu Right. What can be done, therefore, is to implement the recommendations of the Rangnath Mishra Commission report that are about religious minorities and not exclusively about Muslims. According to the Commission, the intra-community social exclusion among the Muslims and Christians is a reality. The lower caste Hindus who got converted to Islam or Christianity centuries ago continue to face similar kind of social exclusion at the hands of the so-called upper strata of their respective communities as is the case with the SCs and STs. For that reason, the Commission recommended the conferment of Scheduled Caste status to Muslim *arzals* and the low caste Christians. Once these segments of the Muslims and Christians are included in the SC category they would be constitutionally entitled to enjoy benefits of reservations that are available to the SCs among Hindus, Buddhists, Jains and Sikhs.

Similarly, the recommendations of the Sachar Committee must also be implemented sincerely. The most important recommendations that need immediate state response are: a) setting up of an autonomous Assessment and Monitoring Authority (AMA) that should do regular audit whether the communities concerned are benefitting from various government schemes and programmes that are launched for their uplift; b) instituting of an Equal Opportunities Commission (EOC) to examine the grievances of socially excluded communities of Indian society; c) exploring the possibility of making available some incentives to a "Diversity Index" in the fields of education, government as well as private employments and housing schemes; d) evolving some kind of 'nomination' procedure for increasing the levels of inclusiveness in governance; e) in the field of education the Committee's recommendations include institutionalizing evaluation procedure for text-books, alternate admission norms in universities and colleges, cost friendly hostel facilities for minority students, state-run education Urdu medium school for primary education in mother tongue, ensuring appointment of experts from the minority community on interview panels and boards and linking Madarssas with higher secondary schools; f) in order to ensure better representation for the Muslims in politics, the Committee recommended certain measures such as removal of anomalies in Reserved Constituencies in view of frequent complaints that the territorial constituencies with concentration of Muslim voters are usually declared reserved for SCs and STs. The Committee has also observed reported that there were many complaints of Muslims' names missing from electoral rolls. Additionally, it must also be pointed out that we must have a relook at "first past the post" electoral system. In view of experts a proportional representation system can better ensure inclusion of minorities in the institutions of political power. Some scholars have also suggested that a candidate can be declared elected only if he bags at least 25 per cent of minority votes from his constituency.

The simplest corrective measure to improve the lot of the Muslims is to stick to secularism as an operative principle of running administration. The bureaucracy in India is perhaps the most communal section of our society. If the Muslim percentage in employment is abysmally low, the main culprits are the bureaucrats, many of whom have covert affiliations with the RSS. By making the recruitment procedure truly transparent we can attract deserving Muslim youths to join the public services. Another area that needs reexamination is the financial sector. The working of the banks and other financial institutions must be carried on strictly on professional and secular lines. An urgent necessity is to weed out communal elements from the law enforcing agencies.

It is this damaging psychological factor that alienates the common Muslims from the national psyche and forces them to go back in their shells. On that account they fall prey to the intrigues of the wily mullahs and the crooks masquerading as Muslim leaders. The most important exigency, it must be reiterated, is to improve the educational status of Muslims. The unfortunate reality in India today is that political gangsters who run most of the institutions of higher and professional education coerce the Union and State governments to finance their institutions. Obviously, the percentage of institutions that cater to the needs of the Muslims is negligible. If the seculorists are really sincere about helping Muslims improve their socio-economic and educational conditions, they should see to it that the enrollment of Muslims children in schools increases, their drop-out rate decreases and they must have fair and judicious opportunities to join institutions of higher and professional education.

REFERENCES

1. The supreme body of the Sikhs, the Shiromani Gurdwara Parbandhak Committee, advised the Sikhs not to sing Vande Mataram in schools and other institutions when its singing was being pushed as an obligation by the state to commemorate the song's centenary in 2006. SGPC head, Avtar Singh Makkar, expressed the apprehension that "imposing a song that reflected

just one religion was bound to hurt the sentiments of religious minorities. The Delhi Sikh Gurdwara management Committee has also given a call that singing of "Vande Mataram" is against Sikh tenets as the Sikhs sought *'sarbat da bhala'* (universal welfare) and did not believe in *'devi* and *devta'*.

2. A few Christian institutions such as Our Lady of Fatima Convent School in Patiala did not sing the song on the eve of its centenary as mandated by the state. Christian scholars maintain that they make a distinction between 'veneration' and 'worship'. Though the song does not fall into any of these categories, some Christians nonetheless declined to sing the national song because of its intention and content.
3. Quoted by A.G. Noorani in his article, 'How Secular is Vande Matram?', published in *Frontline*, Vol. 16, No. 1, January 2-15, 1999.
4. Ibid.
5. Quoted from letter #314, *Selected Letters of Rabindranath Tagore*, edited by K. Datta and A. Robinson (Cambridge University Press, 1997).
6. Mohammed A. Basith, 'Now a Fatwa to Sing Vande Mataram', *The Times of India*, September 7, 2006
7. Ramchandra Guha, *India After Gandhi: The History of the World's Largest Democracy* (New Delhi: Macmillan, Picador India, 2007), p. 366.
8. Ibid.
9. *Hindu*, November 22, 2002 (online version).
10. Martha Craven Nussbaum, *The Clash Within: Democracy, Religious Violence, and India's Future* (Harvard University Press, 2008), pp. 50–51.
11. Quoted in Cynthia E. Cohen, Roberto Gutierrez Varea, Polly O. Walker, (eds.) *Acting Together: Resistance and Reconciliation in Regions of Violence* (New Village Press, 2011), p. 280.
12. See Moin Shakir, *Muslims in Free India* (New Delhi: Kalamkar Prakashan, 1972), wherein he quoted from *Link* issue of November 9, 1969 and Y.B. Chavan's statement in the Lok Sabha reported in *Times of India*, November 29, 1969.
13. Quoted by Swaminathan S. Anklesaria Aiyar in his article, 'Declassify Report on the 1948 Hyderabad Massacre', *Sunday Times of India*, November 25, 2012.
14. Quoted by Swaminathan S. Anklesaria Aiyar, Ibid.
15. Source: Syed Zubair Ahmad's online article, 'Blanket State Policy to put Muslims within 3% in Civil Services', www.twocircles.net

16. Quoted in Moin Shakir, op. cit.
17. Arvind Kala's online article, 'Muslims in Army: Hiding whats Well-known', www.business-standard.com.
18. ibid.
19. See Asghar Ali Engineer's online article, 'Identity and Social Exclusion: A Muslim Perspective', www.csss-isla.com/arch
20. Dr. Shekh Belal Ahmad's article, 'Indian Muslims and Their Social Exclusion', *International Research Journal*, July 2010. Though the Government of India constituted the National Commission for Religious and Linguistic Minorities (NCRLM) under the chairmanship of Justice Rangnath Mishra in October 2004, its constitution was delayed because of which it became functional only in March 2005. In its report submitted in May 2007, the Commission *inter alia* recommended that lower castes people who embraced Islam or Christianity should be treated as lower castes and be included in the SC list so that they could also get benefit of reservation in employment and educational institutions.
21. Source: *Sachar Committee Report*, p. 370.
22. Iqbal A. Ansari, *Political Representation of Muslims in India 1952-2004* (New Delhi: Manak Publications Pvt. Ltd., 2006).
23. Mushirul Hasan, *Muslims in Secular India: Problems and Prospects in Education* (New Delhi: Academy of Third World Studies, New Delhi, 2003).

2

Indian Muslims and the Question of the Renaissance

Asghar Ali Engineer

It is often asked why Indian Muslims did not go through the Renaissance. By implication it is suggested Islam prevents any such possibility. I think it is quite a simplistic assumption. Religion by itself neither obstructs nor helps the process of Renaissance. To understand possibility of Renaissance or otherwise one has to understand the complex processes at work in society and history.

Europe experienced the Renaissance not because of Christianity, but in severe opposition to Christianity. Once a society, through certain processes is ready for change, religion can no longer stop it. Religion can become a pull to an extent, but not all the way. If society is ready to change, religion may even become helpful to an extent, but not otherwise. Certain social theorists ignore social processes and structural forces at work when they assume religion to be the driving or impeding force of history.

Indian society is highly diverse even though Brahmanical Hinduism has been a predominant force. It would also not be wholly true to maintain that non-Muslim India as a whole has already experienced the Renaissance. It is far from true. What is true is that Indian society itself is highly complex and has to be understood at different levels. Not only a section of India, but South Asia in general has not accepted modernity wholeheartedly. India, like South Asia thus cannot be said to be modern.

In Europe it was the emergence of the bourgeois class that led the Renaissance movement after the 16th century. In fact one can say Mughal India was far ahead of Europe in philosophy, fine arts, architecture and liberal outlook. Indians had far greater achievements in classical learning and sciences. It was left behind only after progress of science and technological achievements in Western Europe that led to the industrial revolution whereby Europe could break from the womb of feudalism.

In fact as far as the Islamic world is concerned, the Abbasid period from 9th century to early 13th century had already experienced a Renaissance. Its achievements in the fields of philosophy, mathematics, classical arts and sciences were par excellence. This era produced great philosophers like Avicena, Averroes (Arabic Ibn Sina, Ibn Rushd) and others. Logarithm and algebra were invented and great progress was made in chemistry and optics. In fact Europe was passing through the dark ages when the Abbasids were encouraging transfer of treasures of knowledge into Arabic from Greek, Persian and Sanskrit languages through *the Dar al-Hikma* ("House of Wisdom") established in Baghdad. In fact, the knowledge from Greece was transferred to Europe through Arabic translations and philosophers like Avicena and Averros were taught in some of the universities established in Europe. Thus it will be seen that Islam did not come in the way of the tremendous progress made by Arab intellectuals in worldly sciences.

It is true that there was some resistance by the orthodox ulema to the dissemination of these sciences and especially to rational philosophy. But it could not become a powerful impediment in the way of the excellent achievements of these illustrious thinkers and scientists. Some of the theologians developed the science of dialectics ("Ilm al-Kalam"). Though there were two streams of knowledge existing side by side, the orthodox stream could not overpower the rational one. Even today eminent thinkers and philosophers like Avicena, Averroes, Ibn Hayyan and others are great names from that period.

Al-Ghazzali, it is true, is also a great name from amongst

the theological thinkers of the orthodox stream, but he himself passed through various phases including the rational phase when he even became an atheist. However, he felt that reason alone is inadequate to understand ultimate reality for which revelation, intuition and inner experiences are necessary. Ghazzali had a great debate with Averroes and wrote to a book denouncing philosophy and called it *Tihafut al-Falasifa* ("Perplexity of Philosophers") to which Averros replied by writing *Tahafut Tahafut al-Falasifa* ("Perplexity of Perplexity of Philosophers"). This shows that opposition of orthodox Ulama could not impede progress of rational sciences in the Islamic world of that period.

However, the decline of this great philsophpical movement of the Islamic Renaissance began after the fall of Abbasids in the 13th century. The factors are historical. One cannot point to the faults of Islam for this downfall. This clearly shows that the cultivation and consequent triumph of philosophical and scientific learning depend on power and prosperity and a sense of security in society, than on religion per se. If society is on decline, such movements cannot flourish; and if society is prospering and has grip over power such movements flourish. Thus it has much greater connection with society than with religion.

After the decline of the Abbasids whose centre of power and whom Toyenbee, the renowned historian, calls the "universal state of Islam", a sense of insecurity gripped the Islamic world and many scholars have suggested that thereafter intellectual decline of Muslims began and the orthodoxy took over. One of the Abbasid caliphs in the period of decline al-Mutavakkil, sided with the orthodox Ulama and severely persecuted rationalists. It would be interesting to note that it were the rationalists (Mua'tazila) who persecuted the orthodox at the beginning of the Abbasid period and the same dynastic period ended with the persecution of the rationalists.

In Europe too, orthodoxy prevailed and kept its tight grip over Christians. A great struggle ensued against the Church only when a powerful bourgeois class appeared on the scene and became confident of its power and grip over the situation.

Europe, however, never looked back since then and science and technology went from strength to strength and religion lost its centrality and grip over the minds of people of Europe.

In case of Muslims though some regional powers like the Fatimids in Egypt, Ottomans in Turkey, the Mughuls in India and the Safavids in Iran did emerge on the scene, they could not regain and continue their achievements what they had achieved during the Abbasid period. Their "universal state" declined and could never look up again. The regional powers could not match the centrality of the Abbasid achievements. The theologians also felt insecure and closed the gates of *ijtihad* (creative interpretation).

It is imperative to understand that Indian Muslims should not be treated as a monolithic bloc. They were highly stratified due to many reasons; the Indian caste system is one reason for their stratification. Muslims in India except those who came from Iran and Central Asia never got the share in economic and political power and remained a deprived lot. Indigenous Muslims were generally converts from amongst the Dalits and OBCs and always remained poor, backward and illiterate. Before we passed any judgement it is very necessary to understand the sociology of Indian Islam. Though the Muslims belonging to ruling class did merge with indigenous society and assimilated Indian culture and languages, they remained a distinct lot and called themselves *ashraf* ("of noble decent") as against those converts from Dalits and OBCs whom they described as *ajlaf* and *arzal* ("of low decent and untouchables").

The *ashraf* never intermarried with the *ajlaf* and *arzal*. These low caste Muslims themselves are divided in various professional castes called *biradaris*. Generally these *biradaris* also don't intermarry among themselves. A large number of Indian Muslims today come from these low caste *biradaris*. Its estimate is anybody's guess. Recently the *Sachar Committee Report* gives their number as 41 per cent. But it is largely underestimated as many Muslims describe themselves as belonging to higher castes of Sheikh or Syed. Anyway we can say that much higher percentage of Muslims belong to these low caste *biradaris*.

The decline and end of Mughul rule was another severe blow to Indian Muslims. They lost power and upper caste Muslims too felt greatly insecure. The failure of the 1857 mutiny (or the "War of Independence" to be precise) was a much greater blow to Muslims of the ruling class. British power completely destroyed Mughal power. It was indeed a death blow to Muslims of the ruling classes in India. Only a few zamindars who chose to support British rule could survive and regain their landed estates and influence with the British rulers. And with coming and consequent instituionlization of colonial education in the Indian subcontinent Muslims were left far behind in the field of modern secular education as they feared alien Western culture and education.

It was the great foresight of Sir Syed Ahmad Khan that emphasized the importance of modern education and founded the first major institution of modern education for Muslims in Aligarh which was known as MAO College (Mahomedan Anglo-Oriental College). Here also mainly the children of Muslim zamindars and jagirdars (feudal lords) came for education though scholarships were available for the deprived sections of Muslim society. It is these scions of jagirdar families who became lawyers, doctors, engineers and other professionals and came to constitute the Muslim middle class. This middle class was quite small in size as the Muslim masses, mainly artisans and small peasants, had no access to modern education and had no incentive to opt for it and they remained, by and large confined to their hereditary professions.

These jagirdars and zamindars were also mostly from Uttar Pradesh and Bihar, both being Muslim minority areas. Muslim majorities lived mainly in the Punjab and Bengal. This jagirdar class in these two regions was very weak and the bulk of the Muslims were poor and downtrodden. Sir Syed, himself a member of the Muslim nobility, was harbinger of the modern Muslim Renaissance in India. He not only promoted modern secular education he also founded Indian Scientific Society and translated various scientific works in Urdu for benefit of North Indian people. He also founded the Educational Congress to popularize modern education among Muslims. He proposed many modern reforms and even advocated westernization to an extent.

He started a magazine called *Tahzib al-Akhlaq* ("Refining Morals") and advocated change of old cultural practices and introducing modern ways in different fields of life. He also disseminated through this magazine modern knowledge, science and technology. This magazine rendered yeoman service to Muslims in North India and introduced them to modernity. This magazine has been revived again a few years ago and is published from the Aligarh Muslim University. Sir Syed Ahmed Khan was an institution himself and he created a band of scholars and followers who acquired eminence in different fields of scholarship. One of his followers and colleague Maulavi Mumtaz Ali Khan wrote a book *Huquq al-Niswan* who, through this book, pleaded the cause of gender equality. This book, I can say, was the beginning of Muslim feminism in India.

Justice Ameer Ali, a product of this movement, wrote several books of which *Spirit of Islam* became very popular. It was an attempt to see Islam and its teachings in the light of modernity. Another leading light of this movement was Maulavi Chriagh Ali who too advocated modern reforms in Muslim Personal Law and also wrote a tract on jihad and tried to show that the *Quran* does not advocate war through this concept but promotes goodness through maximum human endeavours.

Thus Sir Syed and his colleagues made efforts to bring about a Renaissance among Indian Muslims. However, its momentum could not be. In Europe the Renaissance movement went much further thanks to sustained social and scientific changes in society. The main reason was the defeat of the feudals and the retreat of feudal culture in Europe. This did not become possible for various reasons in the Indian sub-continent. The main reason for the retreat of the Muslim Renaissance in contemporary times was political turmoil and politics of identity during the late thirties and fourties of the last century. The political controversies between Hindus and Muslims became serious obstacles in the process of social and attitudinal change. Identity politics, leads more often than not, to revivalist movements with emphasis on an imagined past. These political developments ultimately led to division of the country in 1947 followed by communal carnage on both sides of the division.

Much of the progress achieved by Sir Syed and his colleagues was undone by the communal upsurge of 1947. Many eminent intellectuals had begun to critically examine various past practices. Now their sons and daughters began to sing glories of the past and began to justify all past tradition. Communal politics is a complete antidote to progressive social change. Partition in fact proved to be double blow to the process of change. In Pakistan, the newly created country, orthodox Islamists asserted themselves aggressively. Pakistan was declared to be an Islamic country immediately after the death of Mohammed Ali Jinnah who was architect of that country. Maulana Maududi, founder of the Jamaat-e-Islami in India migrated to Pakistan in the same year and launched a movement for establishing an Islamic state. Though Pakistan got a breather during presidency of Ayub Khan when moderate Islam prevailed, this era proved to be short lived and once again political turmoil took over and Pakistan itself was divided and East Bengal emerged as Bangladesh. Zulfiqar Ali Bhutto who took over from the military dictator Yahya Khan, though moderate Muslim and modernist, had to make serious compromises with Muslim orthodoxy. He declared Ahmadiyas as non-Muslims and began to enforce the Shari'a law. Finally Bhutto was hanged and Zia-ul-Haq declared Pakistan as an Islamic state and enforced Shari'a laws replacing secular laws. It was the darkest period Pakistan had to undergo thanks to political upheavals and Western and American interests. The United States used Zial-ul-Haq to pursue their political interests to defeat Soviet Union in Afghanistan and backed up Islamic militancy for which Pakistani society is paying an extremely heavy price even today.

Not only General Musharraf (the previous dictator) but even the presently elected democratic government will find it extremely difficult to bring about social change in Pakistan. Both Pakistani Military and Islamic militancy have struck deep roots in Pakistan. Continued policies of imperialist American administration in the name of "war against terrorism" will further prop up militancy and violence. Thus Pakistan is fated to live with violence and turmoil for quite sometime to come. Because of these political upheavals the basic problems of society cannot engage attention of politicians. Poverty and illiteracy among vast number of masses in Pakistan is a serious problem. No Renaissance movement can ever flourish in these social conditions. High levels of education and prosperity and sense of security are needed to promote intellectual movements in society.

Let us not forget that Europe immensely benefited from colonial exploitation and transfer of wealth from colonized countries like India. Some economists even maintain that the industrial revolution in England was financed through transfer of wealth from India. Whether it is true or not, one thing is certain, that colonizing countries achieved more economic and political stability to Europe. Today their economies are self sufficient. But this was not so until the Second World War. I am not reducing the significance of struggles which intellectuals waged in Europe to consolidate the gains of the Renaissance and progressive social change. I am only pointing out the brutal benefits of colonial exploitation which accrued to certain European countries and how it aided the process of social change. One should not try to reduce importance of that process either.

Muslims in post-partition India faced a situation worse than Muslims in Pakistan. The ruling feudal class and the middle class (which by and large emerged from these feudal families) almost entirely migrated to Pakistan and poor Muslims mainly artisans and small land holding peasantry were left in India. Muslims in India have inherited this unfortunate colonial past. Educationally and economically, Indian Muslims are far more backward today. This fact has also been very well brought out by the Sachar Committee Report. Due to economic and educational backwardness the Muslim middle class is very weak compared to the Hindu middle class, not to forget also the Sikh and Jain middle class. Hence there is hardly any possibility of progressive social movements succeeding or striking roots in the contemporary Muslim situation in India.

Muslims in India are also faced with security problems. Often communal violence breaks out further dealing economic blows to them. Muslim businesses were ruined in several riots like the ones where Muslims had achieved economic prosperity like in Meerut, Moradabad and Aligarh. The trading communities in Gujarat like Bohras, Khojas and Memons who have achieved a measure of prosperity in post-independent India were dealt a severe economic blow in the Gujarat communal carnage of 2002. Before this terrible carnage, these communities had already suffered an economic setback in post-Babri riots of 1992-93. Many families had fled to Southern states of Tamil Nadu, Kerala, etc.

Also, under communal onslaught of the rising BJP, even secular governments dither in steadily pursuing policies of economic and educational upliftment of Indian Muslims. Anytime the Congress or other government declares any intention (which may or may not be serious), the BJP immediately raises the bogey of "vote bank politics" and "appeasement of minorities". This has been going on for decades since independence. I would also like to point out that cultural factor also plays important role in strengthening or weakening the Renaissance movement. Indian culture, though feudalism is dead and gone, is still feudal and feudal traditions play a very important role among all communities of India. The caste system in India among Hindus, Sikhs and Buddhists, is quite an illustrative example of this.

Caste is becoming stronger both socially and politically and it seems it is here to stay. Even most progressive Hindus cannot escape from its vice-like grip. India has experienced economic and industrial revolution but culturally it is still under the influence of traditional semi-feudal culture dominated by the cultute of casteism. Muslims, as pointed out above, have not experienced benefits of economic revolutions. It is thus extremely sad that it will be too much to expect for any movement for progressive social change to emerge victorious.In this respect the Renaissance, not only the Muslim Renaissance, but the Indian Renaissance will always be an aborted affair.

3

Why We Must Become Muslims

Murzban Jal

It is absolutely necessary that one takes from the rich for giving to the poor, so that all become equal in wealth.

Tabarī on the Mazdakites.

Most of the inhabitants of Paradise are imbeciles. If they had not been imbeciles, how could they have been satisfied merely by Paradise and its streams?

Jalal-ud-Din Rumi.

You have thrown us to the wolves.

Khan Abdul Gaffar Khan to Gandhi.

Philosophy is required to ensure that thought can receive and accept the drama of the Event without anxiety.

Alain Badiou.

Revolutionary Politics as Marxist Dramaturgy

This chapter, which deals with the relation between Marxism and Islam, is on what is being called presently as "politics proper" in a very Marxist-Leninist sense. Logically, it follows the earlier chapter of Zaheer Ali which notes the precarious conditions of the Muslims since independence. Philosophically it argues out from a historical materialist perspective where the imperialist politics of Islamophobia are critiqued along with the communal-fascist politics of the RSS. But along these one also critiques liberal democracy in India for its totaly inability to solve the question of secularism as well as what one may call the "Muslim question".

Politics proper in this very Marxist-Leninist sense is about aesthetics: the *aesthetics of insurrection*. The question of revolution in the form of direct action, along with the questions of the revolutionary party, the dictatorship of the proletariat and the rights of people for self determination remain at the background of this chapter. This chapter is philosophical, to be precise grounded in the Marxist philosophy of praxis of Revolution. The precise nodal point is to articulate the seeking of revolutionary subject positions. It is directly antagonist to economism that Marx had critiqued as "vulgur economics" and later by Lenin especially in his *What is to be Done?* as distorted study of political economy, where political economy, especially class struggle in the realm of politics is completely obliterated. In contrast to economism is historicism and humanism that Gramsci had talked of, which argues out for a dialectical holistic method, where primacy is given to revolutionary action.

There are two parts of this chapter: one that de-colonizes what one may call after Perry Anderson as the "Indian ideology"[1]. It directly critiques the notions of the Indian "self" as articulated since the last century, an articulation that one can call the "liberal Hindu" articulation that is inexòrably bound to colonialism and imperialism. The statement: "why we should become Muslims" is not only against the fascist phantasmagoria of Hindutva where the Minister of Genocide is is now ruling the country. It is also against the idea of Hinduism, an articulation that was carried out to its logical conclusion by B.R. Ambedkar. This radical de-colonization of the idea of being 'Hindu' (governed by imperialism) takes the route as outlined by Samir Amin on the humanist theory of civilizations governed by what Amim calles the "humanist concept of universalism"[2] that starts with a confederation of ideas around 500 B.C.E. with the condensation of Persian, Babylonian, Chinese and Greek philosophies that developed Greek philosophy, alongside Buddhism, Iranian thought and Confucianism, a line of thought that culminated with the birth of Islam a little over a millennia later; which then gave way in the eleventh century C.E. to the Iranian Enlightenment with Ibn Sin, followed by the European Enlightenment and via the French Revolution finally culminating in Marxism. This historical route that we know after Gramsci as the historicist and humanist route is a necessary route to be traversed, a route that is bound essentially to the question of human freedom. Our Marxist question of being Muslim takes this route. Its main critique is Eurocentrism, to be precise the matrix of ideologies condensed as "Romania" where the earlier ideolgy of the Holy Roman Empire governed by the popes and the czars is now realized as the ideology of modern capitalism now hegemonized by the American Empire and its loyal satraps: the World Bank, the IMF, European Union and the Global Military Arms Complex. In order to understand the "Muslim question" one has to understand this mode of Eurocentric reasoning from the ancient Holy Roman Empire to the present American foreign policy.

To be a Marxist, in fact a militant Marxist, is to challenge this hegemonization. But hegemony by neo-liberal capitalism does not follow the reductionist logic of pure economism. Instead the dialectical holistic method claims that the economic base of capital accumulation in the age of late imperialism in permanent crisis is combined with the political and ideological superstructure of what we once knew as "Eurocentrism", now to be redefined as *"Euro-americo-centrism"*. We call this political and ideological superstructure of Eurocentrism and Euro-americo-centrism the speech act of the estranged mind. What this estranged mind does is that it constructs the language of alienation where Islam and Muslims are demonized. What we, in contrast to the estranged mind, do is that we understand the entire discourse of Islamophobia as sadomasochism and fetishism. Fetishism here implies a regression of thinking, not merely regression of critical thinking, but thinking as such.

The question of wanting to become Muslims is bound to this critique of estrangement and sadomasochistic fetishism as also to the logic of historicism and humanism. Yet the question of wanting to become Muslims by Marxists may seem to be rather strange, even frightening. It is to this very "strange" and "frightening" character that we turn our attention. For in the era of imperialist Islamophobia, it also creates a dialectical shock to the ruling establishment. This chapter is on the very real need of a Marxist to address this question. The response is a Marxist philosophical one. The specter of communism that is mentioned in the *Manifesto of the Communist Party* that haunts Old Europe remains central to the question of wanting to become Muslims. There are two issues central to this chapter: that of the figure of the anti-Christ and the question of evil. The specter of communism takes on the apparition of the anti-Christ. This specter is said to be the embodiment of total evil.

Taking this form of evil, the anti-Christ—this is Marx and Engels' idea in the *Manifesto of the Communist Party* where the specter of communism appears as the anti-Christ—re-articulates the idea of world revolution. "Why we must become Muslims" is a dramaturgy of the anti-Christ specter of communism haunting this time not only Old Europe, but the entire world.

Our point of departure is a form of dramaturgy that has been outlined in the *Manifesto of the Communist Party* and *Capital*. However dramaturgy does not mean drama, most certainly not what Marx and Engels called "nursery tales" (*Marchen*).[3] Instead dramaturgy is a form of a rigorous science, albeit a human natural science[4], that is at the same time philosophical. It is scientific since it accurately depicts reality. It is philosophical since the idea of free humanity stands at the basis of its episteme. And as science and philosophy it is the idea of what we know since Alain Badiou as a "logical revolt" that stands at its basis. Philosophy is no longer about praxis, it is thus not about the philosophy of praxis. Instead it is the *philosophy of revolt*. Thus wanting to be Muslims is about this revolt. The anti-Christ will take centre stage. The idea of evil will follow.

To start with a brief note: although the idea of the haunting and taunting specter of communism is our point of departure, a revolutionary understanding of Marx (and his passion for socialist, post-class society), Freud (for his concern of post-neurotic society) and Ambedkar (for an egalitarian, post-caste society) stands at the basis of this work on wanting to be Muslims. Thus the questions of class (Marx), the unconscious

(Freud) and caste (Ambedkar) stand at the centre of this work. Second, to the question: "what ails Indian Muslims?" one says that it is the coming terror of fascism along with colonialism, capitalism, imperialism and the bureaucratic liberal state that torments the Indian Muslims. And since one is presently viewing the rise of communal-fascism in India in the era of late imperialism in permanent crisis where Islamophobia and communal-fascism are inexorably bound to imperialism, one reiterates that the ailment of Muslims is inexorably bound to capitalism, colonialism and the bureaucratic liberal state.

Islam and the Ethics of Equality

To avoid being caught in some sort of platitude—after all one would say that capitalism is the bane of all humanity, then why only put Muslims as the victims of capitalism?—one will have to concretely contextualize our argument. The contextualization follows our earlier reflections: 'Asiatic Mode of Production, Caste and the Indian Left', 'Why we are not Hindus' and 'Why we can never be Hindus'[5] where we tried to identify class struggle in Asia (here we mean West and South Asia) in the larger matrix of the Asiatic mode of production. Now without being bogged down to platitudes this chapter goes into the recovery of the idea of the Indian popular classes with the suggestion that the critique of colonialism takes a route quite different from the hitherto known critiques. To be a Muslim implies the learning of West and South Asian histories that are independent of colonialism and capitalism. It also implies the learning of the politics of equality, a politics that far predates capitalism and industrial civilization. To be an authentic communist is to immerse oneself into this type of radical historization that is able to free itself from colonialism and capitalism.

This chapter on the need to be a Muslim follows, on the one hand, the line of thinking that is outlined by Peter Hudis who talks of understanding the philosophic traditions that unfolded in the non-Western world[6]. It also implies freeing oneself from the prison house of Eurocentric thought, the mode of thinking that claims that only Europe can give rational knowledge.

Eurocentrism also claims that Europe is only and solely rational, the rest of the world being condemned to irrationality. In contrast to this mode of thinking we have not Asian-centrism, but what we know after Marx as world-historical[7], where Samir Amin's humanistic theory of universalism[8] forms the contours of revolutionary historization.

There are two themes in this paper: one is the idea of humanism, equality and democracy running through the works of Marx. The other is the analysis of non-Western societies, an analysis that is not to be equated with the analysis of European history, especially not to be confused with histories emerging since the dissolution of *prior communist* societies (the so-called "primitive communist societies") or the passage of history from this dissolution via slave society, feudalism and capitalism culminating in the struggle for socialism. Whilst the first has been universally recognized, the second—namely Marx's complex understanding of diverse histories and his critique of the unilinear theory of history—is not yet fully known to the world. Presently it is the Marxist Humanist group (as expressed in the works of Peter Hudis and Kevin Anderson[9]) which is writing passionately on the theme of non-Western societies.

Whilst this chapter on wanting to be Muslims may indeed seem strange, especially when posed by a Marxist, it must also be pointed out that one is not trying to implant a normative discourse. Instead it is the Asiatic mode of production, the critique of the unilinear theory of history and the critique of Eurocentrism that remain central to this work. Whilst we have said that Asian history has a different trajectory from the European one, we are also claiming that capitalism did not naturally evolve in Asia, but was transplanted from the outside by colonialism. Being "Muslim" here is a critique of this capitalism being thrust by colonialism. It is also the critique of the Orientalist construction of the Indian "self" as the fictious Aryan-Hindu self—from William Jones and Max Müller to Wilhelm Halbfass—where the Indian is said to be the imaginary Vedic-Upanishadic Indian, the India that is devoid of its subaltern classes. Being "Muslim" here will imply a recovery of this subaltern self. In this sense this critique is not only of

Orientalism, but also Brahmanism. And since equality stands at the heart of Islam and Marxism, a brief look at Marx's response to Islam is necessary. At the outset one must note that Marx was called the "Moor" by his friends, especially by Engels.

Consider Marx's response to the idea of equality in Islam. Marx is in the last year of his life. He is in Algiers where he writes to his daughter Laura on what he calls "absolute equality" amongst Muslims, a form of equality that puts European morality to shame.[10] And it is in this site of the *ethics of equality* that that one goes into Marx's reading of Islam. Note that for Marx there cannot be a blank reading of religions, and in no way does he equate Islam with Hinduism (read Brahmanism, or for that matter with Judiasm and Christainity). Nor does one have to make a general reading of religion as opium of the people (devoid of its philosophical implications), thus debunking the particular contours of religion

There are two issues concretely bound in the argument on the marginalization and oppression of Muslims in India: one is capitalism that is the cause of this predicament, and along with it the liberal democratic state and the emergence of the religious right; the second being the question of caste and along with this question the need for the annihilation of caste and along with this annihilation, the complete eradication of the religious ideology of anti-democracy and dehumanization. In this sense it is not merely the politics of Hindutva (a form of bizarre Christendom as outlined by Savarkar in the 1920s when Mussolini and the Italian fascists had seized power), but the very ontology of Hinduism that we critique. Now those who have followed Ambedkar's writings would know that for him, caste is bound to its ideological superstructure called "Hinduism" and this religious ideology has at its basis: the principles of graded inequality and division of labourers. It is from this perspective that we state that an Ambedkarite revolution precedes a Marxist one.

Besides agreeing with the Marxist and Ambedkarite principles, we also agree with the Hegelian motif of freedom as universality and the overcoming of the self-alienation of humanity.

On the "Muslim Question"

Though the title of this chapter may seem that one intends going into a form of mere parody of the ruling course of things, it is not so. It is not a polemical work. Instead as a critique of the liberal democratic state situated within the terrain of colonialism and imperialism, it transforms the classical critique of political economy into the critique of geo-politics. We also intend to show how the traditional intellectual (in a very Gramscian sense) has not been able to evolve a radical critique of what we may call the "communal problem". Now we all know that this "communal problem" has not existed from time immemorial, but is a very concrete product of British colonialism in the Indian subcontinent. That the political culture of the balkanization of the subcontinent on communal lines and the continuing problems in this region, especially in India, Pakistan and Bangladesh yet persists; implies that this colonial problem yet exists. In this sense we shall be extremely critical of what we know as "post-colonialism". And just as we may say in a very Leninist sense that there is nothing called "post-imperialism" we similarly claim that there is nothing called "post-colonialism".

It is keeping this note of terminology in mind that we turn to what we may call the "Muslim question". As such of course there is nothing called a "Muslim question". And yet like the "Jewish question" that emerged in the early 19th century (recall Marx's 1843 *On the Jewish Question*) this question (the "Muslim question") is both a very real and a burning question. And that this Jewish question could lead firstly to Nazism, Auschwitz and the genocide, followed by the formation of Zionist Israel, the "Muslim question" takes greater importance than ordinarily imagined. And with the problem shifting from the 1857 perspective to the now Zionist inspired one, and the focus of this question being tied down so inexorably to imperialism and the American empire, makes the issue take a much greater dimension. And since this "Muslim question" is tied down to imperialism and the Military Arms Complex, there can be no innocence in the understanding of this "Muslim question".

Keeping this theme in mind one must note that for Marx's

On the Jewish Question there is a deep relation between political emancipation and human emancipation. Now this relation between political and human emancipation is something akin to the two stages of communism that Marx outlined later in the *Critique of Gotha Programme* where socialism as the so-called "lower stage" is said to be political emancipation, whilst communism as human emancipation is noted as the "higher stage" of communism. It must be stressed that because of this deep relation between these two forms of emancipation, one cannot tear one from the other. Both are essential "moments" in the revolutionary and democratic movement. It must be stressed that it is this alienating one from the other, which brings in confusion. The charge that Marx put on the Young Hegelian Bruno Bauer for this confusion seems to live on when dealing with the "Muslim question". Remember Bauer claimed that the Jews in Prussia could not demand rights as Jews. How could Jews demand rights (i.e. rights as a minority), so Bauer's reasoning went, when by and large the citizen of Prussia had no rights? For Bauer this proposal of rights of Jews in Prussia was legitimizing particular interests. Come back to the present period. Do we not hear the same theme? Do we not hear that rights of Muslims (as Muslims) is nothing but appeasement of minorities? Do we also not hear that one should have *rights for all* (i.e. rights of the abstract citizen, or in other words abstract rights), but *not rights of Muslims as Muslims*?

What we say following Marx is that the question of rights in general and the rights of minorities is etched in this dialectical theoretical problematic. What we also say is that if one removes the dialectical and historical materialist character in understanding the question of the rights of Muslims, then one lapses into a form of Islamophobia. It must be noted that Bauer after his sojourn in Hegelianism went over to the anti-Semitic camp. Bauer could not understand the concrete particular (the Jewish minority in Prussia) and thought of the abstract "man" devoid of religion and ethnicity). Bauer thus was an abstract universalist. Those in contemporary India who also talk of "man" in general, i.e. "man" independent of real living people, or those who talk of citizenship devoid of real people (like the voices heard in contemporary France) are doing nothing but mimicking this discourse of the abstract universal. What we just called "politics proper" in the Leninist sense is the understanding of the relation between the particular and the general. One cannot delink one from the other. One cannot delink the particular from the general. In this sense one must recall Marx:

> I have just been visited by the chief of the Jewish community here, who has asked me for a petition for the Jews to the Provincial Assembly, and I am willing to do it. However much I dislike the Jewish faith, Bauer's view seems to me too abstract. The thing is to make as many breaches as possible in the Christian state and to smuggle in as much as we can of what is rational. At least, it must be attempted—and the embitterment grows with every petition that is rejected with protestations.[11]

Caste, the Asiatic Mode of Production and the "Muslim Question"

This leads me to the main focus which I intend to argue out the question. I situate this question of the rights of minorities in the era of late imperialism in the paradigm of the Asiatic mode of production with caste situated as its essential social formation. How the logic of caste stratification also spills into the site that strictly is not under the auspicies of caste is something that needs being seen. Thus what one needs to see is how caste startfication, where the division of people into four *varnas* governed by the totem of purity and the taboo of pollution and determined by the principle of graded inequality; now transgress itself into the domain of religious communities. Thus one needs to see how the high (Brahman)/low (Shudra) binary is now transformed as the innocent (Hindu)/terrorist (Muslim) binary. The Brahmanical totem of purity and the taboo of pollution are retained where the Muslims are relegated as the polluted "hellish other" who are out to harass the 'pure' Hindus. It must be noted that Savarkar in his *Essentials of Hindutva* perfected this macabre technique of transplanting the logic of caste-stratification into the colonial sponsored politics of the Hindu/ Muslim opposition. What he does is transforms the Brahman/

Shudra oppostition into the imagined opposition: "Aryan-Hindu" who is perpetually harassed by the even more imagined "Semitic-Muslims". The precarious place of Muslims in India is because of the combination of the logic of caste-stratification with the colonial invention of the Aryans as the superiour people. Hindu supremacy that the RSS now practises is born out of these two parents: caste and colonialism.

A small note on the historical materialist methodology is now necessary in order to understand the place of Muslims in the Indian variant of the Asiatic mode of production with caste as the basis of this mode of production. We begin with what Marx called caste as "the solid foundation of Asiatic despotism and stagnation"[12]. It must be noted here that when Marx is talking of the Asiatic mode of production, he is not to be understood a Eurocentric thinker in formulating the idea of the Asiatic mode and the oriental despot. Clearly Edward Said was wrong when he classified Marx as a Eurocentric thinker. But not only is Said wrong. Thinkers like Irfan Habib have also made the same mistake.[13]

What Marx said was that European history could not be transplanted onto the whole world[14], that feudalism was not universal and that after the dissolutions of prior communist societies diverse class formations took place. One has to thus take cognizance of these diverse social formations. In contrast to West European history that traversed through slave, feudal and capitalist societies, Asia witnessed other formations. Though Marx christened these as the "Asiatic mode", and also since he operated through what seems like "borrowed categories", it must be recognized that he did not mean the same as was said by Jean Bodin and Machiavelli, and most certainly not what Aristotle said on Persia. Marx did not use normative categories, but intended to have accurate descriptions of societies.

What we now say is that caste would take the forms of community (*Gemeinschaft*) and class, but would be governed by the logic of anti-humanism and also by the cultural politics of purity and pollution. But it would not merely imply this very strange form of class (enclosed and ossified class). It would also take the forms of (1) race (remember that caste as *varna* implies "colour" and thus stratification according to colour-racial lines) and (2) neurosis-psychosis. Remember when Marx claims that castes are those peculiar social structures that "when accidentally destroyed, spring up again on the spot and with the same name" and that they remain "untouched by the storm clouds of the political sky"[15], he is implying a neurosis within this terrain, where caste (like neurosis) eternally recurs. Just as for the neurotic, the trauma is cured only for it to return once again, the tragedy is that for Indian history, caste is negated only to be posited once again. Caste thus decomposes, only in order that it is recomposed.

Thus when we are talking of caste as neurosis, we mean this process of decomposition-recomposition. And when we claim that caste is psychotic, we imply that like the classical definition of psychosis as the "withdrawal from reality", caste also implies a complete negation of reality. Thus when Ambedkar said that Hinduism is a system where people become like rats living in their hellish holes refusing to have contact with one another, except when rioting with Muslims[16], he implies this psychotic practice of Hinduism.

Here what we have done is gone against the reading of those who chose to claim that Marx followed the old logic of classifying non-Western societies as societies devoid of history. Instead what we have done is claimed that a form of neurosis exists in caste that despite the massive changes taking place all over the world, caste as a dominant social structure remains (albeit in metamorphosized forms). What Freud called the "neurotic compulsion to repeat" now proceeds into the logic of caste. Caste thus is not only tied down to the Indian guild system where the Indian form of the unity of manufacture and agriculture took place, but something more. What then is this something more and how would this surplus come into the question of understanding the "Muslim question"?

Since caste as stratification of society by the totems of *varna* and *jati* imply an "alienating cutting people from one another" dominated by an Asian form of race classification, then the theme of alienation that the young Marx talked of would come into the scene of action.

The Pyramid Model of Imperialism and the Estrangement Effect

What we now do is bring in the question of alienation into the domains of the Asiatic mode of production, caste and the "Muslim question". We now talk of the estrangement effect. Now we know that it was Bertolt Brecht who had talked of the theatrics of the estrangement effect. He also claimed that the estrangement effect replaced Aristotle's idea of catharsis. Whilst alienation implies the loss of the self as also the loss of human reality, it also signifies a sense of hostility and feeling of a form of narcissistic power emerging. The estrangement effect critiques and negates this form of estrangement.

If caste as the alienated cutting of one human from the other is the national form of alienation, colonialism and imperialism is its other half. To consider this question of becoming Muslim and the question of the estrangement effect, consider the model of imperialism where the sense of creating fear and the sense of the anti-Christ specter is seen confronting imperialism. Now one knows that the social models of Islam and Christianity are radically different in the sense that the latter is based on the pyramid model, whilst the very idea of the pharaoh is seen as a class enemy by the former.

Consider now the model of imperialism that is based on the pyramid model. One will recall Johann Galtung in this regard. Now for Galtung, the USA though claiming to be a democratic republic, is basically an Empire. According to him (following the Leninist analysis of imperialism) the central aspect of American foreign policy is its expansionist mode. Being centrifugal in mode the American Empire divides the world into two regions: the centre and the periphery. A part of the periphery, the American Empire hopes to occupy by being accepted with consent and other part, or "the margin" which rejects the center and labelled as *"Evil"* has to be destroyed. The theory of the "clash of civilizations" is inherent in the mode of production and foreign policy of the American Empire. According to American state ideology people are not merely things, but *manipulable things* to be ruled over. Instead of the concept of the democratic self, Freud's architecture of psychosis and the theme of the authoritarian personality that Theodor Adorno had highlighted are inserted in the understanding of imperialism and the American Empire. Not only does the authoritarian personality fit in the violent nature of imperialism and the corresponding model of the Yankee person, but also the ideas of neurosis and psychosis fit in this model of imperialism. This American 'Man' in the imperialist celebration of the will to power rules nature and other people. 'He' is on top of the pyramid of life. The Ego is on top of the pyramid architecture of the self, the Elites are on top of society, the Occident is on top of the world. And look at this Occident 'man'and you will find the US marine. Look again at this marine and you will find the Islamophobic imperialist.

Now relate this model of Muslim hating imperialism. Go now to Ambedkar and his critique of Hinduism and relate the theory of alienation where the cutting off one human from another is seen as the totem of Indian society. Move to Galtungean model as see how this alienation takes a more brutal form. But to counter this, we do not deal with catharsis where human emotions are purged off. Instead one is involved in the estrangement effect where the chapter of the metamorphosis of commodities in *Capital* is retranscribed in a revolutionary form. Recall *Capital* where we see how under capitalism we have a *new father of the people, who changes his features, hair and many things besides.*[17] Likewise the political elites are involved in these changes in features, hair and many things besides. It is this alienation that metamorphosizes people into violent things and destructive machines. The estrangement effect has to deal with this brutal from of alienation.

What we have thus is a counter-metamorphosis. In *Capital* Marx notes how humanity losses its humanity in order to produce commodities. The human then itself becomes a commodity. What the estrangement effect does is that it reverses this process of dehumanization. If the imperialists "anxiously conjure up the spirits of the past" (as Marx in the *Eighteenth Brumaire of Louis Bonaparte* once put it), i.e. sprits of the Crusades, etc. "to their service and borrowing from them names, battle slogans, and costumes in order to present this new scene in world history in time-honored disguise and borrowed language"[18]; the revolutionary does not give some sort of rationalist response to this form of bourgeois phantasmagoria.

The revolutionary now gets into this mist of this phantasmagoria without being fooled by it. They get involved in this estrangement effect. One does not get involved in what Marx calls "the language of commodities".[19] Instead it is the historization and humanization that we need to deal with. And with this historicism and humanism, one moves from the language of commodities to the language of people.

Islam and Social Democracy

What historicism and humanism does as a rigorous science is that it seeks solid foundations and firm beginnings. Thus one says that unlike certain sociological theories made most fashionable in Western universities (mostly to counter Revolutionary Marxism) like postmodernity, Marxism seeks origins. And it is in this seeking of origins that we are able to move from the theological rendering of Islam into the terrain of Islamic anthropology. What we firstly do is that we are able to remove the mist of the phantasmagoria of the interpretation of Islam as violent and bent on imaginary terrorist activity. Consider this historical materialist study of the origin of Islam:

> The absence of landed property is indeed the key to the whole of the East. Therein lies its political and religious history. But how to explain the fact that Orientals never reached the stage of landed property, not even the feudal kind? This is, I think, largely due to the climate, combined with the nature of the land, more especially the great stretches of desert extending from the Sahara right across Arabia, Persia, India and Tartary to the highest of the Asiatic uplands. Here artificial irrigation is the first prerequisite for agriculture, and this is the responsibility either of the communes, the provinces or the central government. In the East, the government has always consisted of 3 departments only: Finance (pillage at home), War (pillage at home and abroad), and *travaux publics*, provision for reproduction. The British government in India has put a somewhat narrower interpretation on nos. 1 and 2 while completely neglecting no. 3, so that Indian agriculture is going to wrack and ruin. Free competition is proving an absolute

fiasco there. The fact that the land was made fertile by artificial means and immediately ceased to be so when the conduits fell into disrepair, explains the otherwise curious circumstance that vast expanses are now wastes which once were magnificently cultivated (Palmyra, Petra, the ruins in the Yemen, any number of localities in Egypt, Persia, Hindustan); it explains the fact that one single war of devastation could depopulate and entirely strip a country of its civilization for centuries to come. This, I believe, also accounts for the destruction of southern Arabian trade before Mohammed's time, a circumstance very rightly regarded by you as one of the mainsprings of the Mohammedan revolution. I am not sufficiently well acquainted with the history of trade during the first six centuries C.E. to be able to judge to what extent general material conditions in the world made the trade route via Persia to the Black Sea and to Syria and Asia Minor via the Persian Gulf preferable to the Red Sea route. But one significant factor, at any rate, must have been the relative safety of the caravans in the well-ordered Persian Empire under the Sassanids, whereas between 200 and 600 C.E. the Yemen was almost continuously being subjugated, overrun and pillaged by the Abyssinians. By the 7th century the cities of southern Arabia, still flourishing in Roman times, had become a veritable wilderness of ruins; in the course of 500 years what were purely mythical, legendary traditions regarding their origin had been appropriated by the neighbouring Bedouins, (cf. the *Quran* and the Arab historian Novairi), and the alphabet in which the local inscriptions had been written was almost wholly unknown although *there was no other*, so that *de facto* writing had fallen into oblivion. Things of this kind presuppose, not only a superseding, probably due to general trading conditions, but outright violent destruction such as could only be explained by the Ethiopian invasion. The expulsion of the Abyssinians did not take place until about 40 years before Mohammed, and was plainly the first act of the Arabs' awakening national consciousness, which was further aroused by Persian invasions from the North penetrating almost as far as Mecca. I shall not be tackling the history of Mohammed himself for a few days yet; so far it seems to me to have the character of a Bedouin reaction against the settled, albeit decadent urban fellaheen whose religion by then was also much debased, combining as it did a degenerate form of nature worship with a degenerate form of Judaism and Christianity.[20]

So there is a deeper structure which the historization and humanization of society and religion discovers. This historization and humanization deals with history from an altogether different way than the known idealist and vulgar materialist ways. Instead of the phantasmagorical method, this historical materialist method transforms questions of religion into questions of class struggle. With this post-phantasmagorical method we link early Islam with the Mazdakite movement which broke out sometime in late 5th century C.E. in the Persian Empire. Not much has been said of this movement. That this was a communist movement in the era of classical antiquity (where the abolishing of private property and the family system was said to be its leitmotiv) has to be noted. Even less has been reflected on it, especially in relation to the formation of Islam. It were basically Revolutionary Islamic scholars like Iqbal who brought out the importance of understanding this movement, as also brought out the importance of understanding Marxism for the Muslim world. On the other hand it were European scholars in the 20th century who reflected on this movement from T. Nöldeke, E.G. Browne, A. Christensen and O.G. Wesendonk to G.H. Sadighi, O. Klima and N. Pigulevskaya. The most recent work on the communist Mazdakite movement and its relation to Islam has been studied by Ehsan Yarshater. What Marx called "absolute equality"[21]—unlike Hinduism's "absolute inequality", or "schizophrenic inequality"—is located in this encounter.

What follows is not only what Yarshater calls the study of the survival of Mazdakite doctrines among a number of sects, mostly of "the Islam'īlī tendency, which sprang up after Abu Muslim's murder, and drew parallels between some Mazdakite doctrines and those of the Druze of Lebanon"[22], but also a site discovered from the historicist and humanist perspective. One aspect of understanding the relation between Mazdikism and Islam is that it questions the pigeonholing of Islam as purely Semitic and theological, totally alienated from world history. Our claim of the need of "becoming Muslim" is sketched in this subaltern version of history. In this subaltern rendering of history, the figures of Abu Muslim (the celebrated Abbasid general and member of the Mazdakites) and Ishaq the Turk appear as the vanguard fighters against authoritarianism.

Here we involve a paradigm shift in Marx's understanding of non-Western societies. It is debatable whether Marx was once influenced by a certain form of universal theory of history where Europe (albeit Revolutionary Europe) was seen as the theater of action of world history, where the rest of the world had to faithfully follow. On the other hand more serious reading, following Raya Dunayevskaya claimed that there was an epistemic break between Marx and Engels with relation to the understanding of so-called "primitive societies". In this sense one would have to critique Engels' *The Origin of the Family, Private Property and the State* where a certain form of unilinear history was chalked out where Asian history (along with pre-colonized American and African histories) was not studied adequately. Instead one would have to turn attention to Marx's *Ethnological Notebooks* and the works of the Marxist Humanists to understand Islam in a much more enlightened manner. Take the reading of Peter Hudis:

> Marx's "Notes on Kovalevsky", like many of his writings on non-European societies in his last decade, is a series of notes, not a finished project, and it is difficult to draw generalizations about his views of Islamic society from it. But several things should be clear from our discussion.
>
> First, by the 1870s (and most likely as early as the mid-1850s) Marx did not view imperialist intrusion into the technologically underdeveloped world as "progressive." He instead viewed the imperialist destructive of precapitalist social formations as being *regressive*. In the *Grundrisse* (1853) Marx warned against "the concept of progress in the commonplace (abstract) sense." Earlier, in *The Holy Family* (1845), he wrote: "In spite of the pretensions of 'progress', continuous retrogressions and circular movements occur....the category of progress is wholly abstract and devoid of content." And in his *Economic-Philosophic Manuscripts of 1844* he wrote: "ask yourself whether, for reasonable thought, progression exists as such." In his last decade (1872-83) Marx *concretized* this viewpoint in projecting an intensifying opposition to the notion that imperialism was in any sense historically "progressive." As he wrote in his "Draft Letters to Vera Zasulich" on developments

> in the East Indies, "the suppression of communal land ownership[23] was nothing but an act of English vandalism which drove the indigenous population backward rather than forward." Second, instead of viewing such native communal formations as "backward," Marx embraced such communal forms, albeit critically, in viewing them as a possible basis for creating a socialist society without going through capitalist industrialization.[24]

One important way of articulating this "Muslim question" in a materialist manner is to state the multilinear character of history, which emphasizes that history is not a linear movement towards one direction. Instead the Revolutionary Marxist point of view claims that after the collapse of prior communism (the so-called "primitive communism"), history did not witness only the European version of slave society, but the emergence of multiple modes of production. It must be noted that neither were slave society nor feudalism universal. 'Universality' existed only with prior communist societies; however universality that itself was extremely diverse. It was capitalism that created a new form of universalism with its gigantic productive forces. Universalism of the capitalist type was one where markets that emerged with industrial civilization connected people through this form of "marketized universe". But this universality became a *reified universality* where it converted the poet and the scientist into wage-laboureres.[25] What one needs to do is to critique this form of reified universality, a form of universality where real people and real history are perpetually absent.

The 'turn' to the history of Islam as social democracy will be a 'turn' towards the understanding of history in its authenticity.

Authenticity, Humanism and History

"What, "one may ask", are the necessary components of Islam?" Now we know that the main answer follows the logic of theological hermeneutics where the idea of a unified God and the call for prayer are stated to be its essence. But this claim is a mere theological claim, a claim that one could call a theoretical anti-humanist claim, where humanity is totally erased from the discourse of Islam. One then forgets Ludwig Feuerbach's philosophy of the secret of theology being anthropology and also the claim that God is nothing but estranged humanity.

One must, in contrast to this theoretical anti-humanism (we know that this term is that of Louis Althusser), claim a humanism inherent to world humanism. First, one must turn to the main question; "What are the two essential components of Islam?" The answer is that like Marxism the central motifs are class struggle—in Islam the struggle between the oppressed (*Mostazafan*) and the oppressor (*Mostakharan*)—and humanism. Note in the Sura: 'The Cow' how the angels bowed down before Adam (the first human).[26] Adam in Hebrew means "human" and the Sura states that even the angels bowed down to this "First Human". One thing is clear from this rendering: that world humanism is inherent in Islam.

What we need to do is to retrieve this humanist rendering of Islam. It is important to locate this humanism that went from al-Farabi and Ibn Sina (Avicena) to Europe. Now what we do not know is that the European Renaissance went via the Islamic world to Florence. The Eurocentric model forgets Ibn Sina especially his *The Book of Healing* (1020 C.E.)—that articulates astronomy, chemistry, paleontology, meteorology, mineralogy, music, logic, metaphysics and psychology—forgets Omar Khayyam's *Treatise on Demonstration of Problems of Algebra* (1070 C.E.), forgets that it was this text that was transmitted to Europe from Iran, as also conveniently forgets Khayyam's *On the Difficulties of Euclid's Definitions* (1077 C.E.). For Eurocentrism there is no world beyond Europe. There is no al-Ghazzali for them, no great Iranian Renaissance that far pre-dates the European one. There can be no Kalidasa, no Jalāl ad-Dīn Rūmī (1207-1273). Eurocentrism forgets that even Greek philosophy did not originate in its European cranium that was totally independent of the Asians. After all, why did the Greeks themselves mention ancient Iranian thought as did Theopompous's *On Miraculous Things*, Hermippus's *On the Magis*, Plato in the *Alcibiades* and Aristotle in the now lost *Peri Philosophia*? Why then is modern Western thought silent on these issues? Peter Hudis (in contrast to modern Western thought) reminds us that Rene Descartes was influenced by al-Ghazzali and that Hegel in his *Phenomenology of Mind* incorporated Rūmī.[27] Hudis also mentions how dialectical-negative thinking that was perfected by Hegel and Marx was articulated as far back as the 10th century C.E. by the Iranian thinker Abu Ya'qub al-Sijstani.[28]

What happens is a complex of ideas connecting Asia Minor with Europe, on the one hand, and the Indian subcontinent, on the other hand. Samir Amin's idea of humanistic universalism (that we pointed out earlier) and the relation between the three waves of this unfolding of universalism fits in here where Zarathushtra, the Buddha, Plato, Aristotle, Plotinus, Mohammed, Ibn Sina, al-Ghazzali and al-Sijistani form the components in the production of universal humanism. And therefore we stress that European Enlightenment did not emerge from its own isolated cranium, but in dialogue with Islam. Further it must be noted that if one locates the comings of European Enlightenment and its philosophy of humanism via the Islamic route, one must also note that the state foundations built by Akbar went through the lineages of the Iranian school of the Illuminationists (*Ishraqis*) to Abu'l-Fazl, the celebrated philosopher-advisor of Akbar. The Illuminationist school was founded by the legendary Kurdish mystic Suhrawardī (Shahāb ad-Dīn" Yahya ibn Habash as-Suhrawardī: 1155-1191 C.E.) who founded his theory of philosophical illumination built on the teachings of Zarathushtra, Plato and Mohammed. And it is this historicist and humanist genealogy that is missed out in present times; times that only want to build their ideologies according to their alienated and uncanny imagination.

Whilst the role of Akbar has been recorded as laying the foundation stones of secularism in India (Amartya Sen presently points this out), the role of the subaltern philosophers who came from Iran and settled in India is not so well known (Amartya Sen misses out this point).[29] One must point out the role of the legendary (but now forgotten) Azar Kaivan a Persian mystic (allegedly of the Sipasian sect according to the *Dasatir* a Persian work of confused origins) with distinct Zoroastrian, Hindu and Muslim ideas who came from Iran and resided in North India (Patna) in the times of Akbar the Great. Azar Kaivan was one of the contributors to the foundation of humanist, secularist and composite cultural ideologies in India. This secularism that emerged in Akbar's times was a secularism that is slightly different from the West European one that emerged in the times of the anti-feudal revolutions. The Ishraqi philosophers from Shiraz and Ishafan in Iran who combined Zoroastrianism and Platonism with Aristotle and Islam were the living link between Iran and India, especially after they migrated to Gujarat in early 16th century. Mir Siyyid Rafi'u'din Safavi (the spiritual guide to the Lodhi, Moghul and the Sur dynasties), Khatib Abu'l Fazl Kazaruni and Sheikh Mubarak the father of Abu'l-Fazl (the court philosopher of Akbar the Great) were some of the Ishraqi philosophers in India.

That the underground stream connecting West Asia over the centuries with India remains a strong motif binding subaltern cultures from West Asia to India, as well as being the least known, is an irony. It must be noted that Akbar's idea of *Dîn* as the Sufi practice of *Suhl-i-Kuhl* or Universal Peace that abolished the legal difference between the Muslim and non-Muslim, which bound the entire court to the emperor, as well as the enabled an egalitarian spirit in the masses, had distinct Persian echoes. The Mughal emperor who took on the role of the spiritual guide like the ancient Iranian "king of the kings" (*Shāhān Shāh*) was said to stand above all distinctions. The Mughal theory of the royal court was a replica of the Sasanian court—Akbar becomes a righteous king like Khausrau I (531-579 C.E.), and was thus, a righteous king, as well as world philosopher and collector of world knowledge. This king-regent relation in Mughal India was not only the revival of the Sasanian policy, but the ancient Iranian system itself, since at least Jamshid (or Yima, the Indian Yama), the legendary king-prophet, who ironically hastened not only the fall from grace of not only himself and Iran, but the entire world for refusing to play the role of prophet conferred to him by God. If the theme of king as regent connected Iran with Mughal India, then the theme of the fallen hero formed the crux of Iranian civilization connecting Iran with India. The imperialist idea that Islam cannot secularize and that Islamic state is necessarily anti-secular, forgets that the origins of the theological state go back to pre-Islamic times wherein is stated the state doctrine of the Iranian Shāhān Shāh. The religion then of Iran was Zoroastrianism. The following is the main motif of the Sasanian state policy from whence the ideology of anti-secularism emerged:

> Know that kingship and religion are twin brothers, no one of which can be maintained without the other. For religion is the foundation of the state, and the state is the guardian of religion. The state cannot subsist without its foundation, and religion cannot exist without its guardian. For that which has no guardian is lost, and that which has no foundation crumbles.....Know that there can never be in one kingdom both a secret chief in religion and a manifest chief in kingship without the chief in religion snatching away that which is in the hands of the chief in kingship. For religion is the foundation and kingship is the pillar, and the possessor of the foundation has more claim to the whole building than the possessor of the pillar.[30]

What I am trying to state is that origins are always overdetermined and rooted in political economies and state policies. They do not originate in religions. We of course forget this form of complex historiography and world philosophizing emanating thereon for the bourgeois mapping out of monistic and unilinear consciousness. We know that Georg Lukács in his *History and Class Consciousness* had called this the *reification of consciousness*. The incorrect formulation posed by Eurocentrism is based on the false unilinear theory of history that locates Islam only at the level of feudalism (this is totally incorrect) and also claims that just as Christianity in Europe was sublated for secularism, so too Islam has necessarily to go through the same path. Paths are of course complex. Besides Islam has its roots in the Mazdakite movement and not in feudalism. And just as Slavoj Žižek had once stated that one needs to rescue Christianity from the Christian fundamentalist[31], one needs to do the same with Islam. In missing out this very complex relation between diverse philosophies and cultures (determined however by a form of unconditional humanism), we relapse into not merely the forgetfulness of our humanity, but we also forget that great cultures are always dialogical. Note one form of tragedy when we forget dialogical cultures:

> Two important religions and cultures meet....in confrontation, without any conscious intention to learn from one another and to evolve a common community having a vision for a common future.[32]

And in this forgetfulness of dialogical cultures determined by colonialism—after all did not the colonial ideologists James Mill and Thomas Macaulay chide Asian civilization as inferior to the European one having no value at all—we also forget the composite culture shared in the Indian subcontinent. One needs thus:

> An immense effort for self-transcendence on the part of both the communities alone could help them evolve into a common human community.[33]

To understand how modern secularism emerged in India, one needs to point out this tremendous role of the Ishraqis, Amir Khusrau, Kabir, Ravi Das, Shah Abdul Bhatai, Waris Shah and Bulleh Shah. The contemporary idea of tolerance cannot be understood without this great philosophic, poetic and humanist genealogy. Secularism did not emerge, as if magically, from the cranium of the European colonialists who with the burden of civilizing the whole of Asia thrust secular values onto Asia. Nor did secularism emerge from the self-proclaimed ingenious minds of the Brahmans. There is another route that one must explore and it is Islam in South Asia that gives us this clue.

Paradise Lost

Yet because of the formation of the modern Indian and Pakistani states, and because of the torment of partition and the massacre of innocent people, humanism could only be lost. The will to life and struggle would give way to the will to colonial submission. In an 1888 poem 'Shikwa-e-Hind', Altaf Hussain Hali talks of Muslims as "homeless guests" who stayed in the "autumnless garden" called Hindustan. He mentions how India treated strangers like relations, giving them hospitality, wealth, government and dominion. And yet:

> You've turned lions into lowly beings, O Hind
> Those who were Afghan hunters came here to become hunted ones

> We had foreseen all these misfortunes
> When we came here leaving our country and friends
>
> We were convinced that adversity would befall us in time
> And we O Hind would be devoured by you
>
> So long as O Hindustan we were not called Hindi
> We had some graces which were not found in others
>
> You've made our condition frightening
> We were fire O Hind, you've turned us into ashes.[34]

Ayesha Jalal claims that the sentiments of the poet Hali represents two contradictory positions: one is the elitist *ashraf's* nostalgia based on a "questionable reading of the history of Islam in the subcontinent" and the other is the "spurious representations of Indian Muslims" (that they are all descendants of Afghans). But there is also an essential truth in the above poetic lament (the impact of the upper-caste Hindu elites on what Jalal calls "the dilemma of Muslim identity"[35]). Despite this contradictory perception, the lament of a lost paradise fits well into the condition of the post-partition Muslims in the Indian subcontinent.

For understanding this let us turn to the introduction to Alam Khundmiri's, *Secularism, Islam and Modernity,* where one may talk of the "sandwiching effect" that affected Muslims.[36] What happened to the Indian Muslim consciousness is that became a sort of "rem(a)inder of certain historical process", almost a form of "leftover" that had a "residual presence and a repository of irrationality in the body-politic of the Indian nation".[37] And in this imagery of being "caught in the crossfire"[38], they became the existentialist hellish other. Muslims could never be a part of the rational theory of citizenship. As the hellish other they became an unnecessary burden to bear.

To counter this myth of burden and the image of hell, a production of critical subjectivity is necessary, a point that the liberal variation of secularism in India could not do. What liberal secularism did was that it merely separated religion and state power, without questioning both religion (especially Brahmanism) and state power. The project of the historicist and humanist understanding of secularism was simply not accomplished. But then the historicist and humanist understanding of history was also not accomplished.

Marxism had to encounter Islam, just as Islam had to encounter Marxism. Both had to search for humanity and the proletariat to realize their philosophic dreams. Both had to abolish capital and private property. It is unfortunate that like the two souls in the breast of Faust, Islam and Marxism could never meet. With the patriarchal and feudal interpretations of Islam (best exemplified by Hassan-al Banna, Sayyid Maududi and Ayatollah Khomeini) and with the Stalinist counter-revolution that created a duplicate Marxism (Marxism devoid of Marx, Revolution devoid of Revolution), the revolutionary soul of world history could only be torn apart. And with the tearing off the soul of Faust, the international proletariat and Islam's idea of "absolute equality" (alongside Faust) had to be condemned to hell. Yet even in hell there had to be revolutionary defiance. For in this condemnation to hell, one is also condemned to read the following verse pasted on the gates of hell:

> *Here all distrust must be left;*
> *All cowardice must here be dead.*[39]

REFRENCES

1. Perry Anderson, *The Indian Ideology* (Gurgoan: Three Essays Collective, 2012).
2. Samir Amin, *Capitalism in the Age of Globalization. The Management of Contemporary Society* (Delhi: Madhyam Books, 1997), pp. 80-1
3. Karl Marx and Frederick Engels, 'Manifesto of the Communist Party', in *Marx. Engels. Selected Works* (Moscow: Progress Publishers, 1975), p. 35.
4. Karl Marx, *Economic and Philosophic Manuscripts of 1844* (Moscow: Progress Publishers, 1982), p. 99.
5. See 'Why we are not Hindus. A Reply to the Indian Fascists', *Mainstream*, Vol. LII, No. 1, December 28, 2013, 'Why we can never be Hindus. The Struggle against Fascism in India', in *Mainstream*, Vol. LII, No. 18, April 26, 2014, 'Asiatic Mode of Production, Caste and the Indian Left', in *Economic and Political Weekly*, Vol. XLIX, No. 19, May 10, 2014 and 'Hindutva, the Asiatic Mode of Production and the Indian Revolution',

Mainstream, Vol. LII, No. 34, August 16, 2014. See also my *The New Militants* (Delhi: Aakar Books, 2014).

6. Peter Hudis, 'Marx among the Muslims', in *Capitalism, Nature, Socialism*, December 2004, 15, 4.
7. Karl Marx and Frederick Engels, *The German Ideology* (Moscow: Progress Publishers, 1976), p. 54.
8. Samir Amin, *Capitalism in the Age of Globalization, The Management of Contemporary Society*, p. 80.
9. Kevin Anderson, *Marx at the Margins. On Nationalism, Ethnicity and Non-western Societies* (Chicago & London: The University of Chicago Press, 2010).
10. Karl Marx, 'To Lara Lafargue, April 13 and 14, 1882', in *Marx. Engels. Collected Works*, Vol. 46 (New York: International Publishers, 1992), pp. 54, 57.
11. Karl Marx, 'To Arnold Ruge in Dresden, Cologne, March 13, 1843', in *Marx. Engels. Collected Works*, Vol. 1 (Moscow: Progress Publishers, 1975), p. 400.
12. Karl Marx, 'To Frederick Engels in Manchester, London, June 14, 1853', in *Selected Correspondence* (Moscow: Progress Publishers, 1975), p. 80. See my *The New Militants* (Delhi: Aakar Books, 2014).
13. Irfan Habib is wrong in dismissing Marx's idea of the Asiatic mode of production as a remnant of Eurocentirc-Hegelian thinking. Note what he claims: Marx's idea of the element of the "unchanging" in the Asiatic mode was *unjust*, and that Marx's idea of the village community was "highly idealized". See Irfan Habib, *Essays in Indian History. Towards a Marxist Perception* (New Delhi: Tulika Books, 1997), pp. 35, 234. Also see his introduction to Marx's articles on India: 'Introduction: Marx's Perception of India', in *Karl Marx on India. From the New York Daily Tribune* (New Delhi: Tulika Books, 2006). See my *The Seductions of Karl Marx* (Delhi: Aakar Books, 2010).
14. See Karl Marx, 'To the Editorial Board of the *Otechestvenniye Zapiski*', in *Selected Correspondence* (Moscow: Progress Publishers, 1975), pp. 291-5.
15. Karl Marx, *Capital*, Vol. I (Moscow: Progress Publishers, 1983), p. 338-9.
16. B.R. Ambedkar, 'Annihilation of Caste', in *The Essential Writings of B.R. Ambedkar*, ed. Valerian Rodrigues (New Delhi: Oxford University Press, 2008), p. 267.
17. See Karl Marx, *Capital*, Vol. I, p. 58.
18. Karl Marx, 'The Eighteenth Brumaire of Louis Bonaparte', in

Marx. Engels Selected Works (Moscow: Selected Works, 1975), p. 96.

19. See Karl Marx, *Capital*, Vol. I, p. 58.
20. Frederick Engels, 'To Karl Marx in London, Manchester, June 6, 1853', in *Marx. Engels. Collected Works*, Vol. 39 (Moscow: Progress Publishers, 1983), pp. 335-6.
21. Karl Marx, 'To Lara Lafargue, April 13 and 14, 1882', in *Marx. Engels Collected Works*, Vol. 46.
22. Ehsan Yarshater, 'Mazdakism', in *Cambridge History of Iran, Vol. 3 (2). The Seleucid, Parthian and Sasanian Periods*, ed. Ehsan Yarshater (Cambridge: Cambridge University Press, 1986), p. 991.
23. "Communal" here is not to be confused with the South Asian version of the same term. By "communal", Marx means "social collective", or societies which are community based.
24. Peter Hudis, 'Marx among Muslims', in *Capitalism, Nature, Socialism*, December, 2004, 15,4, pp. 64-5.
25. See Karl Marx and Frederick Engels, 'Manifesto of the Communist Party', in *Marx. Engels. Selected Works*, p. 38.
26. See *The Quran*, trans. T.B. Irving (Tehran: Chap & Nashr, 2005).
27. Peter Hudis, op. cit., p. 53. Also see Catherine Wilson, 'Modern Western Philosophy', in Seyeed Hossein Nasr and Oliver Leaman, eds., *History of Islamic Philosophy* (London: Routledge, 2001).
28. Ibid., pp. 53-4.
29. See Amartya Sen, *The Argumentative Indian. Writings on Indian Culture, History and Identity* (London: Penguin, 2005), pp. 18-9. Though Sen does mention Amir Khausrau's role in the creation of composite culture, the very complex-dialectical relation between Indian and West Asia in the creation of this composite culture is left out.
30. *Ahd Ardaīr*, ed I. Abbas, Beirut, 1967. See also *The Letter of Tansar*, trans. Mary Boyce and the fourth volume of the encyclopaedic *Dīnkard* which narrates the history of the identity of religion and the state in Zoroastrian Iran. Also see 'The Instruments of Religion', in Shaul Shaked, *Dualism in Transformation. Varieties of Religion in Sasanian Iran* (London: School of Oriental and African Studies, 1994), pp. 99-131.
31. Slavoj Žižek, *The Fragile Absolute: Or, why is the Christian Legacy Worth Fighting For?* (London: Verso, 2011).
32. Alam Khundmiri, *Secularism, Islam and Modernity* (New Delhi: Sage Publications, 2001), p. 275.
33. Ibid.

34. Altaf Hussain Hali, 'Shikwa-e-Hind', quoted in Ayesha Jalal, 'Exploding Communalism: The Politics of Muslim Identity in South Asia', in *Nationalism, Democracy & Development. State and Politics in India*, eds. Sugata Bose and Ayesha Jalal ((New Delhi: Oxford University Press, 2012), pp. 76-7.
35. Ayesha Jalal, 'Exploding Communalism: The Politics of Muslim Identity in South Asia', in Ibid., p. 77
36. See M.T. Ansari, 'Introduction: In the Interstices of an Indian Islamic Identity', in Alam Khundmiri, *Secularism, Islam and Modernity*, p. 12.
37. Ibid., p. 16.
38. Ibid.
39. See Karl Marx, 'Preface', *A Contribution to the Critique of Political Economy* (Moscow: Progress Publishers, 1978), p. 23. Marx is quoting Dante.

4

Indian Muslims: Socio-economic Conditions, Political Mobilization and Emerging New Challenges

Irfan Engineer

According to the census carried out in the year 2001, Muslims are the largest minority group in India forming about 13.4 per cent of the total population in India and numbered about 138 million. According to an estimate, by the year 2007, there might be 150 million Muslims in India. India has second largest population of Muslims, next only to Indonesia. There are 930 Muslim women for every 1000 Muslim men.

Socio-Economic Background of Indian Muslims

A vast majority of members of the Muslim community in South Asia was, for various historical reasons, socio-economically backward. Muslims revolted against the British colonial authorities even before what is recorded as the First War of Independence in the year 1857. The Wahabi and the Farizi Movements with significant participation from the Muslims had challenged the colonial rule declaring India as Darul Harb (inimical abode for Muslims) and calling upon Muslims to engage in jihad against colonial rule. Later, Muslims were particularly targeted by the colonial state. Bahadur Shah Zafar, the Mughal Emperor had become the rallying point during the 1857 Rebellion. After the failure of the Rebellion, Muslims became prime targets for the Britishers. From the days of the

Wahabi and Faraizi movements, Muslims had shunned colonial education and consequent modern English education. The feudal forces from within the community declined, but on account of shunning colonial education, the middle class among the community did not emerge as a strong force. Later, with the partition of the Indian subcontinent, a section of the Muslim middle class migrated to Pakistan hoping for better economic prospects. The community left behind was by and large backward socially, educationally and economically.

Even during Mughal rule, most of the *mansabdars* were Hindus, and only a few were Muslims. Conversion to Islam took place before and during Mughal rule from amongst the backward castes or Shudra castes not due to force as propounded by Hindutva ideologues, but on account of the message of inclusiveness, love and equality preached by Sufi saints. The Shudra castes who found themselves excluded from the village social life were attracted to the humanitarian and egalitarian approach of Islam and Sufis with the hope that conversion will liberate them from the oppressive caste system. Even Swami Vivekananda held that conversions to Islam were not due to force or undue influence during the Mughal rule, but as a result of oppressive caste system. The conversions as stated by Richard Eaton, in his study of the Bengali Muslims, took place in four stages:

(1) In the first stage the locals who gathered around the Sufi saints started noticing, due to continuous chanting of qawwalis and praises to Allah, that Allah was one of the deties to be worshipped.

(2) In the second stage, the followers of Sufi saints accepted Islam and worshipped Allah by chanting his name and in other ways in addition to the deities worshipped by him/her. This stage can be called as stage of inclusion.

(3) In the third stage, worship of Allah became more important and prestigious than other deities.

(4) In the fourth and final stage, the convert realizes that he cannot worship all deities and must purge all other religious influences and therefore this stage can be called as stage of exclusiveness.

These stages did not run parallel in all the areas and amongst all those who converted to Islam in the subcontinent. Though it is said that conversion to Islam took place under the Mughal rule by force, this theory can be easily disputed if we take a look at the geographical location of the Muslim population in the subcontinent. The seat of Mughal rule was in Delhi or towards the Northern part of India. However, we can easily notice that Muslim majority provinces were in the Eastern and North-Western periphery of the subcontinent, which are now Bangladesh and Pakistan. If the objective of the Mughal rule was to convert, then they should have converted and ensured a Muslim majority in and around their seat of power in the first place. Secondly, the Mughal rulers could have ensured conversions of the nobles and those from the noble families and upper castes wielding reins of society. However, with a few exceptions, the nobles, notables and the upper castes did not convert. Even during the Mughal rule, the vast majority of Muslims was those converted from lower sections and are even today called as *ajlafs*, or ordinary Muslim converts from backward castes.

As opposed to the *ajlaf* Muslims, the *ashraf* Muslims were nobles and notables, some of whom claimed to have migrated from Central Asia and generally held public offices, including the Mansabdars, Nawabs, landlords, Ulemas, etc. Their last names usually are Sheikhs, Sayyads, Pathans. The *ashraf* Muslims did not consider *ajlafs* as Muslims on account of their being rooted in the local culture and moreover they were converts from Shudra castes. The *ajlafs* were considered as deviants, and in fact not Muslims as they had not completely given up their local religio-cultural practices. In small towns and villages with considerable influence of feudal values, even in present times the *ajlafs* are not allowed to stand in front rows while praying in some mosques and are supposed to be in the rows at the rear.

Conversions to Islam by and large were on account of activities of Sufi saints who embraced all human beings and considered love of God as the highest form of worship. The Sufi saints lived simple lives and believed in *tawhid* or unity of

Being, viz. all humans are God's creations. There is one God and all humans are His creation. Love of all human beings was therefore worship of God. The Sufi saints never disputed or fought over ways of worship and believed that worship in any form and in any manner is a means to reach God. Nizamuddin Auliya, while walking on the banks of River Yamuna along with his disciple the great poet Khusrau told him, pointing to a Hindu woman performing *surya namaskar*, Oh Khusrau! Don't look at that woman with indifference, as she is also worshipping Allah, for Allah had devised as many ways of worship as particles of sand on the bank of River Yamuna. The Sufi saints embraced the poor and backward caste Shudras into their fold and worked for their well being. Richard Eaton, analyzing Bengali folk tales and songs, argues that the Sufis led the landless backward caste peasants in taming the wild jungles for cultivation. When the economic conditions of the landless backward caste improved after taming the wild forests, they longed for a religion and culture which treated them with dignity, respect and equality. They found that Islam, as practised by the Sufis willingly embraced them and treated them with dignity and respect. It is at this stage that they started observing Islam and Allah as one more deity who was worshipped. Social groups and communities, later over a long period gradually entered into other stages in accordance with their socio-religious needs and the religious leadership.

As a result of this encounter and dialogue between various religious communities, we have various syncretic communities following composite culture. Meo Muslims, Pranam Panthis, Rajput Muslims are some of them. Meo Muslims are excellent reciters of *Ramayana* and *Mahabharat*, living in the Mewati belt south of Delhi extending from Haryana to Rajasthan. Though Islam permits even first cousins to marry, the Meo Muslims strictly observe the gotra restrictions of marital relationships. These gotra restrictions prohibit marriage in mother's gotra, grandmother's gotra and so on. Anyone violating the gotra restrictions of marriage is strictly punished. Marriage between Meo Muslims is never complete without saptapadi (seven rounds) around the holy fire just as among the Hindus. Hindu and Muslim rituals must be completed amongst the Meo Muslims before a marriage can be declared to have been solemnized. The holy book of the Pranam Panthis is called *Kulzum Sharif* and has both—slokas of *Gita* (the holy book of Hindus) and ayats (verses) from the *Holy Quran*. The Holy book *Kulzum Sharif* can be touched only by a Pranam Panthi or a Muslim and no one else. Ablutions have to be performed (just as Muslims do) before touching the *Kulzum Sharif*. If there are two sons in a family, one is buried after death and the body of the other is disposed by cremation.

Likewise, a vast majority of Indian Muslims are thoroughly rooted in the local culture through out the length and breadth of the country. A Muslim widow from a village in Kerala was introduced to the Islamic Scholar Asghar Ali Engineer by a Malayali translator for the scholar's study on Kerala Muslims. The widow promptly responded by saying how could the scholar be a Muslim when he didn't even know Malayalam language! The Mappila Muslims from Kerala identify themselves more with the Kerala Hindu, rather than a North Indian Muslim with whom s/he might find very difficult to carry on any conversation due to language barrier. It is practically impossible for a North Indian Muslim to converse without the help of a translator. I myself had difficulty carrying on conversation with Mohammad Ansari, General Secretary of Al Umma, who recently was convicted for carrying out terrorist attacks in Coimbatore. Al Umma states that the entire Muslim community constitutes one community and should be governed by Sharia enforced by an Islamic State. I had to take help of an interpreter with knowledge of English and Tamil. The purpose of the conversation was to probe Mohammad Ansari in the aftermath of anti-Muslim riots in Coimbatore, which were triggered off with the murder of a traffic police constable by Al Umma members in the year 1998. Mohammad Ansari claims that all Muslims are one Muslim community—yet the two of us needed an interpreter to understand each other! One encounters mind blowing diversity within the Muslim community in India in terms of language, culture and even in rituals and religious practices. There is no single language which can act as a link language for all Muslims. Like the North Indian Hindu politicians, the Muslim politicians from North India tend to determine and dominate the political agenda and discourse of the Muslims in India.

Hindus and Muslims in rural areas, small towns as well as in cities actively participate in each other's festivals and live in harmony and cordial atmosphere. Muslims participate in Ganeshotsav festival during which pandals are erected and Lord Ganesha is worshipped for about 10 days and public programmes are organized during the festival in Western India. In Eastern India, Durga Puja is likewise popular and pandals are likewise erected and public functions and cultural events are organized during the nine days when Goddess Durga is worshipped. Muslims contribute to these festivals and are often office bearers in the organizations which organize cultural programmes and events along with pujas i.e. worship of Hindu gods and goddesses. Whenever images of Hindu gods and goddesses are taken in a procession through several villages or long distances, Muslims of the village or locality gather at a spot and welcome the procession or offer water or cold drinks to the processionists. Likewise, when Muslims take images of Karbala (called as Tazias) through various villages or residential areas in cities and towns, Hindus worship these Tazias in their traditional manner. Worshipping Tazias has become a part and parcel of Hindu rituals in many areas. There are many syncretic shrines where people of all religious communities pray together. On every Wednesday, during the sermons held in St. Michael's Church in Mumbai, there are more non-Christians than Christians, due to belief that if one attends nine sermons on consecutive Wednesdays (also called as Navina), God fulfils any wish and cures illnesses. In dargahs or shrines where Sufi saints are buried, e.g. Haji Ali in Mumbai, Khwaja Garib Nawaz in Ajmer, Nizamuddin Auliya's dargah in Delhi, Saibaba in Shirdi, Maharashtra, one finds more non-Muslims than Muslims. In Siddhivinayak Temple in Mumbai, there are number of Muslims who give offerings and walk from their place of residence to the temple, whatever the distance between their residence and the temple may be. In some cases, the distance may be over 30-40 kilometers.

Besides the sectarian divisions within the Muslim community, viz. the Shias and the Sunnis, there are sectarian divisions within the Sunnis, like the Deobandis, the Barelvis, Ahle-Hadith. Shias are largely based in Lucknow, where they form the majority of Muslim population of the city. Lucknow is the only city with history of violent conflict between the Shias and the Sunnis, particularly around the Moharram. The Deobandi-Barelvi and the Wahabi-Barelvi conflict is an instance of internal feud between Sunni Muslims. There have been frenetic pamphleteering outside and inside mosques against the Deobandis by Barelvis and vice versa leading to violent provocations of the religious feelings calling for intervention of police. The Wahabis and the Deobandis denounce religious practices like offering chadars (sheet of cloth) on dargah or visit to dargahs. As majority of Muslims were converted by the Sufi saints, the Dargahs where the pir or the Sufi saint is buried is very popular amongst the Muslims and non-Muslims alike. As the Indian census does not enumerate the sub-sections within the Muslims according to the fiqh (schools of jurisprudence like Hanafi, Hanbali, Maliki, Shafi, Ahle-Hadith etc.) that they follow, their exact numbers will be difficult to determine. However, most ordinary Muslims can hardly tell one from the other.

Those under the influence of the Wahabi Movement try to propagate the tenets of the movement. The Wahabi movement nevertheless, has not influenced many Muslims in India. However, the impact of Wahabi followers is disproportionate to their numbers. The Wahabi Movement was founded by Syed Ahmad of Rae Bareli and was a vigorous movement for socio-religious reforms in Indo-Islamic society in the 19th century with strong political undercurrents. It stood for strong affirmation of *tawhid* (unity of God), the efficacy of *ijtihad* (the right of further interpretation of the *Quran* and the *Sunnah*, or of forming a new opinion by applying analogy and the rejection of *bid'at* (innovation). The movement was active for well over half a century till it slackened in the year 1865 following the arrest of several leaders of the movement by British colonialists. The Wahabi Movement covered the greater part of northern

India. The Wahabis stressed the efficacy of direct reading and understanding of the religious texts as far as possible. The overall effect of the Wahabi doctrines was lessening of stranglehold of worldly minded ulema on the life of common people, and propagation of a simpler and cleaner way of life. The Wahabis today preach simple religious life and oppose Western culture more in the nature of a revivalism. The Wahabis gave the message of jihad against the British colonial rulers and called British rule as Darul Harb (abode inimical to Islam). They therefore propogated the great need and merits of jihad against British colonialism.

The Tablighi Jamat, continued the ideals of Wahabi movement. Started in 1920 by Maulana Ilyasi, the Tablighi movement sends groups and teams to all parts of the country to apparently propagate amongst Muslims to follow Islam and all its tenets. They urge Muslims to pray five times a day, observe fasts during the month of Ramadan, to perform Haj and give Zakat (Islamic tax). They organize *Ijtemas* and mobilize tens of thousands of Muslims to listen to sermons of Ulemas who urge the gatherings to observe all the tenets of Islam. However, this simple sounding message has more than religious agenda. The Tablighi Jamat started their activities from the Mewat area, with the mission to Islamize the Meo Muslims and persuade them to purge all non-Islamic (read Hindu) accretions in their faith. At any given time, thousands of teams of Tablighi Jamat undertake to tour villages in four corners of the country to preach amongst Muslims to purge non-Islamic accretions, i.e. to wear Islamic dress where the lower garment or trousers have to be well above the ankle, to emphasize the virtue of growing moustacheless beards and to wear Islamic skull caps. The message appears simple and religious, but is directed against syncretic traditions. The Tablighi Jamat failed to 'Islamize' the Meo Muslims and persuade them to give up non-Islamic practices. However every year, hundreds and thousands of youth are mobilized to undertake travel for days and even months, visiting various Muslim inhabitants in various localities and urge them to follow rigid Islamic tenets and purge non-Islamic accretions like Tazias. The itinerant preachers exhort the people not to participate in 'sinful' practices such as taking out of processions on the occasion of Muharram, visiting the tombs and dargahs of Sufi saints or supplicating the help of the saints in solving their problems.

The impact of such preaching is telling when Muslims of a particular locality or village come under the influence of the Tablighis. Under the influence of the Tablighis, when Muslims give up the cultural practices of the region, they incur the displeasure of the non-Muslims in the locality, who feel betrayed. It disturbs the harmonious life of the region. If Muslims give up Tazia processions, Hindus feel a great loss since worship of the Tazias in Hindu tradition is understood as one of the religious rituals that they would be deprived of. Hindus of a village in Sangli District in Maharashtra once imposed a social boycott on Muslims following desecration of a Hanuman temple. Muslims were boycotted as they were thought to be the natural and usual suspects. No investigation was thought necessary by the villagers. When Muslims suffered severe economic deprivation on account of the social boycott, they approached the Hindu leaders to withdraw the boycott and were ready to adhere to any condition. One of the conditions imposed on the Muslims of the village to lift the social boycott was that they would continue to take out Tazia procession during the Muharram. Another condition was that men would not wear Islamic skull caps and grow beards and women would not wear veils while in the village. The conditions imposed indicate the hurt feelings that non-Muslims had, on account of changes under the influence of the Tablighis who had been visiting the village lately and the community had acted in accordance with their preaching. Tablighis preaching usually creates disrespect towards the 'un-Islamic' cultural practices and therefore disrespect towards the non-Muslims in the area. 'Islamic' culture and moreover the 'Islamic' practices preached by them create a feeling of superiority of particular practices over 'other' cultural practices. Tablighis therefore keep themselves aloof from other communities and withdraw themselves from all social, religious and cultural life in the village, which creates segregation and at times communal conflicts.

Emergence of Middle Class Elites in the Muslim Community after Independence

The middle class within the Muslim community is very tiny due to a number of reasons. Only about 4-5 per cent of Muslims can be called middle class, which include those in government jobs, other respectable employment and small or medium business enterprises. There are only one or two industrialists— Azim Premji and the Khorakiwalas who could rank as industrialists. After partition, the already small section of elite and middle class amongst the Muslims migrated to Pakistan for better economic prospects and for obtaining larger pieces of land and securing higher government posts and offices. Others migrated fearing discrimination, marginalization and insecurity. The community that was left behind was socially and economically backward consisting of landless labourers or small peasants, urban hawkers and self-employed artisans and petty traders.

However, over period of time, due to their hard work, a small middle class began emerging from amongst the artisans. Some entrepreneurs from amongst the Muslim brassware artisans in Moradabad emerged as traders and financers in the brassware business, particularly with the growing demand for export markets. A section of Muslim weavers of Varanasi similarly graduated as traders and financers in the saree trade with growing demand for Varanasi sarees. Likewise, the workers of the scissor industry in Meerut, the lock industry in Aligarh, beedi industry in Jabalpur took over the reins of trade and emerged as the new middle class. The new middle class that was emerging in the community was from amongst the *ajlaf* Muslims. The emergence of this new middle class brought new aspirations and new dynamics into play for the community. Unlike the old feudal class, which supported Madarssa education and religious symbols, this new emerging middle class supported secular education and emphasized regional identity.

Communal conflicts and riots in all these cities targeted the emerging middle class amongst the Muslims and the competition between the new emerging class from Muslims and the established Hindu traders played no mean role in these conflicts. Properties and businesses of Muslims were the prime targets in communal conflicts in all these towns. The communal riots pushed the emerging middle class to seek refuge in homogenous communal identity and pushing them to support moderate communal leadership of the community. The new middle class became the social base of the moderate communal leadership for another reason. With their newly acquired economic status, the emerging middle class naturally were not happy with their former backward and lower class *ajlaf* identity. They were struggling for a more dignified identity with higher social status. In spite of the syncretic traditions, there was no composite regional identity embracing the emerging middle class with appropriate social status commensurate with their economic status. The emerging middle class therefore adopted Islamization as a strategy for upward mobility to claim higher social status. The emerging middle class therefore started imitating the *ashrafs* wherever possible, even while not completely breaking with their former caste-based *ajlaf* identities. On the one hand the emerging middle class generously contributed towards mosques to control the community institutions, even while relying on caste networks for marital relations and socialization. The Tablighi Jamaat's preachings appealed to the emerging middle class amongst the Muslims in their Islamization process.

Emergence of Moderate Communal Leadership within the Muslim Community

After independence in the year 1947, the community was led by nationalist leaders like Maulana Abul Kalam Azad. Communal harmony, composite nationalism and secularism were the main pillars of Maulana Azad's values and he never compromised on these values. Maulana Azad once wrote that if an angel came to him and promised him the gift of immediate independence but at the cost of partition, he would refuse such a gift, for living under the colonial rulers was loss of Indian people, but partition of the country along religious lines was loss of entire humanity and was not acceptable to him. Maulana

Azad was the president of the Indian National Congress in the year 1946 and had successfully represented the Congress before the Cabinet Mission and entered into a pact with Muslim League for power sharing. The Muslim League and all parties had accepted united India. Maulana Azad after the successful negotiation of the Cabinet Mission Plan resigned from the post of President of the Indian National Congress and Jawaharlal Nehru was elected as the President in place of Maulana Azad. After his election as President of the Congress Party, Nehru in a press conference stated that the Cabinet Mission Plan was not God's work and could be altered. The Muslim League then spared no efforts to achieve their demand of Pakistan as they felt that the Congress leadership could not be trusted. Maulana Azad, in his book, *India Wins Freedom*, regrets that he resigned from the post of President of Indian National Congress. If he had not resigned, Nehru would not have been elected to the post and perhaps partition of the country could have been avoided. Maulana Azad was the Education Minister after Independence. He objected to contesting elections from a predominantly Muslim constituency of Rampura when he was given ticket from that constituency. He wanted to be elected by the people of India and not by Muslims alone. Fielding him from a Muslim constituency, according to him, was affront to secularism, a value so dear to him and the freedom movement.

Immediately after independence, which was achieved at the cost of partition, the Muslim leadership focused itself on laying foundations of a secular state and secular identity for all citizens. The leadership of the Muslim League, emphasizing on Muslim identity, either migrated to Pakistan or lied low. Education was another issue on which the Muslim leadership focused itself. Zakir Husain set up the Jamia Millia Islamia and focused his efforts to get Muslims secular education. Justice M.C. Chagla, who retired as Chief Justice Bombay High Court, Syed Hamid, educationist, were other Congress leaders who worked for secular education of Muslims. Muslims during this period were grossly underrepresented in the legislatures of states and in the Parliament and the elected representatives kept a low profile.

Problems that emerged with the colonial balkanization of

the Indian subcontinent and Hari Singh's (the rules of Kashmir in 1947) accession of Kashmir to India though not being a dominant issue for mainland. Muslims, inevitably laid the stamp for future communal problems. Sheikh Abdullah, supported the integration of Kashmir into India, though he bargained for autonomy within the Indian Constitution. This phase can be called as the "phase of integration" of Muslims into India. This phase lasted till early 1960s. Later Sheikh Abdullah was arrested and kept under detention till 1964 as he was wrongly suspected to be working for independence of Kashmir. One major reason why this phase can be called a phase of communal integration, in spite of partition-inspired violence, is because people were mobilized on the issue of reorganization of the boundaries of the provinces on linguistic basis. Muslims wholeheartedly supported the linguistic re-organization of states. The poet Amar Sheikh wrote inspiring powadas (Marathi folk songs) that inspired the struggle for reorganization of Bombay Province into Maharashtra. This affirmed and strengthened regional and linguistic identity across religious lines. People paid less attention to communal mobilization. By the year 1966, all the states were reorganized along linguistic lines, though some minor problems of borders continue till date.

The phase of integration was over in the 1960s. The phase of mobilization on linguistic basis was more or less over. In the late 60s, there was an economic crisis. The value of rupee had dipped to an all time low by 1966 and there was unprecedented inflation and price rise. The country was dependent for supply of its wheat on America under the Public Law 480. Agricultural production had also hit an all time low. People were agitated and for the first time non-Congress parties were successful in mobilizing people. In many states in North India, the Congress government lost power at the state level for the first time in independent India, though it continued to be in power at the Centre. All the opposition parties formed a united front and formed coalition governments in Bihar, UP, Madhya Pradesh and Rajasthan. The opposition coalition governments were called Samyukta Vidhayak Dal (United Legislature Parties). The Jana Sangh, a right-wing Hindu party was also part of the coalition and it came to power for the first time. The Congress party also split into Congress(S) and Congress (I). All the opposition parties were actively mobilizing people of the country against the Congress and for the first time the credibility of Congress was at its lowest. The Jana Sangh also joined in the coalition governments of Samyukta Vidhayak Dal. They could now use their official machinery to spread the ideology of Hindutva and prejudices against Muslims. Communal riots also became a weapon to consolidate Hindu mobilization across castes and regions, on the one hand; and spreading prejudices against Muslims, on the other hand. The Praja Socialist Party mobilized people on the issue of price rise and economic crisis, and were particularly more successful mobilizing backward classes on the ideology of anti-Congressism on the one hand; and on the programme of opposing the caste-based oppression and domination of upper castes on the other hand. Anti-Congressism however proved to be the main plank of mobilization. However, there were two contesting ideologies underlying anti-Congressism. The anti-Congressism of the socialists was to annihilate caste oppression. The Congress party was seen as the main obstacle to the status-quo. The anti-Congressism of Jana Sangh was to question the ideology of inclusive nationalism in which minorities also were accommodated and given their space, albeit underrepresented and within the dominant ethos of Hinduism. The Jana Sangh called this as "appeasement of Muslims". The Hindutva agenda was to exclude minorities altogether and treat them as second class citizens. The dominance of the Congress party in the political arena was seen as an obstacle to their goal. Communal riots were used as a weapon by the Jana Sangh and other Hindutva organizations to spread hatred against Muslims. Riots always followed by media coverage tending to blame the Muslims for the riots. Prejudices and stereo types against Muslims inevitably strengthen after communal violence.

In the year 1961, there was a major communal riot in Jabalpur in which more than 400 persons were killed. The riot shook the secular foundation of the country. The Congress leadership, particularly, Jawaharlal Nehru was disturbed by the first major riots after the phase of partition-led violence in independent India. The media as well as the state administration was partial and the message was not lost on the Muslims of the country as regards their place and status in the country. No doubt, the main factors behind the riots were economic, social and political rather than religious. There was tough competition between a Hindu bidi magnate and an emerging Muslim baron in the bidi industry who was posing a challenge to the otherwise Hindu monopolist. The local media reported the event of the elopement of the son of a Muslim bidi industry owner and daughter of a Hindu industrialist and their subsequent marriage in a highly coloured, biased and questionable fashion. The media coverage of the incidents leading to the riots and the subsequent handling of the riots in Jabalpur widened the divide between the two religious communities along social and communal fault lines.

Subsequently, there were communal riots in Jamshedpur and Ranchi-Hatia in 1967 in Eastern India. In the year 1969, Ahmedabad, a textile city in Western Indian witnessed another major riot taking toll of over 2000 persons. In the year 1970, there were major riots in Bhiwandi, Jalgaon and Mahad in Maharashtra State. Over 600 people were killed in the riots that shook the confidence of Muslims in Indian democracy. Throughout the 1980s there were series of riots throughout North India and in Western India.

One of the explanations for the communal riots from the early 1980s is that the backward classes had acquired considerable economic clout on account of land reforms in North India. The Jats, Yadavs, Kurmis, Koeris not only became land owning peasants, but were able to diversify into other economic activities supplementing agriculture with dairy industry. Impact of the Green Revolution was bearing fruits in the eighties and cash crops like potatoes, wheat, sugarcane, etc. were highly successful in North India. With the growing economic clout, these backward classes questioned caste-based oppression and nurtured political aspirations.

As pointed out earlier, the socialists mobilized the backward classes by opposing Brahmanical ideology and world view, whereas the right-wing Hindu nationalists promised dignity to the lower castes by providing broader nationalist identity to all Hindus, to which individual caste identities were to be subjugated along with the exclusion of minorities as also targeting of Muslims as enemies of the nation. Both these forces merged into the Janata party post-emergency along with conservative sections of the Congress.

The right-wing Hindutva forces were in power in a number of states as well as at the Centre. The Janata party government at the centre lasted for two and a half years from 1977 till 1980. Post-emergency when elections were declared in the year 1977, Muslims also voted for the Janata party in a significant way. The Muslim votes shifted away from the Congress party on account of enforced family planning by Sanjay Gandhi during the emergency. Muslims suffered disproportionately during emergency and terrible atrocities were committed on them. Amongst many atrocities, bulldozing of Muslim slums without notice and brutally at Turkman Gate in Delhi became symbols of atrocities on Muslims during the emergency. While in power, various factions of Janata party fought amongst themselves, particularly over the issue of former Jana Sanghis' continued association with RSS, the right-wing Hindu organization.

After the Janata party split and lost power, and the Hindu right-wing organizations had tasted power, the RSS and its other front organizations used their positions and resources to carry out more intense campaign against minorities than they were able to carry ever before. Small routine disputes between followers of different religions had the potential of developing into a communal riot.

There was also more intense economic competition amongst the Hindu backward classes and upwardly mobile Muslims over land which was increasingly becoming a valuable commodity. During the eighties, campaign on the issue of Ramjanmabhoomi-Babri Masjid issue was also exploited to the hilt, particularly after 1986, when the gates of Ramjanmabhoomi temple were opened, on the one hand; and Muslim moderate leadership was mobilizing the Muslims against the Judgment of the Supreme Court in Shah Bano case demanding that the judgment be reversed as (according to the Muslim leadership) it was against the Shari'a to give maintenance to divorced Muslim women. Muslim moderate leadership was able to mobilize thousands of Muslim men and women against the judgment of the Supreme Court in the case of Shah Bano.

TheBJP exploited both these issues—Ramjanmabhoomi issue as well as that of Muslim mobilization against the Shah Bano judgment for mobilization of Hindus.

As a result of the mobilization and counter mobilization of the backward classes and the Muslims, there were series of communal riots in 1980s, particularly in Gujarat, Uttar Pradesh, Madhya Pradesh, Bihar and Rajasthan. The moderate Muslim leadership comprised the second generation leaders who grew up in these circumstances. They were bolder and more assertive than the first generation leaders who led cautiously in the aftermath of the partition on the issue of Muslim identity. The new leadership emerged in the late sixties but consolidated in the eighties. In the late sixties, when the position of Congress weakened, and opposition parties grew stronger in their challenge to the Congress, the Muslim leadership had more options to choose from. The political mobilization of Muslims in India consolidated around emotional issues. The three issues around which much of the mobilization of the Muslim community took place were: 1) Defence of Muslim Personal Law or Shari'a, 2) Minority Character of Aligarh Muslim University and 3) Urdu language.

The moderate and more religious leaderships often than not come together on the issue of Shari'a. Article 44 of the Constitution of India (in the chapter on Directive Principles of the State) provides that the state shall strive to enact a Uniform Civil Code. Muslims fear that family laws based on Hindu religion, tradition and customary practices would be imposed on them in the name of Uniform Civil Code. Both, the religious leadership and the political leadership of the Indian Muslims have by and large very assertively and aggressively taken a stand that Shari'a is divine and there can be no human interference in matters of Shari'a. Religious leaders naturally have vested interest in holding that Shari'a is divine and

Muslims should not tolerate any interference in Shari'a. In this way they become sole arbitrators of the Shari'a. Muslim political and religious leadership belonging to all the fiqhs and schools of Muslim jurisprudence have come together and constituted the Muslim Personal Law Board. The Muslim Personal Law Board has acquired much financial and political clout and deliberates on all the issues affecting the community. It strongly resists any effort to reform the Shari'a or even reinterpret the Shari'a according to the needs of modernity. The religious leadership in India has gone to the ridiculous extend of validating divorce which may be sent via SMS by writing the word *"talaq"* thrice or by pronouncing the word thrice over phone, or in inebriated condition, or in a fit of a rage, or even while in sleep. The Quranic way of divorce is of course pronouncement of the word *"talaq"* followed by arbitration by representatives appointed by the husband as well as the wife. The Muslim political leaders find it convenient to rally the community around the issue of Personal Law which has become an issue of its identity with highly emotional appeal. It must be said though that there have been voices from the margins demanding framing of Model Nikahnama where women stipulate conditions for marriage, namely that the husband would not take a second wife without her permission and would delegate the right of divorce to her. However, the voices are extremely weak due to the feeling of insecurity that the community is undergoing.

The minority character of the Aligarh Muslim University is another emotive issue that has the potential of mobilizing the community and bringing them on streets, though now it has lost much of its relevance. The Aligarh Muslim University (AMU) was initially established as the Mohammedan Anglo-Oriental (MAO) College to encourage modern education amongst Muslims during colonial rule. Interestingly, the religious leadership opposed any such attempt to equip Muslims with modern education when Sir Syed Ahmed established it during colonial period. Slowly, the community saw the importance of the college and modern English education. The graduates of MAO College later provided the leadership of the Muslim League which demanded partition of the country. After independence, through parliamentary legislation, the MAO College was converted into a Central University. The community always demanded that the university should be held to be an institution of minority character established and administered by Muslims. After initial controversy, the community had upper hand in administration of the university. The vice-chancellor of the University has always been a Muslim. Majority of the members of the Court, which runs the University also have been from the Muslim community. It is considered quite prestigious to be alumni of the university. The community mobilizes whenever there is a threat to its autonomy or to its hold on the university. The supreme court has categorically ruled that AMU has been established by parliament and not by the minorities, though the MAO College was established by the Muslim minority community. However, the Central Government had through legislation ensured that all the fears of the community in this regards are allayed. The university however, has been in news for all the wrong reasons, due to students' strikes and law and order issues posed due to frequent strikes in the university. Though the moderate leadership of the community has made the minority character of AMU as an emotive issue, it otherwise does not focus itself on matters of getting the community educated or establishing schools and other educational institutions for the benefit of the community.

Urdu is another emotional issue for the moderate Muslim leadership largely drawn from North India to rally and mobilize the community. Muslims from South India, West Bengal and Assam are least concerned with Urdu as they do not speak that language, except a small section in Hyderabad who speak Dakkhani Urdu as they were under Nizam rule. However, Urdu is wrongly perceived as a language of Muslims. Many stalwarts and literatures of Urdu have been Hindus in the past. Premchand, the celebrated short story writer, initially wrote his stories in Urdu. Kishan Chander and Jagannath Azad were other popular Urdu writers. However, during colonial rule, the Hindu right-wing rejected Urdu written in Persian script and mobilized

Hindus to accept Hindi language which shares the vocabulary and grammer with Urdu but written in Devnagri script. With the emergence for the Muslim League and demands for the formation of Pakistan in pre-independent India, Urdu came to be considered in popular perception as the language of Muslims. Since Urdu is also the national language of Pakistan, considered even today as arch rival of India, the perception that Urdu is the language of Muslims has continued in the minds of non-Muslims. Neither all Muslims speak Urdu, nor, even presently, all Urdu speakers and literateurs are Muslims. With this perception, Urdu has been discriminated by successive governments in independent India. The Indian state has stifled Urdu schools with lack of funds, resulting in lack of teachers and poor school buildings. Those who have graduated from Urdu schools have little prospects of higher education or employment. Readers of Urdu language newspapers are also on the decline as there are less and less graduates who have emerged from Urdu medium schools. Urdu newspapers are discriminated by the government in giving tender notices and other paid public information and advertisements. As the middle class, businessmen and entrepreneurs from within the community form a very small section of the community, the Urdu press does not even get revenues from private advertisements. It is only the Bollywood film industry based in Mumbai that relies on Urdu songs and popular Urdu poetry. This is the only factor which helps Urdu survive the sad state of neglect.

Onslaught on Urdu has become synonymous with onslaught on the Muslim community itself. Due state encouragement of Urdu language has therefore been the demand of North based Muslim moderate leadership. However, the fundamentalist sections want Urdu to become the lingua franca of all Muslims in India and encourage Muslims to learn Urdu, and further, without much success, discourage other languages so that Muslims can have not only religious identity but also communal identity with an imagined common culture. Like the right-wing Hindu parties, the fundamentalist sections too want the Muslim community to have not only common religion, but also common and homogenous culture. The fundamentalist leadership struggles to create space for culturally unified and homogenized community which, according to them would strengthen the community and equip it to fight the onslaught of Hindu communal forces.

The moderate leadership during the eighties was led by Syed Shahabuddin from North India and Sultan Salahuddin Owaisi in Hyderabad. The Muslim League with by Ibrahim Sait at its helm led the Kerala Muslims. In the eighties, another issue was added to the aforesaid issues, viz. defence of Babri Masjid. The moderate leadership took up the challenge to defend the Babri Masjid through political processes. Emotional speeches were made calling upon the community to rally around the issue. Except giving emotional speeches to the effect that they would not allow the Babri Masjid to be touched, they had no strategy on ground to activate the democratic institutions and take on the combined might of the Sangh Parivar (RSS). They were never going to succeed on the streets as the Sangh Parivar was known to have far greater strength to mobilize. The RSS also has tacit sympathy of the law enforcement agencies. However, as we all know, the moderate Muslim leadership utterly failed to protect the structure against mass mobilization by the Sangh Parivar. The moderate leadership was badly divided and without any strategy. One of the organizations was Babri Masjid Action Committee and the other organization was Babri Masjid Coordination Committee. They worked at cross purposes. They were competing with each other in occupying the moderate space within the community and posing themselves as champions of the Muslims rather than focusing on saving the mosque.

The overall objective of the moderate leadership was to ensure unity of the community by homogenizing the culture of the Muslim community around Urdu, on the one hand, and religion, on the other hand. They mobilized around communal demands to maintain Muslim identity and for minor concessions like declaring public holiday on Prophet Mohammed's birthday and on other cultural issues, the prime one being non-interference in Shari'a or Muslim Personal Law. It is Muslim women who suffer most due to rigid applicability of the Shari'a and the refusal to reform the Shari'a even in accordance with the Quranic framework. The moderate Muslim leadership did not aim to address themselves to socio-economic issues of the community though the community is educationally and economically backward. The moderate leadership utterly failed in securing justice to the victims of communal riots. None of the guilty were punished and in most cases, not even put to trial, including the instigators, abettors and conspirators. The overt and covert collaborations of law enforcement agencies with the rioters also were not prosecuted and punished. The Congress party was happy to grant symbolic religio-cultural and identity related issues as it did not burden the exchequer and were easy to meet. Each time a moderate politician came up with identity related issues, the government of the day would grant the same, with the hope that it would help mobilize minority votes. The concerned leader who agitated for symbolic issues then demonstrated his prowess and clout with the political set up and continues to enjoy the support of the community. In a way, the Congress party and other parties made it easy for the moderate leadership to enjoy their cheap and easy popularity by agreeing to their demands.

The leaders with alternate visions and ideologies were marginalized, as the state resisted with all its might their just demands. They thus appeared weak and fanciful before the Muslim community. The Congress was not the only party which agreed to the identity related demands of the moderate leadership from the community. The regional parties monopolizing over the votes of sections of backward classes also found it easy to accept the identity related demands of the Muslim community and mobilized Muslim votes. For example, the Yadav-Muslim alliance or MY formula worked wonders in UP and Bihar. Mulayam Singh's Samajwadi party successfully built the MY alliance in UP, while Laloo Prasad's Rashtriya Janata Dal worked the same alliance to be in power in Bihar. Muslims during all these regimes continued to be discriminated: socially, educationally and in government jobs. They were also victimized by the law enforcement agencies. They only managed to get the promise of security—control the communal riots.

A section of the moderate leadership also came from criminal background. The case of Mohammed Shahabuddin in Bihar is an instance of criminals entering the political domain. The criminal elements survive only under political patronage. In addition to symbolic identity related demands, the criminal elements from the Muslims afford marginal protection during the communal riots to Muslims in areas where they predominate. However, their retaliatory action against innocent Hindus only worsen the situation and innocent Muslims face communal onslaught in the name of "retaliation" from the Hindu right-wing. The bomb blasts in Mumbai and such activities are cases in point.

Political Islamist Ideology

The political Islamists are also popularly referred to as fundamentalists. However the term "fundamentalist" is very controversial and can be a misnomer. Many argue that the term fundamentalist means observing and going back to the fundamental principles and values of one's religion and in that sense, every person wanting to go back and follow the fundamental teachings of religion are fundamentalists. The origin of the idea of "fundamentalism" is ironically distanced from its most urgent current associations. As the *Webster's Dictionary* notes:

> Fundamentalism was a movement in American Protestantism that arose in the earlier part of the 20th century. It was a reaction to modernism, and stressed the infallibility of the Bible, not only in matters of faith and morals but also as a literal historical record. It stressed on belief in the *Bible* as the literal word of God.

Fundamentalism, thus, originally referred to certain trends within American evangelism proclaiming the infallibility of the revelations of the *Bible,* but was eventually widened to include all belief systems that asserted or advocated a return to the "fundamentals" of their religion or ideology. It is characterized as a "worldview or movement centred on restoring religious tradition or sacred text as guiding force in society, usually in opposition to ideas or practices considered modern." The fundamentalist ideology developed was a reaction to modernity and modern cultural values and harped on an imagined perfect past. Fundamentalists always aim to return to the past, even using violent methods if necessary.

The Political Islamists on the other hand aim to establish an Islamic State and enforce Islam, or rather rituals of a particular sect of Islam through the state. The moderate Muslim leadership is content with using certain symbols to mobilize Muslims and project Muslim society as one observing a homogenous culture by emphasizing common appeal of symbols, which more often than not are religious symbols that undermine diversity of cultures within Muslim society.

Political Islamists on the other hand, do not only want society to be homogenized, but also establish Islamic State and enforce religious rituals and seek compulsory compliance to religious symbols and rituals through the state. They also seek to reshape all religious laws in accordance with orthodox and conservative understanding of religion. Political Islamists are far more homogenizing than the moderates. Maulana Abu Ala Maududi established the Jamaat-e-Islami on 26th August 1941. Maulana Maududi argued that it was the duty of every Muslim to fight to establish an Islamic State in India. Initially the Jamaat-e-Islami opposed the demand of Pakistan as it was led by secular politicians like Jinnah. Moreover, the objective of Jamaat-e-Islami was to fight for an Islamic State for the entire country. However, as soon as Pakistan was created, Maulana Maududi migrated to Pakistan and established the Jamaat-e-Islami in Pakistan. The Indian branch of Jamaat-e-Islami continued its activities on the Indian side of the border as well. The Jamaat-e-Islami in India lay low for some time after independence and did not have much following. However, it concentrated on building its cadre by training students. The Students Islamic Movement of India (SIMI) was its front organization through which it reached out to the students and recruited its cadre. It emphasized on character building of Muslim students. However, it gave ideological training to a select few. During the 1980s, when India witnessed series of communal riots throughout the country, and with militancy raising its head in

Jammu and Kashmir, the stance of some of the leaders of SIMI hardened with Political Islamist ideology and adopted violence as its credo to achieve its objective of establishing an Islamic State. The SIMI split and those opposing violence as an immediate plan walked out of the organization and formed the Students Islamic Organisation.

The level of violence against Muslims was acting as a catalyst and pushing them towards a Political Islamist dream. After the demolition of the Babri Masjid, the Jamaat-e-Islami mellowed its stance and adopted the road to peace, reconciliation and communal harmony. The Jamaat-e-Islami has formed a platform for communal harmony with prominent secular intellectuals from the Hindu community. It emphasizes and organizes programmes for communal harmony to reach out to all its cadres in all the districts, tehsils, villages and cities where it has its following. It has also formed an organization called Movement for Peace and Justice. The Jamaat-e-Islami cadres working in this organization take up issues of social justice pertaining to all castes and communities.

Situation after the Demolition of Babri Masjid

As pointed out above, after the demolition of the Babri Masjid, there was a lot of churning and realignment within the community and the way it was mobilized. The moderate leadership utterly failed to stop the demolition of the mosque and all its tall and competitive claims before the community to protect the Babri Masjid at any cost also collapsed along with the mosque. The community now does not respond to any emotional issues related to the politics of identity any more. There is a feeling within the community that education is the only salvation. Many organizations focusing themselves on secular education have been more popular after the demolition of the Babri Masjid than before. Particulalry, Muslim girls have topped the Secondary School Certificate examinations in Maharashtra and other states. Recently in Mumbai, two girl students defied the edict of a few conservative elements within the community to attend college and sought police protection for the purpose. There is increased awareness and urge for secular education within the community. The moderate leadership is reconfiguring itself and re-working political alignments. Muslims drifted away from the Congress and for more than a decade did not vote for Congress as it rightly held the party responsible for demolition of Babri Masjid. Though it was in power at the Centre, and could have protected the Masjid, the Narsimha Rao government just twiddled its fingers and watched the Masjid fall. The issue before the community was not the Masjid alone—it was the issue of survival of secularism and democracy itself and more particularly, the issue of security as the demolition was followed by communal riots throughout the length and breadth of the country. The moderate leadership was more actively seeking and working out alliances with regional parties, most of them were anti-Congress alliances while some were merely non-Congress alliances. The social base of Congress before the demolition of the Babri Masjid was social alliance of upper castes (read Brahmans), Dalits and Muslims. The alliance was dominated by the upper castes, but was accommodating Muslims. The Congress was also called a soft Hindutva Party. With the Muslims walking out of this alliance, the social base of the Congress shrank and it lost power. By aligning with the regional parties, the social alignment was with dominant upwardly mobile backward classes. The moderate leaders who aligned with Samajwadi party in UP and Rashtriya Janata Dal in Bihar were realigning with the Yadavs, i.e. M-Y alliance or Muslim-Yadav alliance. Likewise Muslims voted for Telegu Desam Party in AP, Muslim League in Kerala, Samajwadi Party in Maharashtra, Janata Dal in Karanataka, DMK in Tamil Nadu, CPM in West Bengal (as Trinamool Congress aligned with the BJP). In Gujarat, Rajasthan and Madhya Pradesh, the straight contest was between the Congress and the BJP. There was no strong regional party. Hence, Muslims continued to support the Congress party in these states.

The only exception to the situation that Muslims did not get mobilized around emotional and identity based issues was on the issue of Danish cartoons that denigrated the Prophet of Islam. The media, including the Urdu media prominently covered the issue of the derogatory cartoons published in Dutch newspapers. Lakhs of Muslims were on streets to protest against these insulting cartoons in Mumbai, Delhi, Kolkata, Banglore and other towns of India. Mumbai witnessed unprecedented mass of Muslims—according to cautious estimates, about 4 lakh Muslims were on the streets to protest on the issue. Muslim commercial establishments were closed down on that day and employees were asked to join the rally. Imams in most mosques had asked people to join the rally. There was unprecedented mobilization in Mumbai and in even in other cities. The mobilization also coincided with George Bush's arrival in India, and anti-American and anti-Bush slogans were also raised in the rally opposing the war in Iraq and Afghanistan. Actually several issues were combined, but the large mobilization of the Muslim community was to vent the suppressed feelings of their victimization by the law and order machinery and feeling of discrimination and treatment of second class citizen.

The influence of the ISI (the Pakistani Intelligence Agency) increased considerably after the demolition of Babri Masjid and the communal riots that followed in which Muslims were victimized. The infamous underworld don Dawood Ibrahim and the gold smuggler Tiger Memon conspired with the ISI to carry out serial bombings in Mumbai on 12th March 1993. Muslim youth were trained in Pakistan by the ISI to carry out the bombings in which over 287 people died. A small section of Muslim youth was attracted to the concept of revenge for the communal riots and were brainwashed by showing videos of the demolition of the Babri Masjid and communal riots that followed. Anti-social elements amongst the Muslim community in South India were also attracted to religious fundamentalism after 1992 and plethora of communal organizations like Al Umma sprang up in the South for the first time. Muslims in the South always identified themselves with the Dravidian movement. However, after 1992 there was rise of Militant Islam. The RSS headquarters were bombed in Tamil Nadu to seek revenge for the demolition of the Babri Masjid. There were communal riots for the first time in Coimbatore in Tamil Nadu, in which 27 Muslims were killed by police in firing on an unarmed mob followed by an attack by Hindu Munnani in the year 1998. The communal riots in Coimbatore in 1998 were followed by bomb blasts in the same year. In Kerala, Maulana Madani started a militant organization Islamic Service Society to militantly counter the RSS, even resorting to violence. ISS attracted hundreds of youth to its fold. Madani was ultimately jailed and spent several years in prison, for his role in Coimbatore bomb blasts, but was acquitted recently. There were bomb blasts also in Jammu region of J & K State, on Akshardham temple in Gujarat, Shiv temple in Varanasi (UP) and near Jama Masjid in Delhi. There were bomb blasts in a BEST public transport bus in Mumbai and series of bombings in local trains in Mumbai in which 147 people died. Most of these bombing were motivated in the spirit of revenge for attacks on Muslims in Gujarat in the year 2002 and in other communal riots. ISI provides training, weapons and financial resources. The Maharashtra police and Andhra Pradesh police arrested Muslim youth for bombings outside a mosque in Malegaon and in the Mecca Mosque in Hyderabad. However, the Muslim community feels that the youth have been unfairly targeted. HUJI (Harkatul Jehade-e-Islami), a Bangladesh based militant Islamic organization has been accused of bombings in Hyderabad near Gokul Chat Bhandar and a theatre in Hyderabad.

Some fundamentalist or Political Islamist organizations have started rethinking their ideology and are now working for communal harmony, secularism and justice for all. As pointed out above, the Jamaat-e-Islami is one such organization which has reviewed its stand on the issue of Islamic State. The Jamaat fully participated and extended wholehearted support to Marathi Muslim writers to organize a conference of Marathi Muslims. This itself shows a sea change in the Jamaat's ideology, which was unthinkable earlier, for, to them only Islamic identity and no other socio-cultural identity was acceptable. Earlier they had negated all other identities, whether Indian or regional, Maharashtrian or Gujarati for that matter.

Meanwhile, the backward classes amongst the Muslims have been organizing themselves for extension of benefits of affirmative actions. Remember that the backward classes amongst the Hindus rose to the forfront more than two decades back when the Mandal recommendations were implemented. In doing so, the backward caste Muslims emphasize their regional identity over a communal Muslim identity. The Pasmanda Muslim Mahaz (Forum of Backward Muslims) in UP and Bihar is one such organization. It is a welcome democratization of Muslim identity emphasizing plural cultures within the larger Muslim community. Islamic religious identity is only one small but important factor in the identity, but it is not the only factor that shapes their identity. The backward Muslims, by claiming their former Dalit-caste identities are proud of their Islamic identity as well as their local cultural identity. It acts as a bridge between Islam and regional identity. Backward Muslims are proud of both aspects of their identity. It connects them to their Hindu brethren and builds harmonious relations with them. Claiming backward Muslim identity, the backward communities amongst the Muslims also engage with the state to be more democratic and extend affirmative action to them on the ground that they are backward classes too. What they also claim is that the state should not discriminate between Hindu and Muslim backward classes. The Andhra Pradesh government has recently added to the list of backward classes, names of Muslim communities. It has also passed legislation to extend 4 per cent reservation to Muslim backward classes.

Where are the Muslims Today and What should They Do?

We can just list some points on this very briefly

- Education is one key if the Muslims are to have better future in India and take advantage of the growth and development in the country. Two strategies will have to be followed here—availing of secular education on the one hand and on the other hand ensuring that text-books and syllabi are more accommodative and sensitive towards the concerns of minorities, particularly as represented in history texts books. The text books in particular and education in general should reflect the multicultural society aspect of Indian society.
- Struggling for more democratization of the Indian state

with robust institutions monitoring and protecting democratic rights and human rights of all, particularly of the weaker sections. This includes discrimination on the basis of religion, caste, gender or linguistic basis. There is already a constitutional bar against any discrimination, but there is no effective remedy for any violations. The courts are too overburdened and marshalling of evidence to prove discrimination is too arduous a task to be undertaken by an individual from the deprived backward and marginalized sections of society.

Cleaning the house from within. The Shari'a as practised now is discriminatory to women, particularly regarding the practice of polygamy and the pronouncement of triple talaq in one sitting or one breath. Considering irreversible divorce as great blow to the rights of Muslim women. Tripal talaq marginalizes women and is also not in the Quranic spirit of gender equality. Indian Muslims will have to reform their society from within and adopt the best practices of diverse sects and communities. The Muslim community should recognize the rich cultural diversity within Islam.

Restrain the tiny violence-prone sections which are attracted to fundamentalism and Political Islam. Indian Muslims should work for peace, harmony and reconciliation and justice for all sections of society to establish a just and inclusive society. Any instance of discrimination and hate crimes directed against the community should be fought through democratic and non-violent means.

5

Pawns in, Patrons Still Out: Understanding the Phenomenon of Hindutva Terror

Subhash Gatade

On, September 11, 2014, a suspected Hindutva terrorist was severely injured in Kannur when a bomb was prematurely exploded at his house at Kooleri under the Mattannur police station limits in Kannur on Wednesday. The injured suspected terrorist has been identified as 21 year-old Rashtriya Swayamsevak Sangh (RSS) worker Nikhil, son of Kunnummal Pavithran. A large cache of explosives was found at his damaged house after the blast. It is suspected that he was making bombs to carry out terror attacks in the region.

Before this recent event, on April 8, 2001, in Mumbai, the Kolhapur police in Maharashtra discovered a bomb making factory in Lakshmi Hill near the MIDC area of the Kagal town. The Kolhapur police also arrested four suspected Hindutva terrorists, who were in their 20s. They have been identified as Ajinkya Manohar Bhopade (22) and Aniket Bhivaji Mali (22) from Chokak village in Hatkananagale, Nilesh Babanrao Patil (20) from Male Mudshingi, in Hatkanangale and Anil Popat Kharase (26) from Kabnur-Ichalkaranji in Hatkanangale. All four were remanded to police custody till April 14 by a Kagal court on Sunday evening.

Emergence of Hindutva

The ascendance of Hindutva right at the centre, symbolized by the victory at the 2014 National Election of Narendra Modi as Prime Minister of the country, has put the discussion on terrorism engaged in by fanatic Hindutva formations at the backburner. The silent emergence of new fanatic Islamist forces in West Asia represented by the ISIS and the growing media attention it has received has also helped the process in an indirect way. It is a different matter that these fanatics of the Hindutva right-wing seem to be continuously active, as is evident from a random collection of news items mentioned above.

A question can rightly be raised why a discussion about "Muslims and the Politics of Hindu Right" should deliberate on this particular phenomenon of Hindutva terror or how does it implicate Muslims in the whole schemata of things. One would come to details later, but after a cursory glance at many of the terror acts committed by the Purohits, the Pragyas, the Aseemanands and the Panses one notices that there are two aspects of this phenomenon:

- One is the work of executing terror acts—creation of the figure of the "hostile other" and the consequent targeting of this "other". This creation of the figure of the "hostile other' then leads to the actual acts of Hindutva terror, like putting bombs at crowded places or in trains, storing explosives, engaging in targeted assassinations etc
- The second aspect is to camouflage such operations in such a way that they appear as acts by some fanatic Muslim groups. Such methodology then victimizes the victims further and puts the community and its members to further inconvenience.

Before I come to the actual presentation it would be opportune to make few initial remarks.

I am opposed to all sorts of terrorism. It may be executed by state actors or for that matter, non-state actors.I am equally pained if the state kills innocents under a false pretext, or the Talibanis blast a church in Peshawar, or the Jihadis (call them

"Fassadis" if you wish) put a bomb at a Sufi shrine, or the Khalistanis single out non-Sikhs in a bus and massacre them in cold blood, or Hindutva terrorists killing innocents in similar manner.

And I am of the considered opinion that law of the land should be applied in every such case. There should not be any dilly dallying on this front, especially a country which calls itself secular as well as democratic has to take extra care in doing that.

Violence and Terror

Violence and terror are an integral part of any exclucivist organization professing allegiance to a particular faith. This part of South Asia where the unfolding project of democratization undertaken after the exit of the colonialists has faced many hiccups and seems to be a fertile ground for proliferation of such formations.

Today one is witness to the emergence and further consolidation of Sinhala-Buddhist chauvinist groups active in Sri Lanka, the likes of Lashkar-e-Toiba and Jaish-e-Mohammad exerting influence cutting across borders, or the likes of Wirathu, called "Bin Laden of Burma" a Buddhist monk along with thousands of his followers creating havoc for the minorities in Myanamar, or organizations like HuJI, Jamaitul Mujahideen Bangladesh, which were synonyms of terror a few years back, trying to regroup their forces in neighbouring Bangladesh. We have here Hindutva supremacist groups engaged in similar terror acts which are no less deadly or barbaric.

A worrisome aspect of this phenomenon of Hindutva terror is that for long, prejudice has ruled investigations, obscuring the role of organizations and their multiple affiliates in planning and executing of attacks and bombings in the country and despite gaining visibility it has not yet evoked commensurate response from the state as well as what is popularly known as civil society.

Yes, pawns have been caught, actual planters of bombs and explosives have been apprehended, cases have been filed but the real planners and real masterminds of this terror turn in

Hindutva politics are still roaming free. And one does not see any immediate possibility of their getting caught or sent behind bars.

Yes, gone are the days when a conspiracy of silence awaited us when a bomb blast at an RSS activist's house in Nanded, Maharashtra occurred, (April 6, 2006) which killed his son Rajeev Rajkondwar and another RSS worker Himanshu Panse and the police discovered an elaborate plan of organizing bomb blasts in minority populated areas in Maharashtra and could also unearth linkages to some earlier bomb blasts in the state where the culprits were never found.

The stranglehold of the "common sense"—which equated terrorism with Muslims—was so profound then that the whole news was literally blacked out in the mainstream media. It is true that post Malegaon 2008 bomb blast, investigations done by the legendary police officer Hemant Karkare, there has been a partial qualitative change in the situation. The very idea of Hindutva terror is not brushed aside easily—as it was done earlier.

But sadly things have not moved much ahead after that. The planners, masterminds are still roaming free and none those police officials and investigating agencies people who misled the investigations earlier, who were instrumental in hounding the innocents, trampling of the basic constitutional rights of innocents, have received punishment of any sort.

We all are aware of the developments in the Malegaon bomb blast case 2006 where a terror module of RSS workers has been finally chargesheeted, here also many key figures have been left out, is a pointer to the *modus operandi* of the probe agencies. One can notice that the report filed by NIA (National Investigating Agency) has completely discarded the earlier FIRs (First Information Reports) by ATS (Anti Terrorist Cell) Maharashtra and by CBI (Central Bureau of Investigations), which had led to great miscarriage of justice in the lives of nine innocents and their families.

We have number of such examples where the actual perpetrators were never caught and innocents were apprehended, tortured badly and asked to 'confess' to a crime which they had not committed.

Or refer to the expose by Ashish Khaitan (www.gulail.com) which has unearthed

> -[i]nternal documents from more than half a dozen anti-terror agencies that show that the state has been knowingly prosecuting innocent Muslims for terror cases and keeping the evidence of their innocence from the courts...

It is high time we looked into the manner in which investigating agencies function or how an influential section among them is engaged in consciously spreading canards against religious minorities, criminalizing and stigmatizing them further and how a majoritarian viewpoint dominates their functioning which has facilitated the silent emergence of Hindutva terror.

Different Aspects of Hindutva Terror

Definitely, this terror turn of a different kind is not a regional phenomenon. In fact, few things related to the unfolding phenomenon can easily be summarized:

- Not a recent phenomenon

The phenomenon of Hindutva terror, whose danger to secular democratic polity has always been underestimated has had a pan India presence and has been able to build international linkages as well.

The bomb blast at the house of Laxman Rajkondwar, a longtime RSS activist on April 6, 2006, which killed his son and another activist, definitely brought to the fore this phenomenon, but it cannot be said to be the beginning of Hindutva terror. As far as terror acts such as Mhow (1999), Bhopal (2002, 2003), Jammu (January 2004), Nanded I (April 2006) and Nanded II (February 2007) to the likes of Malegaon I (September 2006) and Malegaon II (September 2008), Kanpur (August 2008), Tenkasi (2007) and many of their ilk are concerned, participation of activists of different Hindutva organizations has been noted and first information reports have also been lodged underlining their involvement.

Right from Jammu—where they were found to be involved in bomb blasts in front of a mosque—Ahl e Hadees Masjid—

way back in January 2004, which killed two people and injured more than twenty which was initially blamed on some Teherik Um Mujahideen—to Kanyakumari—it is now history how activists of Hindu Munnani themselves were found to be involved in fake bomb attack on the RSS's own office in Tenkasi, not far from Kanyakumari in the year 2007.

After the Nanded bomb blast (April 2006) the involvement of the RSS in other bomb blasts also came to the fore[1]

- Parbhani blast at Mohammadiya Masjid, Rehmat Nagar, on Friday, November 21, 2003, the main accused Sanjay, Panse, Wagh or Widulkar
- Purna (district Parbhani) blast at Meraj-ul-Uloom Madarssa and Masjid, Siddharth Nagar on Friday, August 2004, the main accused are Sanjay and Tuptewar.
- Jalna blast at Quadriya Masjid, Sadar Bazar, August 27, 2004, Wagh is the only accused
- Nanded blast—the bomb that exploded in Nanded on April 6, 2006 was supposed to explode at Aurangabad Mosque on Friday, April 7, all the above accused were involved in planning that blast.
- Malegaon blasts also occured on Shab-e-Barat, a prominent day for Muslims on Friday, September 8, 2006.

A point worth noting is that all these blasts in central Maharashtra (including the ones in Malegaon on September 8) occurred between 1.45 pm and 2.00 pm at the most prominent mosques in these towns, just after the Friday prayers, when attendance is maximum.

S.M. Mushrif, former I.G. Police, Maharashtra who has written a book *Who Killed Karkare*? explaining what he claims as "the real face of terrorism in India" has given a list of 49 incidents randomly culled from the mainstream media (March 2000—April 2009) providing details of activities ranging from holding of training camps in weapons training, making of bombs or attacks on religious places, or mysterious blasts, all involving activists of RSS, VHP and Bajrang Dal.[2]

- International Linkages

> We asked for four things—continuous and uninterrupted supply of equipmental training, secondly allow us to start our office with a saffron flag in Tel Aviv, number three political asylum and number four support our cause in the United Nations that Hindu nation is born.[3]

The 4,000 page chargesheet filed in Malegaon bomb blasts case by the Anti-Terrorist Squad in the MCOCA court reveals previously less explored dimensions of the Hindutva terror formations. The chargesheet exposes the radical intentions of creating a separate Hindu nation and extensive attempts by the saffron terror brigade to network with Nepal and Israel. According to the Anti-Terrorism Squad (ATS) the transcripts of audio video recordings recovered from the terror mastermind Dayanand Pandey's laptop is evidence enough to prove that Purohit had already kicked off efforts to liason with establishments in Nepal and Israel to set up a separate Hindu Rashtra (nation).

In his testimony, the military personnel with the Army Education Corps—who were persuaded by Purohit to become a part of Abhinav Bharat—shared their plans referring to a meeting which he had attended

> Lt Col Purohit discussed about establishing some progress on some government in exile. Lt Col Purohit also said that for the government in exile contacts were established with Israel and Thailand... Shankaracharya also spoke about government in exile etc. Lt Col Purohit talked about cannibalization of RSS, VHP and forming a pure Hindu organization and need for an academy of ideological indoctrination. [4]

The said chargesheet provides details of some meetings of these terrorists at various places in India. In one such meeting where many of the leading lights of the Hindutva terror were present (namely Dayanand Pandey alias Sudhakar Dwivedi, Delhi based Dr. R.P. Singh, Col. Bappaditya Dhar, Himani Sawarkar and others), Purohit is reported to have said the following:

> I have contacted Israel and one of our captains has been to Israel. There has been a very positive response from their side. They have

> said show us something on the ground because we have just shown them everything on paper right now. They said wait and watch for six months.

In the same meeting Swami Dayanand Pandey is reported to have said:

> I had told you that day that two people from Israel had come to us. They sat here and talked for a while and whatever it is they promised to cooperate first.

The transcripts also talks of the group's efforts to take help of the ousted monarch of Nepal namely King Gyanendra.It is learnt that Purohit had a meeting fixed with King Gyanendra for June 24, 2006 and then again on February 13, 2007. It is worth noting that a Nepal army official who acted as a middleman for Purohit and King Gyanendra, through whom Purohit had almost got a clearance to train cadres in Nepal.

-A Brief History of Terror

All such acts can be said to be the continuing legacy of a more hardcore section within the Hindutva fraternity, which had its genesis say in the assassination of Mahatma Gandhi, at the hands of Nathuram Godse, who could be considered the first terrorist of newly independent India. According to Chunnibhai Vaidya, a renowned Gandhian from Gujarat, there were total six attempts on Gandhi's life during a span of 14 years which involved Hindutva radicals.

In fact, after the assassination of Mahatma Gandhi, this is what the government communique issued on February 4, 1948 said announcing the ban on RSS:

> ...the government has, however, noticed with regret that in practice members of RSS have not adhered to their professed ideals.Undesirable and even dangerous activities have been carried on by the members of the Sangh. It has been found that in several parts of the country, individual members of the RSS have indulged in acts of violence involving arson, robbery, dacoity and murder and have collected illicit arms and ammunitions.
>
> They have been found circulating leaflets, exhorting people to resort to terrorist methods, to collect firearms, to create disaffection against the government and suborn the police and military.

While the role played by Hindu fanatics in Mahatma's assassination is widely known, not much has been written on the other exploits of activists of RSS in bomb making. Refer to this news item at the time of independence.

> Bomb blast in Shikarpur area of Karachi at the time of independence witnessed deaths of two Sangh Pracharaks namely Vasudev and Prabhu Badlani. Their third accomplice was apprehended by the Pakistani police and had to languish in their jail for quite some time. And how come there was a bomb blast in the residential area in a house owned by one Raibahadur Tolaram which was rented by the RSS people supposedly to run tuitions for kids?... The plan hatched by a 21 member team of RSS workers was to organize bomb blasts in different places in Karachi and kill as many people as possible.[6]

It all started with the terror plot discussed by Rajeshwar Dayal, the first home secretary of United Province who in his autobiography[7] exposed the sinister design of the Hindutva workers to organize a pogrom against Muslims in Western Uttar Pradesh in the immediate aftermath of partition.

"Terror of Riot" to "Terror of Bomb"

The investigating agencies suspect involvement of Hindutva activists in as many as 16 major explosions across the country. For laypersons, it may appear that such terror attacks organized in different parts of the country are the handiwork of some disgruntled, rogue elements belonging to different Hindutva organizations who yearn to make India a Hindu Rashtra. Nothing can be farther from the truth.

A careful look at the unfolding dynamic makes it clear that this "terror turn" is a very carefully drafted strategy by the Hindutva formations which some years ago decided to slowly to move from their prime strategy of "terror of riot" to "terror of bomb". They discovered that the older strategy was no longer paying rich dividends at the pan-India level, and the new strategy was more appropriate for the following reasons:

1. It was in tune with the times as 'terrorism' had been made a global phenomenon, and was inculcated in the psyche of the people worldover by the reactionary forces.

2. In the name of security of the country, it was possible to rope in sympathisers in the intelligence, the Executive and the Judiciary for the ultimate project of building Hindu Rashtra, and even blackmail the vulnerable political opponents.
3. It created fear in the hearts of all citizens,
4. It required fewer people's participation, and also carried less risk for the perpetrators.
5. It also helped victimize the victims further through arrests and torture.
6. It helped create wider divides in the name of religion,
7. The tag of terror could be pinned on Muslim community, thereby consolidating the image of the 'evil other'—a must for moving society towards authoritarianism and ultimately to fascism
8. It had wider reach, and helped in faster consolidation of people behind them.

Thus the "terror of bom" was more beneficial for the reactionary political project for promoting fascism.

One can see it as a result of two processes—one national and the other international. The universal condemnation of the Hindutva brigade for aiding and abetting Gujarat carnage 2002 definitely forced the Parivar to revisit the politics of riots. There was growing realization that engineering communal riots would not pay the desired political dividends but would rather nullify the political gains accrued through communal politics. Another factor which favoured this new modus operandi of the Hindutva brigade pertained to the "new common sense" foisted on the people by United States post 9/11. The "war against terror" launched under its aegis had strong overtones of undue targeting of a particular community and its religion namely Islam.

Conflating Hinduism with Hindutva

Definitely a lot depends upon the way the secular and left forces react to the ongoing investigations. Whether they would focus themselves on the role of the state and confine themselves to issuing statements and appearing in talk shows alone, or they are ready to take up the gauntlet thrown by the challenge of Hindutva terror in a more militant and creative way, would be the deciding factor. As anyone concerned with the cause of secularism would agree that the cause would be better served if we are ready to take a radical rupture with the previous approach and are ready to convince people, start mass campaigns, unleash movements to further the cause.

It is evident also from the fact that when Nanded (April 2006) 'inaugurated' this phase for everyone to see, then also they did not get up from the deep slumber they were in. Like ordinary people they also preferred to individualize the crime.

Only when Malegaon (September 2008) happened did they joined the chorus, but then also the emphasis was not on mass actions but talk shows and press conferences etc. We had this spectacle before us where the ATS was going ahead with investigations, the right-wing was protesting on the streets and seculars were far away from the streets. There is no doubt that they lost a historic opportunity to turn the tables on the Hindutva brigade.

As far as dealing with the menace of Hindutva terror is concerned, it is of key importance to engage with questions, clear confusions in the minds of people. A common thing is the way Hinduism is conflated with Hindutva.

One generally notices deliberate conflation of two distinct terms: Hinduism and Hindutva. According to RSS leaders all those people who talk of Hindu terrorism are trying to denigrate the whole community. It cannot be denied that some people did describe the role of Hindu fanatics in terrorist operation as 'Hindu terrorism'. But a large majority of the critics avoided describing it in this fashion and instead talked of Hindutva terrorism which seems to be a more accurate description of the phenomenon.

All those people who are not aware of the debates in the movement would wonder what is the big difference between Hindu terrorism and Hindutva terrorism. Perhaps it would be better to refer to a book by Savarkar, who is considered to be a pioneer of the Hindu right or the Hindu nationalist movement. This monograph which is named *Hindutva* has reached classic status and lays down the guiding principles of the idea.

What does the monograph say? Its key contribution is the way in which it differentiates between Hinduism and Hindutva:

> Hinduism is only a derivative, a fraction, a part of Hindutva. Unless it is made clear what is meant by the latter, the first remains unintelligible and vague. Failure to distinguish between these two terms has given rise to much misunderstanding and mutual suspicion between some of those sister communities that have inherited this inestimable and common treasure of Hindu civilization.[..] Here it is enough to point out that Hindutva is not identical with what is vaguely indicated by the term Hinduism. By an 'ism' it is generally meant a theory or a code more or less based on spiritual or religious dogma or system. But when we attempt to investigate into the essential significance of Hindutva, we do not primarily and certainly not mainly concern ourselves with any particular theocratic or religious dogma or creed. Had not linguistic usage stood in our way, then 'Hinduness' would have certainly been a better word than Hinduism as a near parallel to Hindutva. Hindutva embraces all the departments of thought and activity of the whole being our our Hindu race. It is imperative to point out that we are by no means attempting a definition or even a description of the more limited, less satisfactory and essentially sectarian term Hinduism.[7]

It is imperative that before getting confused with what the leaders of the Hindutva formations want to convey, it would be definitely helpful if one refers to this classic monograph and understand for herself/himself that when we say Hindutva terror, then it does not at all mean all those people who have deep faith in principles of Hinduism. Just as Islam and Political Islam cannot be considered equivalents, Hinduism and Hindutva cannot be measured on the same scale.

Naming the Organization: Beyond Individualizing the Crime

The biggest antidote to control, combat and counter terrorism of any kind is the ability of the law of the land to operate unequivocally in dealing with it. Theoretically speaking at least, the modern state differentiates itself from the earlier theocratic states by being impartial towards violations of human rights and dignity by any actor. As we have seen, a fake encounter killing even by the repressive machinery of the state itself can lead to action on the actual perpetrators and the planners of the act, if the aggrieved party or any third party refuses to accept the 'explanation' offered by the powers that be. Of course, if the masses are not aware and vigilant then the state can very well cover up thousands of such killings by performing all routine formalities even under a formal democratic setup which regularly organizes elections to elect its rulers.

A corollary of this point is to guarantee that different branches of the state—the judiciary, the executive as well as the legislature—are not only made more responsive to the people, but more sensitive towards the issue; and processes are institutionalized which ensure diversity at every level and at every tier. Unless and until affirmative action programmes are undertaken to ensure representation of the marginalized and excluded as well as minorities of different kinds, unless and until transparency and accountability are ensured at every level, the possibility would always remain that any of these wings of the state would seem to be acting unfairly with the aggrieved party. Any dillydallying on the part of the state on this score would provide further legitimacy to such forces who can then convince their followers that the state is discriminating against them because of their faith, colour and origin.

As expected, as far as the actual situation is concerned we notice a great hiatus between the desired and the actual. It has been a general experience of civil liberty activists or legal luminaries that actions by different wings of the state when dealing with issues of terrorism do not inspire confidence. This is especially true when victims come from the marginalized, exploited and minority sections of the population. While dealing with issues of majoritarian communalism and terrorism, one notices a general reluctance of the investigating agencies to name organizations involved whose activities are found to be involved in terror acts.

It would be worth examining the statement by the then director of CBI Ashwini Kumar when asked to comment on the news that few top leaders of the RSS were asked to appear before the investigating agency to "explain their relationship with some of the terrorists belonging to RSS" who were apprehended by the police. According to media reports the director "categorically denied that CBI had interrogated any big leader of the RSS." (July 13, 2010). It was the same time when CBI officials had filed charge sheet against five RSS workers namely Devender Gupta, Lokesh Sharma, Ramji Kalasangra, Sandeep Dange and Sunil Joshi—for their involvement in the Mecca Masjid blasts. The CBI had even declared a reward of 10 lakh rupees to anyone who gave clues about the whereabouts of the two absconding terrorists namely Ramji Kalasangar and Sandeep Dange. There were reports in the mainstream media about the senior leaders of RSS like Ashutosh Varshney and Ashok Beri being called to Hyderabad by the CBI officials to explore their links with the likes of Devender Gupta. But despite every news of the developments being available in the public domain Mr. Ashwani Kumar deemed it necessary to 'officially' deny this news. What must have prompted him to do this?

One witnessed a similar approach of the NIA (National Investigation Agency) also which has been specifically formed to look into terror related cases., when it ultimately filed a charge sheet in the bomb blast in Madgaon and Sancole in October 2009. The bomb blast had witnessed deaths of two Sanatan Sanstha activists—Malgonda Patil and Yogesh Naik. The NIA filed a charge sheet against eleven members of the Sanatan Sanstha. It duly mentioned that the conspiracy to organize bomb blasts in different parts of Goa on the occasion of Narkasur festival was hatched in the Ashram of the Sanatan Sanstha itself but it refused to include the organization as one of the accused.

M.K. Dhar, a senior intelligence official who has written a book called *Open Secrets* based on his experience, mentions that on many occasions one noticed a concurrence of views between the "intelligence officials and the RSS". Should one then say that the reluctance to name the organizations concerned reflects this concurrence?

Where are the Masterminds?

One cannot say that the state does not have enough instruments to deal with issues of transgression of law engaged in by state and non-state actors, but the fact remains that in actual practice it loses its impartiality.

Another important aspect worth emphasizing in this case is that all those people, formations and parties who want that the investigating agency to reach the kernel of truth and catch the real masterminds of these terror attacks will have to continuously remain vigilant. They will have to understand that there is a long chain involved in organizing a terror attack, namely:

1. Planter of the bomb/explosives or executioners of the terror act
2. Masterminds of the terror acts
3. Planners of the terror acts who take care of the finances as well.
4. Constant communalization in society which creates a 'conducive' situation to make terrorist activities.

One can compare this chain with the videos available which show suicide squads or fidayeen squads trained by the likes of Lashkar or Jaish. The likes of Kasabs who was the only live terrorist caught involved in the 26/11 attack can be considered the last link of the chain. The actual planners of such attack may be sitting far away in Karachi in some airconditioned room.

Comparing this chain with the Hindutva terror we can see that most of those people who have been apprehended till date are basically planters or actual executioners of the terror act. And catching the masterminds or planners of the terror acts seems to be the most difficult task at hand. Despite claims by the powers that be that they would not allow any accused, however, high-powered s/he might be—to go scot free, one finds that the higher the authority of the accused the lesser the interest shown by investigating agencies—forget arrest—even to send him/her summons to appear before them for some clarification.

Take a random look at any of the terror acts and one realizes how the authorities develop cold feet when they are faced with the possibility of nabbing/interrogating/naming some high profile individuals/formations against whom some concrete evidence exists or at least who are seen to have facilitated the work or had taken part in a meeting which supposedly planned the terror act

In her write-up on 'Hindutva Terror' leading anti-communal activist and editor of *Communalism Combat* tells us:[9]

> Both the Nanded investigations as well as the Malegaon probe have pointed to the indoctrination/inspiration provided by high profile rabble causing leaders of the VHP Dr. Praveen Togadia and Acharya Giriraj Kishore, in exhorting youngsters towards these acts, both individuals having allegedly visited Nanded on the eve of the blast in 2006. The ATS has been wary of drawing them into the charge sheet as accused or witness however.

When ATS Maharashtra under the leadership of Karkare was investigating the Malegaon bomb blast, they had got reports that Lt. Col. Purohit had met Praveeen Togadia and few other senior leaders of the RSS and VHP. None of these leaders have ever been questioned or called to the investigating office to explain their links (if any) with these terrorists.

Lastly, would it be correct to say that ensuring the rule of law, making the state accountable to people would drive the final nail in (Hindutva) terror's coffin? It would be only partially true.

Administrative measures centred around law or correcting aberrations in the justice delivery system are a necessary condition for combating terrorism. But they cannot be considered sufficient to root out the phenomenon. Prompt action by the police or a proactive judiciary can help snap the long terror chain, it can deter lot of people from resorting to that path but it is definitely not a guarantee that henceforth there would not be groups who would not take to terrorist methods. While "terrorism as crime" could be curbed and perpetrators apprehended, the possibility of new elements taking up this mode cannot be ruled out. It is because the larger politics which engenders this type of violent action has a much deeper basis in society. It is the politics of communalism—an ideology which gives primacy to a particular community and a worldview ensuing from it. Thus in today's world where one can think of an individual bearing multiple identities based on one's sex, nationality, race, choices, beliefs and languages known, it becomes very difficult to bracket two individuals in a particular 'slot'. The ideology of communalism marks out a particular individual on the basis of the (religious) community to which s/he belongs to and very crudely 'simplifies' the process of slotting. In fact, the phenomenon of Hindutva terror could be understood as a new dimension of Hindutva communalism where extremist Hindutva elements have taken resort to terrorist methods.

It is high time that we reboot ourselves for an uncompromising struggle against communalism of various hues. That is the only guarantee to save ourselves from 'terror turns' of various kinds.

Can We Do a 'Bangladesh?'

A question arises whether it will be possible for us to win the battle against Hindutva terror or if we will have to learn to live with it. Looking at the penetration of ideas of exclusion and hierarchy—which find deep resonance with the project of Hindutva—in our society and polity and the multifarious organisations built by executioners of the project to reach out to wider cross-sections of people, immediate victory definitely appears difficult.

Do we have countries in our neighbourhood who had to undergo similar experiences?

Interestingly, a look at Bangladesh, proves exactly the opposite. The transformations through which it has passed since last few years demonstrate that not only can the majoritarian terror be reined in, but processes can be unleashed at both structural and superstructural levels which create conditions for building a robust democracy. For any close watcher of the Bangladesh situation, any such development was unimaginable even a few years ago. The ascendance of fundamentalist forces aided and abetted by the ruling dispensation then was part of its stark reality.

It would be difficult to believe today but just a few years back, its future as a democracy remained bleak. It was a period when one was witness to repeated abuses by Islamist vigilante groups which were engaged in a campaign of attacks on minorities. The rising wave of hate speeches in public rallies inciting acts of violence against the Ahmadiyyas, Hindus and Buddhists had become a regular feature. It was disturbing to note that even cinema halls, Sufi shrines, traditional village fairs and cultural functions were then made targets of bomb attacks. The series of assassinations of respected secular intellectuals, journalists and academics had accompanied assassinations and violence against opposition party Awami league leaders. In fact, Bangladeshi intelligence agencies warned the government back in 2003 about JMB (Jama'atul Mujahideen Bangladesh) and the threat it posed to the state.[10]

Sheikh Hasina, the then leader of the opposition, herself was the target of a bombing attack at the Awami League Headquarters at a massive rally in Dhaka. (September 2004) Incidentally she had a miraculous escape. The situation inside Bangladesh looked so grim that around hundred former civil bureaucrats, diplomats and IGPs jointly issued an appeal to the government in the aftermath of the killing of Kabria plainly stating that, "Bangladesh will suffer the fate of Afghanistan, Darfur/Sudan, and Somalia unless the evils of extremism and intolerance are stemmed immediately" (January 2005).

An unprecedented number of suicide bombings rocked the country in August 2007. On August 17, 2005 there were 350 simultaneous bomb blasts throughout Bangladesh, across 63 of Bangladesh's 64 district headquarters. A wave of fear struck Bangladesh. Bombs exploded almost simultaneously across towns and cities, killing two persons and injuring about 140. The bombs targeted government offices, courts, press clubs and universities in Dhaka and 63 of the country's 64 district headquarters, sparing only Munshiganj. Leaflets left at blast sites, bearing the name of the banned Islamist outfit Jamaat-ul-Mujahideen, asked the government and parliament to establish Islamic rule in Bangladesh. The officially banned terrorist group Jama'atul Mujahideen Bangladesh claimed responsibility for the attack. Bangla Bhai's Jagrata Muslim Janata Bangladesh was also the other principal suspect for the serial bomb blasts. The blasts brought Bangla Bhai back at the centre of discussions on the threat of Islamist jihad in Bangladesh. A former school teacher, whose followers were believed to number over 10,000, he had taken part in the Taliban's jihad in Afghanistan.

Today, Bangla Bhai alias Siddiqul Islam and his brand of fanatic politics is history. As far as dealing with the challenge of majoritarian terror is concerned, it is clearly visible in the ongoing process of 'institutionalization' which has successfully challenged the ongoing process of de-institutionalization when the key institutions of democratic polity, ranging from the judiciary to the police and bureaucracy had become heavily politicized and partisan.

The sentencing of four cadres of the outlawed Jamaat-ul-Mujahideen Bangladesh (JMB) to 26 years of hard labor for throwing bombs at a local court in 2005 returned the focus to Bangladesh's struggle against pressing odds to contain the rise of Islamic extremism.[11]

There are certain important aspects of the process which need to be emphasised and which carry import for countries like us where similar challenges await us. Bangladesh tells us that a combination of political will, proactive judiciary and active citizenry can help rein in the menace of majority terrorism.

- Political will: The powers that be decided that the atmosphere of anarchy and lawlessness need to be changed and it should not appear that crimes against humanity are being condoned. An all out action programme against the fanatics was launched wherein many leaders, activists, ordinary workers of these fanatic formations were jailed or sent to rigorous imprisonment for the crimes they committed against humanity or a few amongst them (including Siddiqul Islam) were given death sentences. The powers that be decided that law of the land should prevail and there should not any one-sidedness in its operation and implementation. The installation of a caretaker government in 2007 under the leadership of Fakhruddin Ahmed, with due support from the military, proved to be a crucial factor in this crackdown against the terrorists. (As it happens in such cases, there were charges of gross human rights violations against the security forces. Nobody can condone such practices.)

It is noteworthy that the drive to clip their wings had started during the BNP regime itself which was supposed to be sympathetic to them. It was forced to take some action against these groups because of international pressure. The group was banned in February 2005 after a key leader—a university professor and ideologue, Dr. Mohammad Asadullah al-Ghalib—revealed the group's plans to overthrow the civilian government through violence (*New Age* [Dhaka], February 28, 2005).

> -Proactive judiciary: Bangladesh's judiciary which has been a beacon of hope in the minds of people for the defence of secularism and which also saw the rise of fundamentalist forces as a grave challenge also saw to it that there are no judicial delays in such cases. In many such cases, special courts were also constituted to dispense justice.
>
> - Active citizenry: Bangladesh happens to be one such third world country where a vibrant public sphere dotted with entry of women in large numbers into the public domain, a large number of civil society organisations covering many important areas of human life and combined with the ongoing social campaigns have created conditions conducive to democracy. Impact of public awareness is very much visible in its rapid and spectacular improvements in human development indicators, particularly since 1990s.

Anybody can see that such politically aware, socially conscious citizenry has always acted as a counterweight to the fundamentalist forces.

REFERENCES

1. 'Nanded Blast: The Hindu Hand', *The Tehelka*, December 30, 2006.
2. S.M. Mushrif, *Who Killed Karkare?* (Delhi: Pharos Media, 2010).
3. Lt. Col. Purohit, vide ATS transcript.
4. ATS Transcript.
5. 'RSS in Sindh', *Economic and Political Weekly*, July 8, 2006.
6. Rajeshwar Dayal, *A Life of Our Times* (Orient Longman, 1999).
7 V.D. Savarkar, *Hindutva* (Delhi: Bharti Sahitya Sadan, 1989), sixth edition, pp. 3-4.
8. Smita Nair, 'RSS leaders from UP questioned in Mecca Masjid Case.' *Indian Express*, Wednesday, 30 June, 2010, Mumbai.
9. *Communalism Combat*, February, 2009, pp. 8-9.
10. *Daily Star*, August 28, 2005.
11. *Daily Star* [Dhaka], May 1, 2008.

6

The 'Muslim' Affirmative Action Debate: Post-Sachar Reflections

Khalid Anis Ansari

Most democracies struggle to address the question of inequalities, whether individual or group-based, as a normative necessity. Broadly, the thrust of affirmative action (AA) or positive discrimination policies is on challenging the monopoly of dominant social sections on power and ensuring the *representation* of historically excluded groups in elite positions in society, especially in prestigious jobs or elite educational institutions. The access of disenfranchised groups to preferred positions in society democratizes the deliberative or decision-making spaces by providing the former with a voice, and thereby ensuring that subaltern aspirations are reflected in the policy domain. In this sense, AA policies must neither be confused with conventional measures of *redistribution* of wealth or assets, land reforms for instance, nor misconstrued as poverty alleviation or employment generation programmes. Rather, their scope is very much restricted and singularly premised on the transformation of composition of elite positions in society. Theoretically, AA can include a number of strategies or instruments and is a broader concept than reservations. However, in the Indian context, reservations or quotas in public employment and educational institutions to subordinated caste groups (and to women in the electoral sphere in a limited sense) have been the dominant form of AA thus far. Moreover, there have been animated debates on the nature of groups to be included within the scope of the extant AA framework.[1]

In this context, since the tabling of the reports of *High-Level Committee on the Social, Economic and Educational Status of the Muslim Community of India* (2005), popularly called the *Sachar Committee Report* (SCR), and the *National Commission for Religious and Linguistic Minorities* (2006), or the *Ranganath Mishra Commission Report* (RMCR), a renewed demand for quota to Indian Muslims has been vigorously circulated in the public sphere. While reservations appear to be a popular desideratum in the community, there is little consensus on the mode of reservation policy to be adopted as such. Broadly, there are two kinds of claims that are being advanced: one, reservations on community qua 'community' basis by those who privilege the dimension of inter-group inequality, and two, reservations for the community mediated on the basis of 'caste' by those who believe that the dimension of internal inequality is far more important. If Muslim quota was merely a 'policy' (technical or procedural) issue, its resolution would have been far easier. What makes the issue vexed is its obvious interpenetration with the political and the status of extant hegemonies in the Indian political sphere. This debate is also interesting because SCR not only did not recommend reservations to the community explicitly but also advocated broadening the scope of AA by recommending measures beyond quotas. However, to read any fundamental conflict between quotas and other measures of affirmative action suggested by the SCR would probably be a grave error and the way forward should be to contemplate a healthy synthesis of various strategies/instruments of AA available. Overall, the objective of this chapter is to map the entangled nature of Muslim quota debate, especially in the post-Sachar scenario, and to propose plausible policy prescriptions.

Identity and Policy: Caste as "Inequality", Religion as "Difference"

Conceptually, the last few decades have increasingly brought into sharp relief what may be termed as the crisis of modern universals. In fact, as Ernesto Laclau suggests, what is usually paraded as the 'universal' is basically the dominant 'particular' produced by hegemonic practices in a social field crisscrossed by antagonism and power.[2] In a similar vein, the liberal ideal of universal and abstract citizenship, located within the imagination of the nation as a civic community, has been vigorously interrogated.[3] It has been argued that difference-blind policies can produce deeply conservative outcomes in highly unequal and stratified societies. This is largely because notions of formal equality or procedural democracy are, more often than not, acutely insensitive to the background and structural inequalities faced by various marginalized communities. Therefore, some form of group-differentiated citizenship, which is capable of grasping inequality both in its symbolic (recognition) and material (redistribution) manifestations, becomes imperative in order to ensure substantive renderings of equality or democracy.[4]

In fact, the domain of policy cannot but be deeply intermeshed with identity claims in modern democracies. As Moya comments, "The significance of identity depends partly on the fact that goods and resources are still distributed according to identity categories. Who are we—that is, who we perceive ourselves or are perceived by others to be—will significantly affect our life chances: where we can live, whom we will marry, (or whether we can marry) and what kind of educational and employment opportunities will be available to us [...] an ability to take effective steps toward progressive social change is predicated on an acknowledgement of, and familiarity with, past and present structures of inequality—structures that are often highly correlated with categories of identity."[5] Since the mainstream public sphere is not a space for participatory parity in stratified societies, it is useful for the disadvantaged sections to form what Fraser calls "subaltern counterpublics". These are "parallel discursive arenas where members of subordinated social groups invent and circulate counter-discourses to formulate oppositional interpretations of their identities, interests, and needs."[6] These subaltern counterpublics have a dual role. They act as enclaves for the subaltern groups where they can articulate their concerns and bring a coherence to their demands without the supervision of the dominant groups which concentrate, in Mansbridge's words, on "absorbing the less powerful into a false 'we' that reflects the more powerful."[7] On the other hand, they also act as training grounds for agitational activities directed at wider publics. It is in the dialectic between these two functions of the subaltern counterpublics that their emancipatory potential can be located. In general, these counterpublics expand the discursive space in stratified societies and enable discursive contestation and so craft a ground for participatory parity which the imagination of a single, comprehensive public sphere is at a loss to address.

In postcolonial democracies like India, a similar tension persists between the adherents of the ideal of an unmarked civic community and those who are usually perceived as practicing identity or partisan politics. In the emergent literature an analytical distinction between "civil society" and "political society" is made to highlight a possible tension between modernization and democratization. Civil society refers to self-organized associations and movement organizations that were set up in the heydays of colonial modernity and are usually governed by elite classes who would like to see India in the club of highly modernized nations. Political society, on the other hand, alludes to contingent and fluid political formations such as community pressure groups, or such other contestants for power, who are generally identified with their ability to represent and work for the realization of the popular demands of the subaltern groups in their struggle for survival. Thus, the former can be seen as a site for *modernization* and the latter as the site for *democratization*.[8] As Elliott puts it succinctly, "whereas the interest of civil society in the United States has been animated by worry about lack of civic engagement and in Eastern Europe by resistance to interventionist states, Indian discussion flows from concerns about the extension of democracy to previously subordinated groups, so-called 'democratic deepening."[9]

In the Indian case too, while universal and equal citizenship was upheld as the constitutional ideal, the domain of state-citizen relationship was mediated by the notion of "community". As a matter of fact, social policy in post-colonial India largely conceived religious identity in cultural terms and recommended symbolic protection for the same. In this sense, minority religions, like Islam or Christianity, became a subject of "minority rights" (cultural protection). Caste, on the other hand, was conceptualized in terms of birth-based disadvantage or stigma and therefore necessitated annihilation or transcendence. Hence, caste became a subject of "social justice" (positive discrimination). It may be logically deduced that while the category of "religion" seemed to be informed by a thin conception of materiality, the category of "caste" seemed to assume a thin conception of culture.[10] However, this consensus—caste as "inequality", religion as "difference"—was seriously interrogated by the significant events of the 1990s (the three M's—Mandir, Market and Mandal) and ascendance of new subaltern counterpublics within entrenched categories like the SCs, STs, OBCs, and religious minorities. The emergence of identities like *Mahadalits*, EBCs, *Pasmanda Muslims*, Dalit Christians, etc., clearly indicate at the internal displacements within the aforementioned categories. Hence, since the 1990s the rational policy domain has been under acute strain from the domain of new social movements and emerging political subjectivities, thereby leading to various productive debates that are forcing a reassessment of old hegemonies and extant policy framework.

The Muslim Quota Debate: Negotiating "Caste" and "Community"

In important ways, the terms of most contemporary debates in India were set by the colonial state and its ethnographers in collaboration with the elite, native interlocutors. Broadly, the process of formation of entrenched communities and various fault-lines one witnesses at present were informed by the colonial classificatory categories produced for the purposes of governmentality. Hence, the production of various identifications can be traced back to the crucible of colonial efforts to govern India and the subsequent contestations and jostling for power by various groups inscribed unarguably by an unequal and differentiated colonial development policy. One of the most pervasive effects of colonial ethnographic efforts was in homogenizing and systematizing social identities. Even in pre-colonial times, allegiance to particular communities was considered valuable. But these communities were fuzzier, ambiguous and fluid.[11]

Colonial modernity and the operations of the decennial census on the other hand introduced a "new community" by its efforts at enumeration and classification of subject population.

> The new 'communities' were now often territorially more diffuse than before, less tied to small locality, less parochial, on account of changes in communications, politics and society more generally. They were at the same time historically more self-conscious, and very much more aware of the differences between themselves and others, the distinctions between 'Us' and 'Them'. The new 'community', or 'enumerated community'...also became increasingly a part of a rationalist discourse—centrally concerned with numerical strength, well-defined boundaries, exclusive 'rights' and, not least, the community's ability to mount purposive actions in defence of those rights.[12]

Hence, colonial knowledge system craftily laid out "ethnographic plots" which also quite often "encouraged the census takers to transfer the authority of self-classification from their subjects to themselves."[13] Thus, while on the one hand an all-India "Hindu" and "Muslim" community was constructed, on the other hand, caste continued to interrogate the overarching religious categories from within. As far as Indian Islam is concerned, this negotiation between "caste" and "community", systematized during colonial era, continues to manifest itself in contemporary politics/policy domain.

However, before engaging with the contemporary debate on Muslim quota a few opening remarks would be in order here. Firstly, one has to be aware of the discursive background when the dominant notion of the 'Muslim' as an all India community—monolithic and unmediated by caste, region or sect—was produced by the colonial modes of governmentality. In this context, the genealogy of the conflation of the 'Muslim' with 'backwardness' can be traced back at least to Sir William Hunter's *The Indian Mussalmans* (1871), wherein a claim for the subalternity of all Muslims was spuriously made on the basis of the exceptional data of Bengal.[14]

Secondly, the ensuing discourse of Muslim backwardness offered the background rationality for demands like the separate electorate (1909) and reservations in government services for Muslims (1925) to be legitimized in the colonial period. The naturalization and resultant competitive relationality of religious identities, informed by the interests of the colonial regime and that of the native religious elite, were chiefly instrumental in the Partition of the country in 1947. It is this historical association with secession that was instrumental in framing 'religion' as a suspect category for policy purposes in independent India.[15]

Thirdly, there is sufficient sociological evidence to suggest that "caste" could be delinked with "religion" and framed as the main axis of social stratification in South Asia that determines social status across religious communities. In this sense, caste is not merely a 'Hindu' phenomenon but rather its stamp is present in all religious communities, including Indian Muslims. In the case of the latter, even when the central text, the *Quran*, is silent on this question due to its obvious geographical roots, the theological/hermeneutical production on Islam in South Asia has largely legitimised caste-based hierarchies.[16] In this context the SCR remarks quite unambiguously: "Thus, one can discern three groups among Muslims: (1) those without any social disabilities, the *ashrafs*; (2) those equivalent to Hindu OBCs, the *ajlafs*, and (3) those equivalent to Hindu SCs, the *arzals*. Those who are referred to as Muslim OBCs combine (2) and (3)."[17] In the literature produced by the Muslim anti-caste movements in the last two decades, the subordinated caste Muslims, both so-called *ajlaf* and *arzal*, are generally referred to as *Pasmanda Muslims*, while the term *Dalit Muslims* is specifically reserved for those sections that are pejoratively termed as *arzal*. Broadly, the so-called *ashraf* Muslims either trace their origins to foreign lands like Arabia, Iran, Afghanistan or Turkey or are converts from high-caste Hindu locations (the Ranghars for example); the *ajlafs* include the converts from Shudra locations whose occupations are generally considered to be ritually clean, like the Julaha (weaver), Dhunia (cotton-carder), Kunjra (vegetable-seller), Hajjam (barber), Darzi (tailor), etc.; the *arzals* refers to converts from the so-called "untouchable" castes, like the Halalkhors (sweepers), Lalbegis (scavengers), Jogi (mendicants), Dhobi (washer-man), Nat (acrobats), etc.

Fourthly, as the SC and ST categories were largely settled ones and due to the Supreme Court's ceiling of 50 per cent for reservations, it was the ambiguity of the OBC category that offered space for Muslims to make a claim for reservations in the post-colonial phase.

So can Muslims as a whole be included in the category "Other Socially and Educationally Backward Classes" (OBC)? As per the Constitution, there are only two relevant factors for including a group in the OBC category. Firstly, it should be underrepresented in the services under the State [Article 16 (4)]. Secondly, it must meet the criterion of being "socially" and therefore an "educationally" backward community [Article 15 (4)]. So, let us apply these tests to the *ashraf* sections within Muslims because the case for the inclusion of Pasmanda Muslims is broadly a settled one and most of the subordinated caste Muslims are already included in the Central OBC list. So is the *ashraf* section underrepresented? Can it be said to be socially backward? These questions must merit our attention now.

In this context, Table 10.10 of the SCR deals with the representation of Hindu OBCs (H-OBCs), General Muslims (M-Gen) and Muslim OBCs (M-BCs) in public employment (Sachar 2006, 210). The relevant figures are reproduced below:

Department/Undertaking/ Institution	*H-OBCs (%)*	*M-Gen (%)*	*M-OBCs (%)*
Central Security Agencies	11.4	1.0	3.6
Railway	9.3	4.5	0.4
Central PSU	8.3	2.7	0.6
SPSC-Recommended for Selection	27.0	0.9	0.9
University Faculty	17.6	3.9	1.4
University-Non Teaching	24.9	3.0	1.7

According to NSSO 61st round (2004-05) the population of OBC Muslims (Dalit Muslims included) was 40.7 per cent of the total Muslim population (the population percentage for General Muslims in that case turns out to be 59.3 per cent). If the total Indian Muslim population is 13.4 per cent of the national population (2001 Census) then the General Muslim population would be 6.76 per cent of the national population. If one keeps this figure (6.76 per cent) in mind and compares it with the figures in the shaded column (M-Gen) then it can be clearly inferred that the *ashraf* Muslims are underrepresented in public employment in most of the sectors.

However, if we probe further we find the case is not as simple and clear-cut as that. As we know the SCR has derived the population data for Muslim OBCs (Dalit Muslims included) from the 55th (1999-2000) and 61st (2004-05) round of NSSO returns wherein for the first time since Independence the data pertaining to OBC category was obtained. Moreover, most of this data suffers from the limitation of 'self-reporting'. From the 55th round returns, the population of Muslim OBCs was estimated at 31.7 per cent of the Muslim population (for General Muslims it was 68.3 per cent) and from the 61st round returns the estimate of Muslim OBCs was 40.7 per cent of the Muslim population (for General Muslims it was 59.3 per cent). This shows a growth of about 9 per cent in Muslim OBC population in just five years. In the case of Uttar Pradesh the growth in Muslim OBC population was from 44.4 per cent (55th round) to 62 per cent (61st round)—a jump of 17.6 per cent in five years. In the case of Bihar, the growth in Muslim OBC population was from 40.6 per cent (55th round) to 63.4 per cent (61st round)—a jump of 22.8 per cent in five years! While the official estimates of Muslim OBCs show an ascending trend, the Pasmanda Movement in Bihar and elsewhere had always estimated the population of subordinated caste Muslims to be about 85 per cent of the Muslim population.[18] Interestingly, this figure is also accepted by the National Movement for Muslim Reservation that campaigns for Muslim reservations in the country: "Only 10 to 15 per cent of the Muslim community belongs to the so called *ashraf* while 85 per cent to 90 per cent are non-*ashraf*. Due to ignorance and inattention Muslim Backward Classes have not been surveyed comprehensively and that is why with every successive statistical survey, the percentage of Muslim OBC's goes on increasing to levels, higher than that of Hindu OBCs."[19] So there is a consensus on the break-up of the Muslim population in caste terms by both the *ashraf* and *Pasmanda* groups.

Now reworking the Indian Muslim population according to these estimates (15 per cent *ashraf* Muslims and 85 per cent *Pasmanda* Muslims) the Muslim population of 13.4 per cent (2001 Census) can be broken into 2.01 per cent General Muslims (instead of the earlier 6.76 per cent) and 11.39 per cent OBC Muslims. If we revisit the shaded part of the table then we can gauge that given the reworked population of General Muslims as 2.01 per cent they now turn out to be over-represented in at least four sectors and almost represented half of their population in the remaining two sectors. In striking contrast, the OBC Muslims are grossly underrepresented in all sectors. Similarly, if we take the case of political representation then out of seven thousand five hundred members from the first to fourteenth Lok Sabha only about 400 members belonged to the Muslim community. Out of these 400 Muslim members, about 340 have been General Muslims and only 60 have been OBC Muslims. Hence, the representation of General Muslims in Lok Sabha works out to 4.5 per cent that is way beyond their population percentage of 2.01 per cent. Even here, they are not only adequately represented but rather are doubly represented.[20]

Let us consider if the upper caste Muslims do actually constitute a socially backward group. However, what does social backwardness mean in the Indian context? What are the criteria for declaring a group as a socially and educationally backward class? It is interesting to note that while the Scheduled Castes (SC) and Scheduled Tribes (ST) were coherently defined in the Constitution, the Other Backward Classes (OBC) remained a vague category and was relegated to the backburner for decades (except in certain states). When, in the early 1950s, the Constitution of India prescribed affirmative action benefiting OBCs, however, it was unclear who these classes were. Though

Dr. B.R. Ambedkar was clearly of the opinion that, "[what] are called the backward classes are nothing else but a collection of certain castes."[21] In this respect, at least since the 1990s, the Mandal judgment (*Indra Sawhney vs. Union of India*, 1991) has apparently informed most debates around reservations. The Mandal judgment expresses quite clearly that:

> The expression 'backward class' in Article 16(4) takes in 'Other Backward Classes', S.Cs, S.Ts and may be some other backward classes as well. *The accent in Article 16(4) is upon social backwardness.* Social backwardness leads to educational backwardness and economic backwardness. They are mutually contributory to each other and are inter-twined with *low occupations in the Indian society.* A caste can be and quite often is a social class in India. *Economic criterion cannot be the sole basis for determining the backward class of citizens contemplated by Article 16(4).*[22]

Further, the judges have opined:

> A caste can be and quite often is a social class in India. If it is backward socially, it would be a backward class for the purposes of Article 16(4). *Among non-Hindus, there are several occupational groups, sects and denominations, which for historical reasons are socially backward.* They too represent backward social collectives for the purposes of Article 16(4).[23]

Besides, the following extract would lay to rest any ambiguity with regard to the meaning of the term 'backward' used in the Constitution:

> Further, if one keeps in mind the context in which Article 16(4) was enacted it would be clear that the accent was upon social backwardness. It goes without saying that in Indian context, social backwardness leads to educational backwardness and both of them together lead to poverty which in turn breeds and perpetuates the social and educational backwardness. They feed upon each other constituting a vicious circle. It is a well known fact that till independence the administrative apparatus was manned almost exclusively by members of the 'upper' castes. The Shudras, the Scheduled Castes and the Scheduled Tribes and *other similar backward social groups among Muslims and Christians* had practically no entry into the administrative apparatus. It was this imbalance which was sought to be redressed by providing for reservations in favour of such backward classes [...] We are,

> accordingly, of the opinion that *the backwardness contemplated by Article 16(4) is mainly social backwardness. It would not be correct to say that the backwardness under Article 16(4) should be both social and educational*.[24]

Quite clearly, if 'caste' is the key category for defining socially and historically accumulated backwardness, then the case for *ashraf* Muslims becomes extremely fragile. It is on the basis of the aforementioned logic that about 80 Muslim groups were recognized as 'backward' castes by the Central OBC list in 1993 and most high caste Muslims were duly excluded. Interestingly, the Central OBC list includes both the *ajlaf* and *arzal* sections as the latter, who should ideally be clubbed with the Hindu SCs, were controversially ejected from the SC list through the Presidential Order of 1950 (Clause 3). If we follow the logic of the Mandal judgment closely then it is only the occupational groups within the Muslims, in other words the Pasmanda Muslims, that can be defined as socially backward and hence brought within the ambit of reservations under the OBC category. Consequently, the case for *ashraf* or high caste Muslims, which according to the SCR itself, are "without any social disabilities" turns very weak. Even historically, apart from the exceptional states of Kerala and Karnataka which included all Muslims (sans the creamy layer) in the OBC list, the first and second Backward Classes Commissions, various court judgments and state OBC lists have all recognized only the subordinated caste Muslims for reservation purposes.[25]

And, this line of reasoning is exactly the basic impediment that those making a claim for Muslim reservations on the basis of "community" have sought to overcome in recent times. So, the first point in the terms of reference of the RMCR was: "To suggest criteria for identification of socially and economically backward sections among religious and linguistic minorities".[26] Indeed, the insertion of the term "economically" here is notorious to say the least as the phrase used in Article 15 (4) is "socially and educationally" and there is no mention of the term "economically" there. Further, the first recommendation of the NCRLM report curiously demands a blanket reservation of 15 per cent for religious minorities including a 10 per cent separate quota for all Muslims. The report suggests:

> Since the minorities—especially the Muslims—are very much under-represented, and sometimes wholly unrepresented, in government employment, we recommend that they should be regarded as backward in this respect within the meaning of that term as used in Article 16 (4) of the Constitution—*notably without qualifying the word 'backward' with the words 'socially and educationally'*—and that 15 per cent of posts in all cadres and grades under the Central and State Governments should be earmarked for them as follows: (a) The break up within the recommended 15 per cent shall be 10 per cent for the Muslims (commensurate with their 73 per cent share of the former in the total minority population at the national level) and the remaining 5 per cent for the other minorities.[27]

While the members of the Commission appear to have laboured hard to arrive at this recommendation yet they themselves seem to be sceptical of their position when they write further: "We are convinced that the action recommended by us above will have full sanction of Article 16 (4) of the Constitution. Yet, *should there be some insurmountable difficulty in implementing this recommendation*, as an alternative we recommend that [...]" before going to the next recommendation. What exactly is the "insurmountable difficulty" if not the fact that the recommendation is against the spirit of the Mandal judgment as is evident by the extracts from the judgment mentioned above?

Post-Sachar Developments

The contentious site of Muslim reservations has witnessed an interesting journey since the tabling of the SCR and the RMCR. Spurred by the deepening of the discourse of Muslim backwardness and electoral arithmetic, the UPA government announced on December 22, 2011 a 4.5 per cent sub-quota for backward sections within minorities in the overall Central OBC quota. As we know a number of backward caste groups from the minority sections were already included in the Central OBC list and were availing the benefits of reservations from 1993 onwards. What the UPA government did was to club together all these already recognized and enlisted backward caste groups within minorities (especially, Muslims, Christians and Sikhs) into a 4.5 per cent sub-quota, thereby by default reserving the remaining 22.5 per cent for OBCs within the majority community.[28] However, in May 2012 the Andhra Pradesh High court struck down the sub-quota citing, among other reasons, that the Centre had acted in a "casual manner" and that the creation of the sub-quota was based on "religious grounds". Further, when the Centre challenged the order in the Supreme Court it failed to get interim stay as "the Bench felt the scheme of 4.5 per cent reservation was supported neither by constitutional nor statutory provisions" (PTI 2012). The Bench also asked, "Can you make classification on the basis of religion?"[29]

In separate but related moves the AP High Court had earlier quashed twice the attempts by the state government to chalk out a quota for Muslims. When the state government announced a quota of 5 per cent for Muslims in 2005 it was struck down citing absence of consultation with the Backward Classes Commission. When in 2007 the AP government set up a Backward Classes Commission and announced 4 per cent quota—1 per cent less in order to keep within the 50 per cent ceiling set by the Supreme Court—it was axed citing the absence of relevant criteria to identify social and educational backwardness and inadequate representation in government services. However, the Supreme Court stayed the order and the AP government continued to give 4 per cent quota to subordinated caste groups within Muslims. In 2010 the Left Front government in West Bengal announced a 10 per cent quota for economically weaker sections among Muslims in jobs and education. However, the plan was challenged in the High Court and the case is still pending. Similarly, on June 25, 2014, the INC-NCP government announced 5 per cent reservations for Muslims in Maharashtra. The move has been subsequently challenged and the verdict of the Bombay High Court is awaited.

Concluding Comments and Policy Inferences

Overall, due to the Supreme Court's ceiling of 50 per cent on the quantum of reservations and the treatment of "religion" as a suspect category owing to its historical association with secessionism, the demand for a separate quota for all Muslims (10 per cent according to RMCR) or even a separate sub-quota exclusively for backward caste Muslims, is not a feasible one as the recent court wrangles amply demonstrate. Such a scenario calls for a fresh approach to Muslim quota. As we know, while the dominant castes among Muslims are not recognized, the backward (*ajlaf*) and Dalit (*arzal*) Muslims are duly included within the Central OBC list. Consequently, the dominant caste Muslims, in their bid to be recognized, have either raised the demand of a separate quota for all Muslims or have attempted to sneak into the existing OBC lists.[30] Also, while the backward caste Muslims have complained that they are not receiving a fair share inside the existing OBC quota, the Dalit Muslims have demanded that they be shifted to the SC quota from the OBC quota by scrapping the 1950 Presidential Order (Para 3). How do we navigate and negotiate between these various competing claims? In this context, P.S. Krishnan offers a valuable suggestion:

> It is true that Muslims have not received a fair deal in the field of social justice, including reservation. But it is desirable that the leaders of the community move for remedial action in a manner that is constitutionally valid and judicially sustainable. This means they should try to secure reservation and other measures of social justice for BC Muslims, along with a scheme of categories that will ensure BC Muslims cease to be exposed to competition with BCs who are less backward. In matters like religious freedom, cultural freedom and freedom from violence, all Muslims and other minorities have the same entitlement. But in the matter of reservation and other measures to ensure social justice, it is only the socially and educationally BCs of Muslims and other minorities who have valid entitlement. Protecting these rights of Muslims as well as of all minorities requires unity among them and among those who do not belong to minority religions but believe in constitutional and human values. By espousing the cause of Muslim BCs in the matter of social justice, the advanced communities among Muslims will help build up such unity.[31]

In the light of the above discussion the following policy options are suggested:

I. Sub-categorization within the Central OBC quota

Let us take the issue of the marginalization of OBC Muslims within the Central OBC quota. The argument often made is that the dominant Hindu OBC groups corner most of the benefits thereby leaving Muslim OBCs with an inappropriate share and therefore the latter should be accommodated in a separate sub-quota. However, this logic applies to non-dominant Hindu OBCs as well because arguably only about 20-25 castes out of more than 2500 Hindu OBC castes included in the Central OBC list can be assumed to be dominant. Hence, the best recourse is to raise the issue of internal inequalities within both the extant OBC category and Indian Muslims on the basis of caste, and to club similarly placed caste groups across religions in the various sub-categories chalked thereby. Drawing significantly from P. S. Krishnan's suggestions, one can propose at least three sub-categories within the Central OBC list: Most Backward, More Backward and the Backward. The "Most Backward" may refer to those sections that have no asset base but have skills. The "More Backward" castes may include castes of small peasants, especially tenants without rights. Moreover, the "Backward" may refer to those castes with relatively substantial asset base but who are nonetheless backward.

In this context, most Muslim artisanal groups (*ajlaf*) can be included in the "Most Backward" and "More Backward" sub-categories along with other similarly placed caste groups from other religions. Also, while the case for inclusion of *ashraf* Muslims in the OBC category—whether in terms of representation in services, social or educational backwardness—is far from conclusive and seems fairly weak prima facie, they may be eventually accommodated in the "Backward" category if they qualify the necessary tests of social backwardness. It must be mentioned that such sub-categorisation of the OBC quota is not entirely novel and is already in place in states like Karnataka, Kerala, Bihar and Andhra Pradesh. This scheme also has an additional merit of safeguarding us from any communal polarization on religious lines and is more judicious.

II. Inclusion of Dalit Muslims within SC Quota

The Dalit (*arzal*) Muslims must be delisted from the OBC list and incorporated in the SC list. In the pre-independence period, the Dalit Muslims benefited from the reservation policy in the SC list. After Independence, by the Presidential Order of 1950 (Clause 3), most non-Hindu dalits were ejected out from the SC list. However, in 1956 the Sikh dalits and in 1990 the neo-Buddhists were integrated thereby debarring only Dalit Muslims and Dalit Christians from the SC list. This violates the principle of secularism enshrined in the Constitution and the RMCR has properly advocated the scrapping of the 1950 Presidential Order (Para 3). In terms of identification of Muslim caste groups that should be included within the SC list the RMCR clearly recommends "...that all those groups and classes among the Muslims and Christians, etc. whose counterparts among the Hindus, Sikhs or Buddhists, are included in the Central or State Scheduled Castes lists should also be covered by the Scheduled Caste net. If any such group or class among the Muslims and Christians, etc. is now included in an OBC list, it should be deleted from there while transferring it to the Scheduled Castes—placing the same persons in the Scheduled Caste list if they are Hindu, Sikh or Buddhist but in the OBC list if they follow any other religion—which is the case in many States—in our opinion clearly amounts to religion-based discrimination."

III. Affirmative Action beyond Quota

The SCR had stressed on innovative policies in the domain of affirmative action and suggested the formation of a National Data Bank (NDB), an independent Assessment and Monitoring Authority (AMA), and an Equal Opportunities Commission (EOC) in order to address the equity-related concerns of marginalized communities. While some progress has been made on these fronts, yet a lot needs to be done. Some policy analysts have argued in favour of a 'diversity index' and to link it to certain incentives for educational institutions, the private sector, etc. There are other recommendations in the SCR relating to education, employment, credit and infrastructure that may be appropriately considered in this context. More recently, the Planning Commission has suggested a number of measures in the 12th five year plan for the development of minorities, especially Muslims.[32] There is a need to take these suggestions seriously.

REFERENCES

1. Ashwini Deshpande, *Affirmative Action in India* (New Delhi: Oxford University Press, 2013), pp. 8-10.
2. Jacob Torfing, *New Theories of Discourse: Laclau, Mauffi and Žižek* (Oxford: Blackwell, 1999).
3. Charles Taylor, 'The Politics of Recognition', in *Multiculturalism and the Politics of Recognition,* ed. A. Gueman (Princeton: Princeton University Press, 1992), Gurpreet Mahajan, *The Multicultural Path: The Issues of Diversity and Discrimination in Democracy* (New Delhi: Sage Publications, 2002).
4. Will Kymlicka, *Multiculture Citizenship* (Oxford: Clarendon Press, 1995), Nancy Fraser, A 'Recognition without Ethnics', in *Theory, Culture & Society* (2001), 18 (2-3): 21-42.
5. Paulo Moya and Michael R Hames–Garcia, *Reclaining Identity: Realist Theory and the Predicament of Postmodernwon* (Hyderabad: Orient Longman, 2000), p. 140.
6. Nancy Fraser, 'Rethinking of Public Sphere. A Contribution to the Critique of Actually Existing Democracy', in *Civil Society and Democracy: A Reader,* ed. Carolyn M. Elliot (New Delhi: Oxford University Press, 2003), p. 91.
7. Ibid., p. 90.
8. Partha Chatterjee, 'On Civil Society and Political Society in Post Colonial, Democrates', in *Civil Society: History and Possibilities,* eds. Sudipta Kaviraj and Sunil Khilnani (New Delhi: Cambridge University Press, 2001).
9. Carolyn M. Elliot, 'Civil, Society and Democracy: A Comparative Review Essay' in *Civil Society and Democracy : A Reader* (New Delhi: Oxford University Press, 2003).
10. Niraja Gopal Jayal, *Citizenship and its Discontents: An Indian History* (New Delhi: Permanent Black, 2003), Zoya Hasan, *Politics of Inclusion: Castes, Minorities and Affirmative Action* (New Delhi: Oxford University Press, 2009).
11. Nicholas Dirks, *Castes of Mind: Colonialism and the Making of Modern India* (Delhi: Permanent Black, 2001).
12. Gayenendra Pandey, 'Communalism as Construction', in

Sudipta Kaviraj (ed.), *Politics in India* (New Delhi: Oxford University Press, 1997), pp. 305-6.
13. Gauri Viswanathan, *Outside the Fold: Conversion, Modernity and Belief* (New Delhi: Oxford University Press, 1998).
14. Sumit Sarkar, *Modern India: 1885-1947* (New Delhi: Macmillan, 2005), p. 77.
15. Laura Dudley Jenkins, *Indentity and Identification in India: Defining the Disadvantaged* (London: Routledge, 2003), p. 110.
16. Masood Alam Falabi, *Hindustan Mein Zaat Paat aur Musalman* (*Caste and Muslims in India*, in Urdu), (Delhi: Al Qazi Publishers, 2007), Yoginder Sikand, *Islam, Caste and Dalit-Muslim Relations in India* (New Delhi: Global Media Publications, 2004).
17. Rajinder Sachar, *Social, Economic and Educational Statues of the Muslim Community in India: A Report* (Government of India, 2006), p. 193.
18. Ali Anwar, *Masawaat Ki Jung* (*The Battle for Equality*, in Devanagari) (New Delhi: Vani Prakashan, 2001).
19. Syed Shahabuddin, 'National Movement for Muslim Reservation, Working Paper No. 1', February 10, 2010, http://www.syedshahabuddin.com/documents.html (accessed March 18, 2014).
20. Ashfaq Husain Ansari, 'Reservation for Muslim Backwards' November 16-30, 2004. http:\\www.milligazette.com/archives2004/16-30, Nov 4- Print Edition/163011200463. htm (accessed January 24, 2012).
21. Frank de Zwart, 'The Logic of Affirmative Action: Caste, Class and Affirmative Action in India', in *Acta Sociologica* 43, No. 235 (2000).
22. B.J. Reddy, 'Indra Sawhney etc. vs. Union of India and Others, etc.' (16 November, 1992), November 16, 1992, http://indiankanoon.org/doc/1363234 (accessed January 22. 2012).
23. Ibid.
24. Ibid.
25. Zoya Hasan, op. cit., p. 171.
26. Justice Ranganath Mishra, *Report of the National Commission for Religious and Linguistic Minorities* (Ministry for Minority Affairs, Government of India, 2007), p. 1.
27. Ibid., pp. 152-3.
28. Ministry of Minority Affairs, *Statement of Minister of Minority Affairs in Lok Sabha on 28 December, 2011*, December 28, 2011. http://www.minorityaffairs.gov.in/sites/upload_files/moma/files/statement_LS_minister.pdf (accessed January 19, 2011).

29. Ibid.
30. Ashok Yadav and Khalid Anis Ansari, 'Traversty of Social Justice: The Curroles case of Inclusion of Upper Caste Syed 'Mallicks' in Bihar Backward Classes List', June 4, 2011, http://countercurrents.org/ansari040611.htm (accessed January 22, 2012).
31. P.S. Krishnan, 'On 4.5 Reservation for BCs of Minorities', unpublished, 2012.
32. Planning Commission (GoI), *Twelth Five Year Plan (2012-2017): Social Sectors*, Vol. III (New Delhi: Sage Publications India Pvt. Ltd., 2013).

7

Rights of Groups and Differentiated Citizenship: The Case of Indian Muslims

Asghar Ali Engineer

India, since its remote past, has had a pluralist society. There have been not only several major religious groups in Indian society like those of Hindus, Muslims, Buddhists, Jains, Christians, Sikhs and Parsis, but also many linguistic, ethnic and cultural groups. This has been the historical heritage of India.

During the feudal era these groups had distinct identities of their own. In the democratic period these diverse people are treated as equal citizens, despite their respective distinct identities. One does, however, find tension between group rights and the concept of citizenship and this tension might even assume violent proportions. Thus demands for rights by different groups become causes of conflict.

In the case of India ever since the struggle for freedom from British rule began, there has been conflict between Hindus and Muslims. A section of Muslims called *ashraf* (i.e. of noble origin) constituted the ruling class for more than 500 years. This class of Muslims lost its power and privileged position to the British through the East India Company. The Muslims also became the targets of wrath of the British rulers ever since the Mutiny of 1857.

Prior to 1857, the Hindu and Muslim ruling classes were fairly integrated throughout the Muslim rule. In fact the ruling class during this period was composite though the Muslims had the predominant position. The Hindu and Muslim kings did often fight, but so did Hindu and Hindu kings and Muslim and Muslim kings. It was not a fight between two religious groups, rather a fight for power between two rulers.

However, after the establishment of the British rule, a serious conflict developed between Hindus and Muslims partly because of the British policy of divide and rule and partly because of failure of any agreement between the Hindu and Muslim elite for sharing power in a democratic set up. This conflict proved to be so serious and irresolvable that ultimately India was partitioned in 1947 on the eve of its independence. The division, it is interesting to note, was brought about by the secular elite of the two countries and not by the religious elite. The demand for Pakistan was raised and won by M.A. Jinnah who was a thoroughly Westernized and secularized person. And it was vigorously opposed by a person like Maulana Abul Kalam Azad who was an eminent religious leader of Muslims in India. Not only Maulana Azad but also several other Muslim religious leaders opposed the demand for the partition. This clearly shows that the partition was caused not by religious conflict but by power-sharing conflict.

It has often been seen that such group conflicts remain suppressed under authoritarian regimes, but emerge under democratic ones. The best example in recent times is that of Indonesia. The conflict between Muslims and Christians was suppressed by General Suharto who was a military dictator. But once a democratic regime was ushered, not only East Timur seceded from Indonesia but also the rest of Indonesia was thrown into turmoil due to violence, which broke out between Muslims and Christians. While authoritarian regimes seek solutions through suppression of aspirations of different groups, democratic societies try to solve the problems by balancing between demands of different groups though the balancing act proves quite difficult to achieve. The balance is often upset by emerging conflicts. A successful democracy is one which manages these group conflicts skilfully and avoids confrontation between them. Tensions can persist though. With proper conflict management tensions can be kept within manageable limits. However, sometimes politicians manoeuvre these group tensions to their own advantage. Such manoeuvrings accentuate the tensions. The tensions can easily explode in countries riddled with poverty, backwardness and illiteracy.

Even the partition of South Asia in 1947 did not resolve the Hindu-Muslim problem, as the politicians on both the sides of the divide continued to manoeuvre issues for their own political purposes. The tensions remained simmering not only between the two countries resulting sometimes in war but also riots between the two communities in India. The religious right exploited religious sentiments and raised highly controversial issues between the two communities. There were tensions not only between Hindus and Muslims but also between secular Hindus and communal Hindus (communalism in India is a strongly negative term. Those who exploit religious sentiments for political purposes are termed as communal and those who believe in keeping state neutral to different religious groups are termed as secular).

The tension between secular and communal groups from the same religious group increases and political battles are fought between regressive (i.e. communal) and progressive (secular) groups sometimes with intense emotions. The whole decade of eighties of the last century (i.e. 20th century) saw intense emotions being raised between the secular and communal forces in India. We will throw more light on this a little later as the clash of group identities during this decade reached its climax.

Before discussing this climactic communal situation we would like to throw some light on the Constitutional provisions for group rights. It must be said that the Indian Constitution is fair to minority religious groups. In this respect, it must be said, it is one of the best documents in the world. It ensures all—religious, cultural and linguistic rights of minority groups. As pointed out above, there are, besides religious minority groups, linguistic, cultural and ethnic minority groups dispersed throughout India in different states. It is also interesting to note that a religious, ethnic or cultural group, which is in majority in one state, is in minority in certain other states.

Thus Muslims are in majority in Kashmir while they are in minority in all other states of India. The Hindus are in majority throughout India but they are in minority in Kashmir. The Christians who are a tiny minority in all other India states are in majority in two states of North East India i.e. Mizoram and Nagaland. The Sikhs while in minority throughout India are in majority in the Punjab.

Thus in view of these complexities, group rights and the differentiated concept of citizenship becomes extremely important in India and the Indian Constitution seems to meet this challenge of group rights fairly evenly. We would like to highlight some of the provisions of the group rights in the Indian Constitution. One finds provisions for minority rights, be they religious, linguistic or cultural, in the Articles 25-30 of the Indian Constitution. Article 25 is the most fundamental for religious minorities. This Article in fact represents the secular essence of the Indian Constitution. The Article is captioned as under: Freedom of conscience and free profession, practice and propagation of religion. Then Article 25(1) goes on to say, "Subject to public order, morality and health and to other provisions of this Part, all persons are equally entitled to freedom of conscience and the right freely to profess, practise and propagate religion."

Article 26 relates to *Freedom to manage religious affairs* and goes on to state that subject to public order, morality and health, every religious denomination or any section thereof shall have the right (a) to establish and maintain institutions for religious and charitable purposes; (b) to manage its own affairs in matters of religion; (c) to own and acquire movable and immovable properties and (d) to administer such properties in accordance with law.

Article 28 prohibits imparting of religious education in any educational institution wholly maintained out of state funds. Thus the government run schools and colleges cannot impart religious education pertaining to any group or community. This progressive character of the Constitution is being violated today under right-wing regimes by introducing majority religious and cultural practices in school curriculum. Some minority groups especially Muslims develop some aversion to send their children to government run schools because of this. In the state of UP in North India the Bhartiya Janata Party Government which belongs to the religious right in India introduced an outright Hindu religious practice called *Saraswati Vandana* (worshipping the goddess of knowledge) in mid-nineties. Both the Muslims and secular Hindus raised strong objections as it clearly violates the Constitutional provision stated above.

Article 29 also makes equally important provisions for minorities. It is entitled protection of interests of minorities. It states, "(1) Any sections of citizens residing in the territories of India or any part thereof having a distinct language, script or culture of its own shall have right to conserve the same. (2) No citizen shall be denied admission into any educational institution maintained by the state or receiving aid out of state funds on grounds only of religion, race, caste, or language or any of them." Thus according to this Article all citizens are free to conserve their religion, language, its script and culture of their own without any let or hindrance.

Article 30 is also of seminal importance for religious, cultural and linguistic minorities. It is about rights of minorities to establish and administer educational institutions:- (1) All minorities, whether based on religion or language, shall have the right to establish and administer educational institutions of their choice.

(2) The state shall not, in granting aid to educational institutions, discriminate against any educational institution of their choice.

Thus it will be seen that Articles 25-30 are very important from the point of view of preserving and promoting the rights of differentiated religious groups in India. Hence today (in the era of rising fascism) they are under attack from the religious right. That is why those against special religious or cultural rights oppose these constitutional provisions and target them in their propaganda. The members of the Sangh Parivar (i.e.

the Saffron family led by the main ruling coalition party BJP) like the Vishwa Hindu Parishad, Bajrang Dal and others are now openly demanding deletion of these articles from the Constitution. However they were cautious enough not to demand publicly their deletion.

In the early eighties the BJP first floated the theory of "appeasement of minorities". This theory, based on certain rights of minorities including the separate personal law, was swallowed uncritically, by a large section of Hindu middle classes. The BJP was anxious to come to power and it craved for the Hindu votes. However, since the Hindus are highly stratified along caste lines it was difficult for it to appeal to all Hindus across caste lines. It was, thus, in search of issues which would enhance its appeal across caste lines.

However, there was a stumbling block. Like communalism, casteism was also politically gaining ground. Before we proceed further it is important to throw some light on the social and political developments during the decade of the eighties. The decade of the eighties was quite critical in many respects. Firstly, democracy, which began in early fifties in India, had struck deeper roots by the seventies. Different sections of population, including minorities as well as low caste Hindus (known as Dalits i.e. the oppressed) were becoming increasingly aware of their rights and privileges.

This awareness on the part of minorities, oppressed and marginalized sections of society posed threat to the rights and privileges of upper caste ruling classes of Hindus. For centuries the upper caste Hindus had enjoyed all the privileges at the cost of lower caste Hindus. Even during the so-called 'Muslim rule' the upper caste Hindus constituted the composite ruling class with Muslim rulers and enjoyed all these privileges.

However, in democracy with the concept of citizenship and equal rights for all, maintaining these privileges are not a viable proposition, at least in theory. And increased awareness on the part of low caste Hindus created political tensions. Some economic developments during the sixties and seventies added to these political tensions. Success of the green revolution led to the demands for increased wages by the farm labour and it was mainly Dalits who constituted farm labour; upper caste Hindus owning large tracts of fertile land.

During the medieval ages the Dalits were under obligation to perform free labour known as *begar.* The upper caste Hindu landed gentry, which expected *begar* from these Dalits, was aghast at their demand for increased wages. Many Dalits were burnt alive for daring to demand increased wages during mid-sixties. The privileges of the caste Hindus were directly threatened by the increased awareness on the part of Dalits.

And increased caste tensions in India lead to increased communal tensions. The upper caste Hindus, in order to defuse caste tensions, encourage communal tensions by raising some communal controversy so that Dalits, as 'part of Hindu society', can be silenced into submission. And in the event of outbreak of communal violence Dalits can also be used for the dirty job of killing members of the minority community and looting their houses. In all the communal riots, I have observed, Dalits are used for killing and burning and looting properties. Thus it will be seen that caste and communal tensions are clearly inter-related.

During the eighties both caste and communal tensions were assuming violent proportions. It was during this decade that scores of major communal riots took place resulting in killing of thousands of people. It was during this decade that the BJP thought of making a serious bid for power and to expand its political base among the backward caste and lower caste Hindus. The BJP had been essentially a party of upper caste urban Hindus who constituted about 15-18 per cent of the total Hindu population. With that narrow political base no political party could come to power at the Centre. The Congress party had been ruling over India with about 37 to 45 per cent of the votes cast. It could manage to get votes of topmost caste i.e. Brahmans (who always managed to monopolize all top jobs and key ministries under the Congress rule) along with the votes of minorities and Dalits. That magical combination always saw the Congress party in power at the Centre.

The BJP, which was making a serious bid for power could do so only by breaking this combination and in order to do so it wanted to create as sense of alienation and injustice among the upper caste Hindus and then to win over the lower castes by creating a sense of "Hinduness" among them. Thus the BJP decided to raise series of controversial issues pertaining to minorities and secular polity of India. And it did help tremendously by delegitimising the Congress rule.

The BJP put the question mark on the very concept of secularism, which was, according to it, the very problem. The concept of minority and group rights was the product of secularism. Thus one should strike at the very root of the problem. Thus it began to describe "Congress secularism" as "pseudo secularism" based on what it called "appeasement" of minorities. And the best example given of the appeasement was allowing Muslims to marry four wives whereas Hindus could not marry more than one. In other words the Muslim personal law came under direct attack.

Muslims have been practising their personal law in India ever since the advent of Islam in India. The criminal law of Islam, however, was rarely applied even during the so-called Muslim rule in India. But notionally it did exist through the period of Muslim rule. It was finally abolished by the British government and they enforced the Criminal Procedure Code of their own which was obviously secular in character. Abolition of Islamic criminal law was accepted unanimously by all Muslims including the Ulema and there was no sign of protest.

But the British government did not touch the personal laws of various religious communities, as it was a very sensitive issue. Personal laws cover areas of marriage, divorce, inheritance, custody of children and other related areas. These are too personal to be easily abolished. In India where religion and religious laws are so highly respected and considered of divine origin it is all the more difficult to change them. Let alone the government, even eminent social reformers like Sir Syed, Nawab Muhsin-ul-Mulk, Justice Amir Ali, Maulavi Khuda Bakhsh and others did not succeed in bringing about reforms in Muslim personal law. There has been strong resistance even to the idea of reform in personal law, let alone any interference from governmental agencies.

Also, the leaders of the Indian National Congress which was in the forefront of the freedom struggle assured the Muslim Ulema that Muslims would be free to practise Islam and Islamic laws of marriage, divorce, etc. It was on this solemn assurance that the organization of Muslim divines Jami'at-ul-'Ulama-i-Hind lent unqualified support to the Indian National Congress (INC) and its struggle for freedom. Mahatma Gandhi was accepted as the leader by this premier organization of Muslim divines. The Ulema, on the solemn assurance, refused to support the Muslim League, as pointed out above, in its efforts to create Pakistan which was projected as the Muslim homeland. The Ulama stood behind the INC for creating a composite nation.

The INC fulfilled its assurance while framing the constitution and left Muslims free to practise Muslim personal law. Article 25 gave fundamental right to the citizens of India to "profess, practise and propagate" their religion. The Muslims interpret Article 25 as the Constitutional right to practise their personal law. Some Supreme Court Judgements also support this viewpoint. The Articles 14 and 15 of Indian Constitution refer to equality of rights for all citizens and non-discrimination on grounds of religion, race, caste, sex or place of birth. When some people challenged existence of the personal laws, particularly the Muslim personal law on grounds of violation of Articles 14 and 15, the Supreme Court did not agree.

But the BJP chose to attack Muslim personal law and depicted it as an attempt to "appease Muslim minority" for their votes. The educated Hindu middle class which was already resentful of permitting Muslims to marry up to four wives lent their support to the BP and justified its demand to abolish Muslim and other personal laws and enforce a common civil code. Thus enforcement of common civil code became one of the most important issues in the mid-eighties of the last century.

When the BJP, the party of religious right, was carrying on political propaganda to enforce the common civil code one development took place, which shook the whole country. A Muslim woman called Shah Bano from Indore (state of Madhya Pradesh) filed a case against her husband claiming maintenance under the Section 125 Criminal Procedure Code (Cr.P.C.) which is obviously a secular law. Under this law, a husband who has divorced his wife is obliged to maintain his divorced wife if she has no wherewithal to maintain herself until she remarries or dies whichever be earlier.

Shah Bano who was divorced by her lawyer husband was awarded maintenance under Section 125 of Cr.P.C. by the Madhya Pradesh High Court. Her husband challenged the MP High Court judgement in the Supreme Court on grounds that it is violative of Muslim personal law, which is the law of the land applicable to Muslims and that in matters of personal law, secular law will not be applicable to Muslims. Thus he prayed to the Supreme Court to set aside the judgement of the lower court and that he should not be obliged to pay maintenance to her divorced wife.

Shah Bano's husband, being a shrewd lawyer, also made Muslim Personal Law Board (MPLB) a party to the case in the Supreme Court. The lawyer husband argued, supported by the MPLB lawyer that Muslims had their own personal law, which allowed maintenance to the divorcee for three months of *iddah* (waiting period after divorce). And he had already paid to his divorced wife three months' maintenance and he therefore, had no further obligation towards her. Shah Bano's lawyer, however, argued that she had claimed maintenance under a secular law (i.e. Section 125 of Cr.P.C.) which was applicable to all the communities.

Shah Bano's lawyer, Daniel Latifi, being a Muslim placed before the Supreme Court, the Abdullah Yusuf Ali's English translation of the *Holy Qur'an* and the relevant verse 2:241 which is as follows: "For divorced women maintenance (should be provided) on a reasonable (scale). This is the duty on the righteous." The Supreme Court thus referred to this Qur'anic verse also while pronouncing its judgement and upheld the lower court's decision that Shah Bano's former husband should pay maintenance to her for life time under the secular law as the relevant Qur'anic verse also provided for it.

This judgement unleashed a storm in India. Muslim leaders condemned the judgement as interference in Muslim personal law and appealed to Muslims to protest against the judgement and stage demonstrations. Muslim leaders said that the Supreme Court judges had no right to interpret the Qur'anic verses. It is for the Ulema to do it and according to the latter interpretation, the period of maintenance should be not more than the *iddah* period. This is the Shari'ah rule and no secular court can violate it through its judicial pronouncements.

The leaders were not sure how Muslim masses would respond to their appeal for protest. But there was massive response. There were two principal reasons for this huge response. Firstly, the religious and political leaders provoked Muslim masses into believing that if they do not protest now Islam would not survive in India. Even mosques would be locked. Obviously this was an overdrawn picture.

Secondly, Muslims were feeling terribly insecure during the mid-eighties as a number of major communal riots had taken place in which hundreds of innocent people were killed. In this insecure environment Muslim masses believed what their leaders told them. Some progressive and liberal Muslims did support the Supreme Court judgement including this writer but they were hopelessly outnumbered. Their voice was naturally drowned. Rajiv Gandhi was the Prime Minister when the Shah Bano movement took place. He initially brushed aside Muslim protests and showed determination to uphold the judgement. However, he soon showed signs of nervousness and could not face the massive protest movement.

He announced that a new law would be drafted for Muslim women upturning the Supreme Court judgement and that Section 125 of Cr.P.C. would no more apply to Muslim divorcees. Thus a law was enacted in February 1986 called Muslim Women (Protection of Rights on Divorce) Act. According to this Act, a Muslim woman would be entitled to a one time provision (called *mata'*) at the time of divorce in addition to her *mehr* (gifts from the husband's family to a woman at the time of her marriage) amount and three months' maintenance. Thus she would get some lump-sum amount while being divorced.

Muslim leaders mainly raised two issues at the time of agitation: 1) The Article 25 of the Constitution gives them the fundamental right to practise their religion and Muslim personal law is integral part of religion. No court judgement should interfere with this fundamental right. 2) It is the question of protecting their Islamic identity and no one can tamper with their religio-cultural identity. Liberal Muslims, on the other hand, argued that fundamental right to religion should not preclude common secular laws particularly relating to women's rights and that the right to religious identity should not be at the cost of women's privileges. Thus the Muslim community was polarized between liberals and orthodox.

Thus for liberal Muslims, women's rights were as important as the fundamental right to religion. Religion should either be re-interpreted or secular laws pertaining to women should be upheld even if the *shari'ah* laws were not in conformity with the former. However, needless to say, the liberals were numerically too weak to press their point and lost out to the orthodox Muslim leaders. However, this debate generated a lot of heat not only between progressives and orthodox among the Muslims but also between the secular Hindus and orthodox Muslims.

It is important to note that the Muslim leadership while pressing for their group rights in a differentiated society did not exercise balance and wisdom. They even antagonised well meaning secular forces among the Hindus on this question who had otherwise always stood by the rights of minorities, specially Muslims. All secular forces were one on the question of upholding the Supreme Court judgement as it involved upholding women's rights. Muslims lost considerable sympathy of these secular forces by taking a very rigid position.

The BJP which was already propagating that the Congress was indulging in the policy of "appeasement of Muslims" had one more issue in its basket to prove its point. It could now easily convince the Hindus that Congress secularism was pseudo-secularism and based on appeasement of minorities and the Congress enacted a new law throwing away the Supreme Court Judgement to appease Muslims. It (the BJP) gave a new slogan of "positive secularism" which meant, "Justice for all and discrimination against none". This slogan greatly appealed to the majority of Hindus but there was clear trap in it: denial of minority rights and religious identity. No wonder then that all secularists rejected this deviation from well-defined path of secularism.

The decade of the eighties proved to be disastrous speaking from the perspective of the group rights, specially of the Muslims. As a result of the BJP propaganda, the two communities i.e. Hindus and Muslims, were almost polarized along religious lines. India had never witnessed such polarisation before in the independent India. The BJP went on intensifying anti-Muslim feelings with a view to monopolize the Hindu votes. Though the Hindus are stratified against caste lines, they closed ranks against Muslims, and behaved politically as if the Muslims were against Hindus and also were anti-national.

This resulted in outbreak of communal violence repeatedly during the decade of the eighties. It was during this decade that maximum number of major communal riots occurred in middle sized towns of North India. The chain of riots began from 1980 onwards. In these riots nearly 400-500 persons were killed, eighty per cent of whom were Muslims. In 1980, a major riot took place in Moradabad in UP wherein more than 1,000 persons were killed mostly by police firing while Eid prayers were going on. In 1981 a major communal riot took place in Biharsharif in the northern state of Bihar in which more than 400 persons were killed.

In 1982 communal riots broke out in Meerut in UP, and Baroda in Western India in the state of Gujarat in which 150 persons were killed. In Meerut more than 50 persons were killed either in stabbing incidents or in police firing. In 1983 communal violence erupted in Nellie in Assam in the North East of India. In Nellie riots more than 4,000 Bengali Muslims were killed by rioters.

In 1984, communal violence flared up in Bombay-Bhivandi region in Maharashtra in which about 200 persons were brutally done to death. In the same year, anti-Sikh violence broke out after the assassination of Indira Gandhi in which about 4,000 Sikhs were killed. Most of the Sikhs were killed in the capital city of India, i.e. in Delhi. Many Sikhs were killed in other parts of UP and MP.

The state of Gujarat was particularly under the strong influence of the BJP and was experiencing communal violence repeatedly. In 1985 communal disturbances flared up in Ahmedabad, the capital city of Gujarat and lasted for a record of 18 months. In this violence both Dalits and Muslims were killed. It is very difficult to estimate number of deaths in these disturbances as no consolidated figures are available. But the number of deaths was certainly upward of five hundred.

Then Meerut in UP once again witnessed the worst kind of sectarian violence in 1987 in which again more than 400 deaths occurred. In the Meerut riots the Provincial Armed Constabulary (PAC) killed innocent Muslim young men, about 23 in number and threw their bodies into a nearby canal. So far no action has been taken against these guilty policemen. The Meerut riots of 1987 were followed by the Bhagalpur riots in 1989 in which 900 persons were done to death brutally, most of them in surrounding villages. And in 1990 when L.K. Advani took out the infamous Rath Yatra to campaign for the construction of a Ram temple, more than 300 riots broke out along the route in which heaven knows how many people were killed.

Thus it will be seen that the decade of eighties was highly explosive and claimed the lives of thousands of innocent people so that politicians could grab power easily. There was unprecedented degree of communal violence during this unfortunate decade. And all this was motivated primarily for politics, and not for religion as such. Religion, it is important to note, is only an instrument and not a real cause. The real cause is political in nature.

There was yet another negative fall-out of the Shah Bano movement which was much more grave in its implications. Rajiv Gandhi was already apprehensive of reaction of the upper caste Hindus to the new legislation on Muslim women. He, therefore, in order to appease the upper caste Hindus and traditional supporters of the BJP ordered opening of the doors of the Babri Masjid for Hindus to worship Ram Lalla (i.e. child God Ram). The right-wing Hindus led by the BJP was pressing their claim on the Babri Masjid, a mosque built during Babar's reign in the 16th century. They maintained (without any historical proof) that Babar, a destroyed a 4th century Ram temple and built a mosque there. This brings out clearly that one should maintain some balance in pressing for the group rights lest it should become counter-productive.

All noted secular historians refuted such claims and maintained that there was absolutely no proof of existence of any Ram temple on the site of the Babri Masjid. However, the BJP leaders, desperate for consolidation of Hindu vote-bank totally ignored all such protests and went ahead, creating religious frenzy among the Hindus. This gave rise to competitive communalism. Muslim leaders created religious fervour among the Muslims in the name of Shari'a and the BJP leaders were bent upon creating similar religious fervour among Hindus.

The BJP also remarkably succeeded in creating religious frenzy among the Hindus cutting across caste lines. The liberal secular Muslims, in case of the Shah Bano movement, were hopelessly outnumbered. The movement went on for a few years and the BJP went on increasing the number of its seats in parliament. It had won only two seats in the 1984 General Elections. In the 1991 elections it gathered 119 seats in Parliament. Babri Masjid was demolished on December 6, 1992. The demolition was followed by a terrible outbreak of communal violence in Mumbai and several other places in India. More than thousand people were killed in the riots in Mumbai alone and several hundred more in other towns and cities.

Thus the BJP has derived maximum benefit by inciting communal passions. It now demanded that the land belonging to the Babri Masjid trust be handed over to it to construct a grand Ram temple. Though the Ram temple could still not be built (it would lead to more bloodshed if it were ever built) the BJP achieved its goal of coming to power in 1999, though in alliance with 22 other parties. Building the Ram temple was not the real goal of the BJP, but to capture political power was its real goal.

Since the BJP was in power in expedient and opportunistic alliance with 22 other heterogeneous and ideologically contradictory parties, it could not talk of building a Ram temple. And since a construction will be in clear violation of all Constitutional provision and in breach of the law of the land, it cannot afford to do that. But other members of the Sangh family like the Vishwa Hindu Parishad (VHP) and Bajrang Dal are publicly pressing for the construction of the temple.

The temple issue could still be explosive as it earlier was. The BJP is maintaining mysterious silence and the VHP is issuing declarations that the temple be constructed precisely at the place where the mosque stood.

Thus it will be seen that in a country with the presence of several religious, linguistic and cultural groups, serious problems are bound to arise even when the Constitution takes care of the minority group rights as does the Indian Constitution. Jawaharlal Nehru, the first Prime Minister of India, was a great champion of secularism and he used all his moral and political authority for acceptance of secularism and made it the basis of Indian polity. Yet, in his own lifetime grave challenges to secularism arose and he witnessed major communal riots in Jabalpur in Central India, which greatly shook him. He never expected such communal frenzy to arise in the independent India.

Post-independence India witnessed series of communal riots in which thousands of people lost their lives. The communal problem, thanks to vote-bank politics in India, remains as precarious as it ever was. There seems to be no way to solve it unless politicians resolve in all seriousness to shun politics based on communal and caste sentiments and engage themselves with issue-based politics. There are no such signs in the Indian political arena. More and more extremist and fundamentalist socio-political formations are springing into action intensifying the communal threat and promoting religious frenzy. What is worse even educational curriculum is getting increasingly communalized under the present political dispensation.

No doubt that majority chauvinism is the main cause of communal tensions in the society. But experience shows that minority groups also have to show wisdom and restraint. The Shah Bano agitation clearly shows that minority aggressiveness can be very dangerous for its own security. For peaceful co-existence, moderation and restraint on the part of all groups are highly necessary. Unfortunately, in India some elements think that being different is being enemy. Democratic polity, however, can succeed only when being different is treated with respect.

Also, one should recognize difference between assimilation and integration. Assimilation treads on the right to be different whereas integration stresses unity with the right to be different. The right to be different is the most important right in democracy. No democracy can successfully function without conceding the right to be different. And right to be different should embrace all fields, religious, cultural as well as political. The right to be different is the hallmark of democracy and the right to be different can be promoted only through dialogue, not through violence. Democracy, diversity and dialogue go together.

8

Economic Problems of Muslims in India

Asad Bin Saif

The hallmark of a functioning democracy and just order is to see how its inhabitants, particularly the most vulnerable sections including minorities, are treated. It is aptly felt that democracy and economic justice are inextricably linked as without democracy, economic justice cannot be achieved whereas without economic justice, democracy cannot be sustained. The economic betterment of the people is the crux of a functioning democracy. Through economic security, people can be empowered to participate in the democratic process in a forthright manner and they cannot be hoodwinked from the realization of their democratic aspirations. In this way, democracy is strengthened; further society and the nation get enabled to put themselves on the salubrious and healthy path and achieve much sought-after enduring peace and all-inclusive growth. Contrary to such a vision, the largest minority, the Muslims of India, are lagging far behind in all the developmental indicators—social, economic, and educational. Their economic and social backwardness is best projected by the Justice Rajendra Sachar Committee, constituted by the then Prime Minister Manmohan Singh in March 2005 to prepare a report on the social, economic and educational status of Indian Muslims. The seven member-committee submitted its report in November 2006. It covered 13 States where the Muslim population is sizable in some districts.

One of the findings, the high level of economic deprivation

of the Muslims was an eye opener, and a source of great consternation for the policy makers. The idea behind constituting such a committee was to collect necessary data as the lack of substantive data proved to be problematic in addressing the issue of Muslim backwardness. More so, the obtained data has the official stamp which would endow it with legitimacy to execute it. The one lacuna in the formation of the committee was the absence of representation of women, despite the fact that backwardness of Muslim women is very acute. The findings of the committee also debunked the notion of appeasement of the Muslims propagated by the communal groups like the BJP. The data contradicts the propaganda onslaught. In fact, Muslims are trapped between two aspects related to their well-being: "Muslim appeasement" propagated by the communal groups and the Congress policy of taking refuge in "There is no alternative" (TINA) syndrome. It is appropriate to mention here that the Congress always plays emotional politics without paying much heed to the real uplift of the Muslims. The Congress depends on local satraps who, more often than not, treat the people as clients rather than citizens.

The data revealed the shocking testimony to six decades of institutional neglect and bias perpetuated against the Muslims in the fields of education, employment, access to credit, access to social and physical infrastructure and political representation. If it is implemented with sincerity, it would help in the amelioration of the problems of the community in the same manner that Mandal Commission did for the uplift of the Other Backward Castes (OBCs). The idea behind such recommendations is to address the socio-economic conditions of 170 million (2011 Census) people and ensure equity and fair-play for them. It is obvious that the stability of the nation can only be achieved through the involvement of all, including the Muslims, in the developmental process. It must also be underscored that the problem of socio-economic deprivation is not merely a Muslim problem, but it is a question of survival of democracy itself. The problem is long-standing and quite a few governments had initiated the studies and tried to address the issue in the past. In the 19th Century, Mountstuart Elphinstone, a perceptive British administrator, put it on record that special measures were required to uplift the backward sections of the Muslims. Studies conducted by the British Administration led to the passage of a Government Act in 1935 offering the Dalit Muslims reservation facilities along with Dalit Hindus. Later, nearly three decades ago, Indira Gandhi constituted a 10-member high-powered panel on Minorities, Scheduled Castes (SC), Scheduled Tribes (ST) and Other Backward sections, headed by Dr. Gopal Singh. In its report submitted on 14th June, 1983, Dr. Gopal Singh Committee maintained that there was a "sense of discrimination prevailing among the minorities and that it must be eliminated, root and branch, if we want the minorities to form an effective part of the mainstream."

The Sachar Committee findings brought back the debate and discussion veered around deprivation and marginalization of Muslims; and it is rightly construed as the continuation of earlier efforts but more significant and relevant than the past initiatives. Sachar Committee focused only on Muslims because it was made known in its terms of reference and examination processes whereas earlier initiatives had been for different segments of the society like SC/ST and other weaker sections. The Sachar data was not a startling revelation as the Centre for the Study of Developing Societies (CSDS) on class formation in different communities had put forth similar information. But Sachar Committee had the advantage in terms of thoroughness and, therefore, it is difficult to reject its findings. The wide range of specifics covered by the committee such as perception about Muslims, the size and distribution of the community's standard population, indices of the community's income, employment, health, education, poverty, consumption and standard of living, and the community's access to social and physical infrastructure indicate the diligence that went into the collection of statistics. The committee also made a meticulous study of the perpetuation of the caste system among the Muslims and hence deprivation remained intact for those who had crossed over from one religion to another centuries ago. The committee collated data from across the country and received detailed oral and written presentations from states that have significant Muslim populations.

It is quite clear that social churning and protracted political contestation are going on vis-i-vis socio-economic deprivation of the Muslim community. The committee is also divulged that the economic condition of the Muslims is worse than Dalits and just above the Other Backward Castes. The committee tried to link three aspects relating to identity, security and equity, but it is the issue of equity had been delved deeply. It is beyond doubt that economic betterment is the desiderata for democratic empowerment. It is economic security which gives a person confidence. It means economic amelioration is a necessary trait for a functional democracy. So, economic betterment of the people and sustenance of democracy are symbiotically linked and both are inextricably bound together.

It is beyond doubt that Muslims face all round deprivations. The average household of a Muslim spends merely Rs. 800 per month which is the equivalent to the lowest caste Hindus and much lower than the upper caste Hindus which is Rs. 1,400. It is well-known that worker population ratio of Muslims is significantly lower than all other SRCs in rural as well as in urban areas. The low aggregate work participation ratios for Muslims are essentially due to the much lower participation in economic activity by the women of the community. In comparison with 44 per cent of women at the national level in the prime age group of 15-64 years in India, workforce participation rate among Muslim women is only about 25 per cent. In rural areas 70 per cent Hindu women comprise the workforce whereas Muslims women are merely 29 per cent; even Hindu upper caste women's percentage is 43. Work Population Ratio (WPR) among Muslim women folk in urban areas is merely 18 per cent as the work opportunities within the household for them are very limited. It must be mentioned here that gainful employment particularly of women folk boost people's self-esteem, and helps in the decision making process which is a sign of empowerment. The lack of resources in the hands of women among the Muslims is also a sign of the community's economic and social backwardness.

It is also established that Muslims due to lack of opportunities and rampant discrimination against them are overwhelmingly dependent on self-employed enterprises. They prefer it also because it generates regular income rather than the erratic gains through casual jobs. Within the Muslim community the reliance on self-employment is higher among the OBC Muslims (64 per cent) than general Muslims (59 per cent). For Hindus, relatively lower i.e. 43 per cent and higher among the upper caste Hindus (55 per cent). It is important to understand that given the high percentage in the self employed category, Muslims should have access to credit facilities. In this respect too, Muslims are deprived of credits facilities and other bank facilities as they are declared as residents of "negative zones", Johupura, a ghetto of Ahmedabad, mostly populated by Muslims is a case in point.

Muslim participation in salaried jobs both in public and private sectors is very low. Barely 13 per cent Muslims are engaged in these jobs whereas upper caste Hindu workers constitute 25 per cent. Lack of job avenues in public sectors for the Muslims is a source of great concern. The participation of Muslims in regular jobs is quite limited as compared to even the traditionally disadvantaged SCs/STs. Only about 27 per cent of Muslim workers in urban areas are engaged in regular work while the share of such workers among SCs/STs, OBCs, and Hindu workers is 40 per cent, 36 per cent and 49 per cent respectively. Less than 24 per cent of Muslims regular workers are employed in the public sector or in government jobs. This proportion is much higher for other SRCs. It is important to note that about 39 per cent of the regular SC/ST workers are engaged in such jobs. The share among the UCs Hindu and OBCs are 37 per cent and 30 per cent respectively. Muslim workers have the lowest presentation in such coveted jobs. The large number of participation by SCs/STs is obviously for the positive discrimination policy of job reservations for these groups. Likewise Muslim representations in government jobs and Public Sector Undertakings is very low at around 5 per cent.

As already mentioned, Muslims are mainly engaged in the

informal self-owned proprietary enterprises and their engagement in formal sectors is much lesser than the national average. It is also true that participation of Muslims workers in PSUs or with the government is the least among the SRCs. As compared to other SRCs, the participation of Muslim workers in the informal sector enterprises is much higher. For example, less than 8 per cent of Muslim workers in urban areas are employed in the formal sector as compared to the national average of 21 per cent. The share of the Hindu OBCs and SC/ST in such jobs is as high as 18 per cent and 22 per cent respectively. The same pattern prevails in rural areas. The vulnerabilities of Muslim workers engaged in informal sectors are exposed. The male workers who are engaged in street bending businesses is 12 per cent higher than the national average of 8 per cent. Two types of industries where the sizeable sections of them are involved are tobacco and textile/garments related industries. More than 41 per cent and 35 per cent Muslim male and female workers respectively are engaged in tobacco production. Similarly 30 per cent workers engaged in the manufacturing of garments and apparels, etc. are Muslims; the corresponding figure of women workers is 17 per cent. The share of Muslims workers engaged in textile industry is more than 21 per cent and 28 per cent respectively for males and females. The other industries where Muslims constitute significant proportion of the workforce are: sales, repair and maintenance of motor vehicles (Muslims constitute 26 per cent of the total workers in this sector) and some segments of electrical machinery and apparatus manufacturing (more than 23 per cent of the male workers in this sector are Muslims). Muslims workforce is also found in large numbers in retail electrical machinery where it is around 22 per cent.

An interesting comparative study was done in 2001 by the Centre for Study of Social and Exclusive Policy: Maulana Azad National Urdu University, Hyderabad comparing Gujarat and Andhra Pradesh where Muslim populations are almost similar i.e. 9.1 per cent and 9.2 per cent respectively. Moreover, the frequency of communal riots is also the same. The figures are interesting because they may help us assces the well-hyped

"Gujarat Model", vehemently propagated by the Prime Minister, Narendra Modi. On the educational front, at basic level, the Muslims in Gujarat are better than the Muslims of Andhra Pradesh. But they lag behind in subsequent educational endeavours. At primary level, school attendance in Gujarat is 74.9 per cent whereas in AP it is 68.5 per cent. In the middle school level Gujarat's figure is 45.6 per cent whereas in AP it is 52.6 per cent. As they move on, the Muslim constitute 26.1 per cent at the matriculation in Gujarat whereas 40.6 per cent in AP. At graduation level the figures are 9.6 per cent and 5 per cent for AP and Gujarat respectively. The data showed that the better wage employment had not accrued in Gujarat compared to the AP. In Gujarat 13.3 per cent workers are Muslims whereas in AP 19.6 per cent are in the workforce. Gujarat being a more industrialized state, the Muslim percentage in the workforce should be higher. Likewise in trade, Muslim involvement is around 22.7 per cent in Gujarat whereas in AP it is 20 per cent. In the self-employment business, both present similar percentages. They are involved in family business, cycle and other vehicle repairs and other such lowly-paid jobs. But in this category child labourers are also involved which shows that their future prospects have dwindled. In terms of state employment in sectors like education, health, police transport and judiciary, Gujarat is far behind AP. In AP the advantage for the Muslims is that their political class is well articulated and they have the communitarian and communications tools like their own political parties, newspapers, TV channels which have been the source of empowerment. These are utilized for community mobilization and upward mobility. It is because of the continuous harsh communal biased situation in Gujarat, the Muslims have limited opportunities for upward social mobility. They fall behind in education which affects their mobility in other sectors. In small scale employment sector, the Muslim representation in Gujarat is 5.8 per cent whereas in Andhra Pradesh it is 6.8 per cent. In the state employment Muslim percentage in Gujarat is 5.4 whereas in AP it is 8.8. In the education sector (teachers, lecturers, university professors and other tertiary jobs) Muslims in Gujarat constituted 1.5 per cent whereas in AP they are 7.9 per cent. In health sectors the community's share in Gujarat is 1.5 per cent whereas in AP it is 6.4 per cent. In the Police Department AP is the only state where Muslim representation is way ahead to its population percentage i.e. 14.5 and 5.6 per cent respectively. Here it shows that Gujarat administration indulged in prejudiced recruitment. The only sector where Muslims are better represented in Gujarat is in the transport business as it is dominated mostly by the low paid jobs of drivers and cleaners. The Muslim representation in the two categories is 16.3 per cent and 10 per cent respectively. The statistics plainly reveal that because of the biased policies of the Government of Gujarat, Muslims lag behind in employment in comparison to AP. In spite of communal riots that frequently break out in the Telangana region, the upward mobility of the Muslims has been remarkable, whereas in Gujarat despite the presence of Muslim business communities, they lag behind.

In Maharashtra the percentage of Muslim workers is 32.5 compared to non-Muslim workers who constitute 43.5 per cent. Here also the disparity between Muslim male workers (49 per cent) and female workers (12 per cent) is very marked. Among the workers nearly 70.7 per cent are engaged in semi-skilled and unskilled informal sectors, which means they have insecure job opportunities. The job seekers among Muslims are very high according to the National Sample Survey Office (NSSO) 61st Round. In 2004-05 the unemployment rate among Muslims was found to be much higher, i.e. twice than among the Hindus.

Muslims are also acutely calorie deprived people; for instance a quarter of their population in Maharashtra and their children face stunted growth. They also lack resources, so they have to take shelter in rickety structures and slums where they are compelled to live a miserable existence. It is also true that the major reason for socio-economic deprivation of Muslims are the communal riots which are perpetrated with the avowed intention to destroy their source of livelihood and properties and push them into ghettoes. The Muslim majority areas like Malegaon, Bhiwandi and even parts of Mumbai are permanently discriminated against by communal forces. They are earmarked as communally sensitive areas where the Muslims are kept under constant surveillance and many of them are perpetually harassed. In the recent past Muslims, in particular the youth, are implicated in false cases; they are detained, tortured and incarcerated for long. Consequently, the prime learning and earning age is lost, during which they could have got educated and gained employment. During 1908 to 2009, Mumbai alone witnessed 83 communal riots. The draconian laws like POTA, TADA and MCOCA have been bluntly misused and abused against the community. Maharashtra had faced 1,192 communal clashes form 1998 to 2008 the highest in the country. Throughout the 10-year period, Maharashtra witnessed 10 per cent to 23 per cent of the total number of communal riots in India. Muslim population in Maharashtra is 10.6 per cent whereas their percentage among the inmates 32.4! They are subjected to complete economic annihilation through the biased implications in cases. After spending long terms in jails they are not even allowed to be rehabilitated as they carry stigma.

It is true that Muslim enclaves, where they were engaged in gainful businesses, had witnessed huge communal riots as in Moradabad (brassware), Aligarh (lock manufacturing), Bhiwandi and Malegaon (textiles) Bhagalpur (silk and sericulture). It must also be put on record that in 1989, in the aftermath of communal flare-up, Pupul Jayakar known as the Czarina of Indian Culture, visited the riot affected areas and she was very much disturbed. After coming back from her tour, she resigned from her coveted post and reported to Rajiv Gandhi, the then Prime Minister how 10,000 power-looms and handlooms belonging to Muslims weavers were destroyed and consequently they were reduced to becoming daily wage earners. She stated that the government was not creating jobs and it also did nothing substantial to stop the communal onslaughts which led to the destruction of poor Muslims' sources of livelihood. This is the epitome of the biased role of the administration where it has failed to protect the lives and properties of Muslims. Yet, the government talks about schemes and welfare measures which looks quite strange.

Muslims are subjected to persistent communal bias, their localities are earmarked as "negative zones", "red zones" and "mini Pakistans". They are not allowed to avail loan facilities. There is deficiency of infrastructure and other amenities.

According to Paul Brass, there is a tangible case of "Institutionalized Riot System" which is legitimized by taking refuge in "Islamophobia". It is beyond doubt that the communal flare-ups destroyed Muslim owned business establishments and different state governments failed to rein in such forces. It is documented that there is complete nexus between the perpetrators of violence and government agencies. In the aftermath of the 1992-93 communal riots in Mumbai, Muslim delegates led by Rafique Zakaria met Balasaheb Thackerey, the Shiv Sena Chief (whose party members had been in the thick of the violence) and requested him to rein in such forces in lieu of protection money (*jizia*). Even in the course of Bhagalpur riots in 1989, Muslim youths pleaded for security even at the cost of surrendering the benefits of welfare measures. These cases are a harsh indictment of the democratic regime of the country. There is also the problem of emerging neoliberal economic policies because of which most of the Muslims are bearing the brunt in the name of competition. Neoliberalism has brought about unemployment and displacement of workers. In fact, the paradigm has created a yawning gap between policy and equity. Gandhiji stated long back: "capitalism is the monster God of Materialism". This God is the harshest under neoliberal capitalism. As business is mostly conducted in the informal sector where there is no protection of any kind whatsoever for workers, the adverse impact of economic liberalization has been disastrous for them.

The traditional occupations wherein Muslims are engaged in sizeable numbers like silk and sericulture, hand and power-looms, leather industry, automobile repairing and garment making are facing immensely tough times under the neoliberal policies. The import of the silk yarn from China and its debilitating impact on the silk industry is a well known fact. Likewise, the emergence of the ready-made garment industry has thrown a lot of tailors, mostly Muslims, out of buisness. They have to face problems related to infrastructure, by way of expensive power, expensive raw materials (due to lack of subsidies) and non-availability of credit and absence of marketing support. In the absence of such facilities artisans get exploited by middlemen. The wages given for job work by the middlemen are usually very low. Diversification of skilled training, credit and appropriate marketing support are some of the critical needs of the hour. Even the apparel business where Muslims are involved as tailors are facing decline because of the invasion of the ready-made cheap garments that flood India. There is strong demand for affirmative action to deal with the abysmal economic deprivation of the community. It must noted that there is a tradition of affirmative action even practised by the colonial masters in the form of reservations and quotas in order to give fillip to the deprived sections. The quota system is used as a niche for empowerment. The practice of giving reservations in jobs and in the emerging representative bodies for those who lagged behind in terms of economic betterment was guaranteed in the Government of India Act of 1935. It is beyond doubt that affirmative action, quotas and empowerment had been used to surmount social and economic backwardness. As is well established, the bulk of Muslims belong to the low caste category of *arzals*. Centuries ago the lower caste Hindus broke free from the ignominious caste system and embraced the egalitarian religion of Islam. But their economic and social condition remained unchanged and they were mired in poverty and privations. Nevertheless, unlike the SC/STs among Hindus they are bereft of the reservation facilities as they were the victims of the biased Presidential Ordinance of 1950 that deprived Muslims and Christian Dalits of the facilities of reservations which had been till then available to them. Christianity and Islam notionally do not subscribe to casteism. The point to ponder is that Buddhism and Sikhism, the adherents of which are allowed to avail the reservations, also do not accept the caste system. In fact, their very origins are based on the negation of casteism. It must also be remembered that according to the *Kumar Singh Report*, there are 35 Muslims castes which belong to the Scheduled Caste category, as these people do the same sort of traditional work which is associated with the Dalit Hindus. It is interesting to mention here that according to the *Ranganath Mishra Report*, the caste system should be recognized as forming the general social characteristic of Indian society as a whole, without questioning whether the philosophy and teachings of any particular religion recognizes it or not. He suggested that "para 3" of the

Constitution (Scheduled Castes) order of 1950 be fully made redundant by appropriate action so as to fully disassociate Scheduled Caste status from religion Because any religion-based discrimination conflicts with the letter and spirit of the Constitution. In order to address Muslim backwardness one should demand their bracketing within the SCs rather than the OBC Hindus. Since quite a few of the Hindu OBCs have landholdings and substantial political clout, they get represented in different elected bodies and their representation is substantial in the Services. Presently, Muslims have to compete with the resourceful OBCs castes under reservations scheme which is not giving them commensurate benefits. So, it is reasonable to demand inclusion of Dalit Muslims in SC category. Although some Muslim leaders demand reservations for the whole community, it would be difficult to get reservation on the basis of religion. Muslim Dalits face similar societal exclusion. But there is no provision for positive discriminations for them like their Hindu bretheren.

The Sachar Committee recommended the constitution of the Equal Opportunity Commission (EOP) to address the concerns of the deprived minority groups including Muslims. It would deal with the institutional bias which is widely prevalent and is one of the causes of Muslim deprivation. Till now, the government has been proclaiming that it is dealing with the recommendations. But one of most important recommendations of the Committee is the constitution of EOP, which is conspicuously absent from government agenda. An identical body had been formed in USA viz. Equal Employment Opportunity Commission (EEOC), which gave "Affirmative Action" real teeth in dealing with the deprivation of the black people. We need bold and visionary leaders like Lyndon B. Johnson, the President of USA, a "Determined Realist" who brought the Civil Rights Act in 1964 and the Executive Order 11246 that had created Affirmative Action in September 1965. Here laws had been activated with the creation of necessary "enforcement mechanism" like EEOC. What is required in India is the political will which is necessary for achieving equity and reclaiming the space for democratic citizenship. It is aptly mentioned in the landmark speech of Martin Luther Jr. in 1963 in Washington:

> I have a dream that one day on the red hills of Georgia sons of former slaves and sons of the owners of former slaves will be able to sit down together at the table of brotherhood. I have a dream that one day even the state of Mississippi, state of sweltering with the heat of injustices, sweltering with the heat of oppression will be transformed into the oasis of freedom and justice...I have a dream that my four little children will one day live in a nation where they will not be judged by the colour of their skin but the content of their character. I have a dream...

The dream was fulfilled as a lot of black people had been ameliorated through legislation where the dream of the suffering people became the creed of the nation.

Muslims face double whammy when communal flare-ups which destroy their economic resources, make them insecure and push them into the ghettos. But they are also discriminated against in many other fields. They are not provided basic amenities as many of them reside in ghettos; they are not given even proper jobs. It is the "vicious circle" in which Muslims are trapped. They are in a mess that keeps them alien to the system which creates hopelessness and in the process destroys future prospects. According to a report (Source: *Times of India*, September 16, 2013) released by the Council for Social Development shows how the previous UPA government had failed to implement the Sachar Committee recommendations with its "cautious and minimalist" approach. The report also stated that most benefits intended for the minorities were being cornered by either the majority population or non-Muslim minorities. The report also divulged the lost focus of the minority oriented programmes, lack of funds and fear of "minority appeasement" as the reasons for the government's failure to fulfil its promises. The report also focused on how government is helping modernization of Madarssas where only 4 per cent of Muslim population is availing education. Recently the Maharashtra government had earmarked Rs 10 crore for the Madarassa education. It is one more case of misdirected priority as there should be emphasis on mainstream education that may lead to empowerment of the community.

It must be mentioned here that the Multi-Sectoral Development Programme (MSDP) which has been brought in with the declared intention to remove disparity has failed. The MSDP was launched after the Sachar Committee Report in 90 districts with around 25 per cent Muslim population for infrastructural development. The accrued benefits for the Muslims in these areas were only 30 per cent. The irony is that in states like Bihar and UP (with high concentration of Muslims) infrastructural projects got diverted to non-minority areas. The Report also divulged the lack of banking facilities in Muslim dominated areas. The Reserve Bank of India's efforts to extend these facilities ultimately helped other minorities whose socio-economic status is comparable to upper caste Hindus. "Diffidence at the policy level to clearly focus on Muslims' deprivation translates into active reluctance by the implementing agencies on the ground to target the Muslims even in districts with high Muslim concentration." One of the members of the team that filed the report, Prof. Mushirul Hasan, blamed the previous Minority Affairs Ministry for such failures. He said: "The Ministry has become liability. It is devoid of ideas and lacks social commitment." According to the Report both funding and its utilization have been problems.

The historical backdrop of marginalization of Muslims are: Muslim elites had ruled the country for more than 600 hundred years and due to loss of power, they also lost their economic clout under the British regime. They lost the language of communication, Urdu. They also lost the status of the landed gentry due to abolition of jagirdari system. The partition of the Indian subcontinent was a big blow for the Indian Muslims. Common people had to suffer because of partition of the country. As most Muslim intellectuals migrated to Pakistan, there is paucity of enlightened Muslim leadership. Last but not the least, during the last three decades strident communalism brought in its wake displacement and economic marginalization of the community. They are forced to live in ghettoes where they are not provided adequate infrastructure. They are easily subjected to stereotypical discriminations which help the communal people to heap atrocities at their own will. There is no expression of outrage against such violence either in the media or by the government because Muslims themselves are held responsible for their victimhood. It is the vicious circle which keeps the community on the edge of alienation and disillusionment which is certainly not a healthy development for the nation.

So, there is need to provide security for Muslims. There must also be sincere implementation of the welfare measures. First of all, the law and order machinery must be brought under "accountable mechanism". The right step in the direction would be to bring about police reforms which would give functional autonomy with the police forces and demand accountability in accordance to the guidelines of the Supreme Court. The Prevention of Communal Violence Bill, 2011, should be immediately passed. It would help the community to get much needed institutional safeguard. It is rightly felt that the high magnitude riots which brought economic deprivation to the community were made possible because of lack of such mechanism. For instance in 2002 Narendra Modi, is alleged by many to have instructed high echelon police officers "to let the people vent their spleen". Lastly, for the efficacious implementation of the recommendations of the Sachar Committee Report, there is a need to institute the Equal Opportunity Commission.

REFERENCES

1. *Sachar Committee Report*.
2. *Frontline*: December 2-15, 2006.
3. Vibhuti Patel, 'Socio-Economic Profile of Muslims in India', in *Economic and Political Weekly*, September 7, 2013.
4. Kancha Ilaiah, 'Development of Muslims, Comparing Gujarat and Andhra Pradesh in the Early 2000's, in *Economic and Political Weekly*, September 7, 2013.
5. John Meacham, 'One Man', *Time Magazine*, August 26, 2013.
6. Christophe Jeffrelot, 'The Sense of a Community', in *Outlook*, July 23, 2012.
7. Meera Nanda, 'Affirmative Action and Caste Dilemmas', in *Frontline*, June 14, 2006. The largest religious minority community of India, October 11 and 12, 2013.

9

Review of Implementations of Development Schemes for Minorities: A Study of Muslims in the State of Maharashtra

Sandhya Mhatre

Introduction

The poorest communities in almost any region tend to be minority communities. They have been targets of prejudice, discrimination, exclusion, and violence resulting in inequalities which circumscribe every aspect of their life. Their situation is worsened by numerous and complex factors. They are often denied equal access to education, employment opportunities and their rights are violated along with and poor representation in decision making bodies and political structures. In India, Scheduled Castes and Scheduled Tribes are often considered to be the most backward social groups. Religious minority communities in India comprise Muslims, Buddhists, Christians, Jains, Sikhs, Parsis, and Jews. Of these religious minority communities, the largest minority is the Muslim community followed by the Buddhists.

This chapter intends to review the implementation of minority schemes, focusing on Muslims as a minority group, taking the case study of Maharashtra. For this purpose, the chapter reviews various national Five Year Plans and their approach towards development of minorities at the national level. The chapter also contextualizes the gradual shift and changes in them in a larger socio-political scenario.

The chapter then takes the specific case of Maharashtra to do a comparative and detailed review of the various policies and funds allocated for those policies, up till the district level, for different marginalized social and religious groups. Further, the chapter looks at the policies made for minority groups and glances at the specific areas into which the minority funds are directed. This inquiry helps in understanding the larger question of the approach towards development of minority communities, especially the Muslims.

Why Muslims: An Overview of the Status of Muslims in India

As it has been pointed out above, this chapter intends to review the implementation of minority schemes focusing on the Muslims in India. Though this chapter takes a broader review of developmental policies, the focus remains on Muslims. Therefore, it is imperative that the reason behind such a focus be spelled out.

The Constitution of India identifies two kinds of minorities —linguistic and religious minorities. A religious minority is an umbrella term used to identify social religious groups which are numerically less in comparison to the majority religious group (Hindus in India). At present, this umbrella comprises of seven religious communities specified above. Even though all seven communities have a smaller share of population in comparison to the Hindu majority, one cannot say that all of them are on equal footing, socially and economically. Depending on their histories and equations with the other communities, and most importantly the majority community, different communities face different kinds of pressures and insecurities. For instance, Muslims, which are also the largest group amongst all the all minority groups, have faced severe discrimination right from partition and therefore have had to face insecurities regarding security, identity and equity. There have been instances of gruesome violence against the community in which the community has been socially and economically targeted. The interplay of these dimensions is from the core of the socio-economic and political processes of deprivation that the community is exposed to on a daily basis.

The deprivation of the Muslim community is well documented, through the reports of commissions which propelled the Muslim community to the centre of the development debate. One of the most prominent committees in this regard was the Sachar Committee. The High Level Committee of six members (popularly known as Sachar Committee) was appointed by Manmohan Singh in 2005. The committee presented its findings in 2006 which brought out the performance social, economic and educational backwardness of the Muslims community, in comparison to other social and religious groups in India.

The report pointed out that the Muslim community was deeply impoverished, suffered from a higher rate of illiteracy, a high drop-out rate, a depleting asset base, below average work participation and lack of stable and secure employment. The report also revealed that the Muslim community had limited access to government schemes and other facilities. As a consequence, the Muslim community performed even worse that the worst performing social groups like the SCs, STs and the OBCs.

The Sachar Committee Report was one of the most significant reports in regard to the status of Muslims in India, it was not the first committee to come up with similar findings. Tanvir Fazal lists out two other reports which came to somewhat similar conclusions, although in a different framework.

Tanvir Fazal first talks of the NCAER study (1994) which shed light on the economic position of the Muslim community. According to Fazal, this study showed the impact of liberalization on the Muslim community which mainly consisted of the traditional artisans. It pointed out that the decline of the prospects of the artisanship-based vocations had been causing increase in the unemployment rates amongst the minorities. Further "Muslims lag behind when compared to the other Minority Groups in terms of both household and per capita income with a wide gap between Muslims and other Minority Groups. The gap in the per capita income is as wide as Rs. 2,242 between Christians holding the highest per capita income of Rs. 5,920 and the Muslims with the lowest of Rs. 3,678." The NSS data on monthly per capita expenditure (MPCE) 2009-10 showed Muslims and the SCs/STs amongst the poorest.

The second report is of the Commission on Linguistic and Religious Minorities, popularly known as Ranganath Misra Commission (2007). This commission also reached a similar conclusion (similar to Sachar Commission's Report) regarding the status of Muslims in India.

Several other studies have clearly shown the huge development deficit that the Muslim community is facing in the social, economic and education sectors. The question then is: what has the state done to address the lack of development of the Muslim minority? Therefore it is to examine the attitude of the state towards the Muslim minority groups and look at how the state has addressed the question of the development of Muslims minority within the larger question of development policies of minorities.

It is important to note that while the chapter focuses primarily on the Muslims, the attitude meted out to other socially and economically backward groups is not ignored. Rather, that has been one of the prime ways in which the differential treatment of policies and policy makers has been brought to light to bring out the contrast in the policy formulations.

Policy Approach towards Socially Disadvantaged Groups in India: A Review of the Five Year Plans

The Planning Commission and the Five Year Plans hold one of the most fundamental positions in the Indian planning process. Therefore it is absolutely necessary to look at the Five Year Plans to understand the policy approaches towards minority groups. One also analyzes the way in which issues of particular communities have been ignored when benefits of development should have been distributed equitably amongst all the sections of society. It is important to look at the implementation of minority schemes in the larger background of these Five Year Plans and their approaches towards the development of minorities.

In the post-independence period, development schemes were formulated and incorporated in five year plans according to Article 46 of the Constitution in order to bring backward classes into the mainstream.Hence, the Five Year Plans had various objectives and approaches such as "grow more food", "infrastructural development", "social justice", "equality of opportunity", "reduction in disparities in income and wealth", "even distribution of economic power", "rapid increase in the standard of living of the people", "promote equality and social justice" in order to 'reach the un-reached' sections through equitable distribution and social justice."

The focus of the Five Year Plans (till the Seventh Plan) was on the Scheduled Castes (SCs) and Scheduled Tribes (SCs). However, not much attention was given to other marginalized communities like the religious minorities in these development plans. Though different plans advocated "equality of opportunity" (3rd Five Year Plan (1961-66) or promotion equality and social justice like the 4th and the 5th Five Year Plan, there was no major shift in the approach towards minority communities.

At the outset, it should be clarified that the purpose here is not to draw an unhealthy comparison between the socially marginalized SCs, STs and the religious minority groups. It is believed that all marginalized communities require affirmative action by the state to help promote their development. One would like to show the differences in the approach taken by the state, by analyzing the reasons for the differences and to address the deprivation of different communities by the way of comparison.

The idea during the 1st Five Year Plan (beginning from 1951) was to benefit all communities and reduce inequalities. However, the plans were more GDP centric. After the 5th Five Year Plan, the planning became more centered on human development. The shift in approach was seen in the approach towards development of SCs in the 6th Five Year Plan (1980-85) which followed through the 7th Five Year Plan (1985-1990). Thus, there was a special emphasis on implementation of the Special Component Plan(SCP) for the Scheduled Castes and Tribal Sub

Plan (TSP) for the STs. Efforts were also attempts made to converge resources from all other developmental sectors according to their population proportion for the SCs and the STs. As a result, there was substantial increase in flow of funds from the State Plans, Central Plans, Special Central Assistance (SCA) and Institutional Finance. All these measures resulted in the expansion of infrastructural facilities and enlargement of SC and ST coverage.

The minorities continued is to be marginalized and it was only in the Eighth Five Year Plan (1992-97) that the word *minorities* was used for the first time in the planning documents. The objective of this plan was to bridge the gaps between different marginalized sections of society and bring them on par with the rest of society.

This significant shift in the planning process was not an isolated incident. The Mandal Commission (1979) emphasized the importance of including Other Backward Classes (OBCs) in the development paradigm. Because of this, provisions were made for OBCs in 1998-99 particularly in the field of education. This was the first time in the Indian scenario that affirmative actions were being taken on the basis of caste across religious communities. Thus the benefits of Mandal commission's recommendations could be extended to all social and religious Communities. It has to be noted that even while the Mandal commission could benefit other marginalized groups who were not taken into planning consideration yet, it did not focus on the specific problems of minorities, as did the *Gopal Commission Report* (1982).

In the context of the Mandal Commission, people came out to demand their rights and fight against oppression beyond their religious identities. As a result, various communal forces sought to polarize the population on the basis of religion. They used identity politics to create an atmosphere of communal disharmony, targeted the religious minority, especially Muslims and Christians, resulting in instances of communal violence throughout the country. In the light of such communal politics, the need arose for sustained approaches to address the issues faced by minority communities like the Muslims and to recognize their rights as individuals.

Though the term "minorities" was first used in the 8th Five Year Plan, there were no specific development programmes formulated for the minorities. The focus was on economic development of OBCs through the creation of National Backward Classes Finance and Development Corporation (1992, National Safai Karamchari Finance and Development Corporation (1996-97).

The 9th Five Year Plan (1997-2002), however had a more holistic approach concentrated on an all-round development through social, economic empowerment and social justice. Efforts were made for an inter-sectoral development programme through various welfare related ministries as well as through non-governmental and governmental agencies. Despite this, schemes for minorities were not implemented during this plan period as well.

It was only during the 10th Five Year Plan (2002-07) that the implementation of provisions for minorities began. The plan focused on the socio-religious development of different marginalized groups including women and minorities.

The 11th Five Year Plan (2007-12) which highlighted more on inclusive growth and equal apportunity for all, identified six categories, viz, (i) income and poverty; (ii) education; (iii) health; (iv)women and children (v) infrastructure and (vi) environment.

A review of FYP plans shows that the important policies like the Five Year Plans did not address the question of the developmental lag of minorities, let alone the lag faced by Muslims which took centre state only, as late as the 8th Five Year Plan (1992-97). Though there has been a gradual change in focus of plan from GDP to Human Development to Inclusive Growth, it is important to note that it was due to political and social pressure created in the wake of Mandal Commission. Thus, while the question of minorities has been brought into the development paradigm, the extent to which religious minority groups have been incorporated in the mainstream policies is yet to be seen.

The Case of Maharashtra:

The chapter examines Maharashtra state as a case study to do a comparative and detailed analysis of the various policies and funds allocated, utilization upto the district level, to different marginalized social and religious groups. Further, this chapter analyzes the specific areas into which minority funds are directed. Such an inquiry will help in understanding the larger question of the approach towards the development of religious minority communities, specially Muslims.

After the *Sachar Committee Report* (2006), various announcements were made by the central government to implement the recommendations of the report. Consequently the Ministry of Minority Affairs was created at the national level on 29th January, 2006 to ensure a more focused approach towards issues relating to minorities. Besides the formation of the ministry, various schemes such as pre-matric, post-matric scholarships, merit cum means scholarships, PM's new 15 point program, etc. were also introduced.

Sources of Data

This chapter uses secondary data available at various administrative levels as well as data from Census of India, 2001. The religion-wise data fo the 2011 Census is yet to be published. Further, 2001 is said to be the first census of India where religion-wise data was compiled right up to the district and sub-district levels. Thus the Census 2001 data has been used to understand the demographic profile of minorities in Maharashtra. Further religion-wise data up to the district and sub-district level is available from 2001 census.

Data that has been used to analyze outlays, expenditure and physical performances of minority development schemes obtained from the Planning Commission, Ministry of Minority Affairs and National Minority Commission. State and District level data have been taken from Economic Survey of Maharashtra State (2012-13), and *Zilla Samajik Arthik Samalochan* (2011-12), publish by Directorate of Economics and Statistics, GoM.

Demographic Profile of Minority Population in Maharashtra

According to the 2001 census, the minority population in Maharashtra is 17.9 per cent of the total population of the state or 17.38 million. From the population of Muslims, Christians, Sikhs and Buddhists, Muslims constitute 59 per cent or 10.60 million, hence are the largest minority religious group in the state of Maharashtra.

Table 1: The Region-wise Classification of Minority Population in the State of Maharashtra: 2001

(Percent)

	Percentage Share in Total Population				*Percentage Share in Minority Population*				
Region of the State	*Total*	*Hindu*	*Muslim*	*Buddhist*	*Muslim*	*Buddhist*	*Jain*	*Christian*	*Sikh, Parsi, Jew & Others*
Konkan	12905380	82.27	9.69	4.25	54.6	23.9	7.2	11.8	2.3
Marathwada	15629248	77.57	14.17	7.29	63.2	32.5	2.0	1.1	1.2
Mumbai	21322871	68.42	17.67	5.34	56.0	16.9	11.9	12.0	3.2
North East	5378248	83.56	2.58	11.46	15.7	69.7	0.8	2.0	11.8
North Maha.	15736784	87.32	9.32	1.69	73.5	13.3	6.0	3.9	3.3
Vidherbha	15252739	74.56	10.37	13.65	40.8	53.6	2.1	1.4	2.1
Western Maha.	19997778	87.20	6.98	2.81	54.5	22.0	14.7	6.1	2.7
Maharashtra	96878627	80.37	10.60	6.03	54.0	30.7	6.8	5.6	2.9

Source: *Census of India: Religion 2001*

Table 1 shows a region-wise distribution of Muslims, who constitute around 10 per cent of the total population, in the state of Maharashtra. The state can be divided roughly into eight regions listed in the table. Out of these, Muslims are mainly concentrated in the regions of Mumbai, the suburbs of Mumbai, Marathwada, Konkan and Vidarbha. The remaining three regions have below the state level Muslim population. But even within these regions, some districts have a higher percentage of Muslims. For instance, in Western Maharashtra region, Solapur and Dhule districts have a higher concentration of Muslims as compared to the region on the whole.

Minority Development Schemes in the State of Maharashtra

In Maharashtra, as in the entire country, pre 2006 or before the formation of the Ministry of Minority Affairs (MOMA), the welfare schemes for development of minority groups have been few and far between. Out of these few schemes, one of the welfare schemes to address the financial and social development of minorities was the Maulana Azad Alpasankhyak Arthik Vikas Mahamandal which was established in 2000.

This corporation was established as an autonomous body by the state of Maharashtra for financing loans for self-employment, education etc. and was incorporated under the Company's Act, 1956. It was for implementation of many schemes like Maulana Azad Direct Loan Scheme, Unnati Term Loan, Mahila Samruddhi and education loan. The authorized and paid up share capital of the corporation is Rs. 170 cr. and 166.31 cr. respectively (*Maharashtra Economic Survey 2010-11*). However, this corporation did not accomplish much and can be looked at as pacification of the Muslim community in lieu of their demands and requirements.

During the period from 2004-05 to 2012-13, National Minorities Development and Finance Corporation (NMDFC) in Maharashtra State disbursed Rs 3,940 lakhs to 8,926 beneficiaries for the Term Loan Scheme (www. indiastat.com).

Under Priority Sector Lending (PSL) to minorities in Maharshtra during 2010-2011 to 2011-2012) the target was Rs. 39,862.44 crore, but only Rs. 24,841.4 crores were disbursed, which means 37 per cent amount was unspent.

Further, even when the Ministry of Minority Affairs (MOMA) was formed at the Center in 2006, the Minorities Development Department was formed as a separate Administrative Department by the Government of Maharashtra only in February 2008 to implement the Prime Minister's New

15 Point programme for minorities and other related schemes.

Despite this, there has been an increase in the development schemes targeting minorities. The Maharashtra State Minority Department implemented schemes for the development of minorities such as various scholarship schemes for students, PM's 15 Point Programme Multisectoral Development (2008) in minority concentrated districts through the concerned state departments such as School Education and Literacy, Women and Child Development, Housing and Urban Poverty Alleviation (HUPA), Labour and Employment, Finance Department, Drinking Water and Sanitation, Human Resource Development since 2008-09. The funds for each scheme were shared between the Centre and the State.

Table 2: Budget Allocation to Respective Communities in Proportion to Their Population: Maharashtra State

Category	*Share of the State's Total Outlay*	*11th Five Year Plan (Rs in Crore)*		
		Outlay	*Expenditure*	*Number of Schemes*
Schedule Caste Sub-Plan (SCSP)	10.2%	28050.00	13271.90	172
Tribal Sub-Plan (TSP)	8.9%	24474.99	10530.04	ITD-24 MADA-43 Mini MADA-24
Minority Community	Not specified for 2011 Census but as per Census 2001- it was 10.6%	Provision = Rs. 1685.00 Received amount = Rs. 986.00	-	26

Source: *Economic Survey of Maharashtra 2012-13*, pp. 203-205.

However, in comparison to the various development schemes for the other socially marginalized communities like the SCs and the STs, the number of schemes as well as the budget allocated for religious minority development schemes was extremely low. Table 2 shows a comparative picture of the budget outlay, expenditure and the number of schemes that have been implemented for SC, ST, and minority communities. The allocation of funds is according to their respective population shares.

From Table 2 it can be seen that there is a vast difference in the number of schemes formulated for the SCs and the STs and those for minorities. As a matter of fact, a huge number of schemes even out of the 26 schemes (as shown in table 2) were formulated only during the 11th Five Year Plan (as explained in the first part of the chapter). Further, of the 26 schemes, several were formulated during 11th FY period.

Further, unlike the SCs and STs, there is no provision of a special component plan for minorities because of which the funds allocated are much less than warranted.

The budget outlay under the 11th Five Year Plan for SC is Rs. 28,050 Cr. and to ST is Rs. 24,474.99 cr. respectively of 263 schemes. However, in contrast, the provisional outlay for the minority development was only Rs. 1,685 cr. and out of that received amount was limited to only Rs. 275 cr. As a direct consequence of such limited allocation and even lower amount received, was that various programs for development of minorities had to be pruned to fit the provisional outlay.

Through this comparative analysis, it becomes clear that even when the numbers of schemes for minority groups have increased since 2006, the measures taken by the state for the development of minorities are extremely inadequate in comparison to steps taken for development of other marginalized communities. It is important again to reiterate that the intention here is not to say that the measures taken for the development of other marginalized groups should be reduced, rather the intention is to say that equal measures should be taken by the state for the development of all marginalized groups.

Approach Towards Development of Minorities

Development of any community is never a unilateral process and thus has various aspects to it. Therefore, despite the minimal budget allocation for minority development, it is important to also see the different areas for which the budget is allocated and the percentage of outlay for each area. Thus, in order to understand the division of the outlay for various areas, that outlay has been categorized into six parts. These parts are: Administration, Education, Employment, Finance for Institutions, Multi-sectoral Development Programme and Welfare. This division helps in not only understanding the outlay distribution but also the approach taken by the state towards development of a community. Table 3 shows the division of the outlay for the year 2009-10 to 2012-13 which is based on Annexure II

Table 3: Grant-in-aid for Minority Schemes 2009-10 to 2012-13: Maharashtra State

Category of Schemes	*Grant-in-aid (Rs. in Lakhs)* Total Outlay	Total Expenditure	Unspent Amount	*Percentage of Unspent Grants*
Administration	1959.00	570.00	1389.00	70.9
MsDP Schemes	39316.72	31603.10	7713.62	19.6
Education	65156.28	49521.11	15635.17	24.0
Finance for Institutions	13572.62	12359.10	1213.52	8.9
Welfare	3576.00	1285.90	2290.10	64.0
Employment Oriented	410.00	0.00	410.00	100.0
Grand Total	**123990.62**	**95339.21**	**28651.41**	**23.0**
Actual Received Amount	109161.00			

Source: Based on Annexure II

Chart 1: Outlay for Minority Schemes 2009-10 to 2012-13

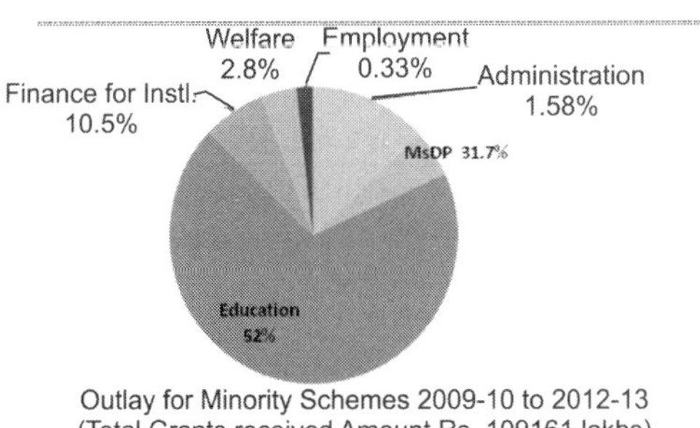

Outlay for Minority Schemes 2009-10 to 2012-13
(Total Grants received Amount Rs. 109161 lakhs)

Source: Based on Annexure II

The total grants-in-aid amounted to Rs 1,23,990 lakh. However expenditure was only Rs 95,339 lakh, which means

23 per cent of the amount sanctioned was unspent during the period of 2009-10 to 2012-13.

Through Chart 1 and Table 2, it can be seen that a major share of the outlay, 52 per cent, was earmarked for education but 24 per cent amount was unspent. These grants-in-aid amount to roughly Rs. 65,156.3 lakhs which included funds for uniforms, incentive to parents for attendance, higher education scholarships, free coaching, starting 2nd and 3rd shifts trainings in existing ITI, opening of ITI, polytechnics, hostels, starting of short term trade base courses, providing bicycles and provision of basic infrastructure etc.

The second major share 31.7 per cent allocation was for Multi-sectoral Development Programme (MsDP), a special area development programme for minority concentrated areas. However 19 per cent was unspent amount in this category.

10.9 per cent of the total grants was allotted as a share capital to finance institutions such as Maulana Azad Alpasnkhyank Arthik Vikas Mahamandal (MAAAVM) and state branch of National Minorities Development and Finance Corporation (NMDFC).

2.8 per cent of the total outlay was for welfare schemes which included allocation for Wakf Board, Haj Committee, Urdu Ghar, Communal Harmony, widows, abandoned women, aggrieved women and NGOs. 64 per cent amount of this grant remained unspent.

Remaining 1.5 per cent allocation from the total outlay was for administration. This includes grants for Minority Commission, help line research, training, publication, publicity and e–governance. 71 per cent of the amount was not spent.

Finally, the last category of employment oriented scheme, the amount received under was a very small grant of Rs 410 lakh, and not a penny of the allotted grant was spent on schemes like the upgradation of power looms and SHGs.

An Overview of the Specific Development Schemes for Minorities

In the previous section, an overview of the budget allocation and the divisions under various heads shed light on some of the basic problems in the approach of the state towards minority development. This section goes further to examine implementation of the specific minority development schemes by examining their performance in the last few years. The three specific schemes that this section looks at are the, scholarship schemes, Prime Minister's new 15 point programme and the multi-sectoral development plan for the minorities.

Schemes of Scholarships for Minority

Within the education sector, various scholarships received from the Maharashtra Minority Department website were distributed. Table 4 is based on the Maharashtra Minority Department Website. Annexure III indicates the proportion of all scholarship amounts and achievements during the period from 2006-07 to 2012-13.

It is to be noted that, 57 per cent of the fund was for pre-matric scholarships, 30 per cent on post matric scholarships and 13 per cent on merit-cum-means scholarships out of the total amount of Rs. 305.92 cr. Allotments for post-matric scholarships were not fully utilized. Allocation was also very less as compared to pre-matric scholarships. Actually the allocation for post-matric scholarship needs to be more because of the higher cost of post-matric education. It is to be noted that dropout rates are higher after 10th standard. It is also to be noted that there is nearly 12 per cent shortfall in the post matric scholarships target.

Table 4: Performance of Scholarships for Minority: 2006-07 to 2012-13

	Amount		*Beneficiary Students*			
Scholarships	*Rs Crore*	*Percentage to Total*	*Target (Numbers)*	*Achievement (Numbers)*	*Percentage Share Achievement*	*Percentage Change Between Achievements & Targets*
Pre- Matric	174.72	57.1	1039887	2295063	93.1	120.7
Post Matric	91.77	30.0	175914	154970	6.3	-11.9
Merit cum-means	39.43	12.9	11880	15637	0.6	31.6
Total	305.92	100.0	1227681	2465670	100.0	100.8

Source: Based on Annexure III

Table 5: Schemes of Scholarships for Minority: 2006-07 to 2012-13

		Number of Students				*Per cent Share in All Minority*			
Minority Group	*Target & Achievement*	*Pre-Matric*	*Post Matric*	*Merit Cum*	*All Scholarships*	*Pre-Matric*	*Post Matric*	*Merit Cum*	*All Scholarships*
Muslims	Target	607041	103909	7588	718538	58.4	59.1	63.9	58.5
	Achievement	1490083	141454	13090	1644627	64.9	91.3	83.7	66.7
Christian	Target	52643	10737	784	64164	5.1	6.1	6.6	5.2
	Achievement	88307	4832	1386	94525	3.8	3.1	8.9	3.8
Sikh	Target	12880	2214	161	15255	1.2	1.3	1.4	1.2
	Achievement	23105	1431	317	24853	1.0	0.9	2.0	1.0
Buddhist	Target	344407	58814	3319	406540	33.1	33.4	27.9	33.1
	Achievement	690692	7204	813	698709	30.1	4.6	5.2	28.3
Parsi	Target	1330	240	28	1598	0.1	0.1	0.2	0.1
	Achievement	2876	49	31	2956	0.1	0.0	0.2	0.1
All Minority	Target	1039887	175914	11880	1227681	100.0	100.0	100.0	100.0
	Achievement	2295063	154970	15637	2465670	100.0	100.0	100.0	100.0

Source: Based on Annexure III.

As per the Table 5, within the minority group, Muslim students benefited less from all type of scholarships than the other minority.

Prime Minister's New 15 Point Programme for Welfare of Minorities

The previous Prime Minister's 15 Point Programme for the Welfare of Minorities was first approved by the Government of India in 2006. This program was later amended in 2009. This programme was announced with a view to incorporate programme specific interventions for minorities. According to this programme wherever possible Ministries/Departments concerned had to earmark 15 per cent of the physical targets and financial outlays for minorities (See Annexure IV). Thus the programme covered many areas for the development of minorities. The performance of some of the department and schemes under this program has been looked at in this section.

An attempt has been made in Annexure 2 to provide details of scheme-wise targets and achievements and some of the schemes and pattern of expenditure in creation of various physical assets under different programmes are examined.

- **Education sector:** There were ten schemes implemented by the Department of School Education including Sarva Shiksha Abhiyan which covers literacy for primary, upper primary, pre, post and merit cum scholarship, Kasturba Gandhi Vidyalay, etc.

  It is seen that except pre-matric scholarships, achievements for all other schemes are very poor. Further, in regard to the infrastructure, the construction of more than 70 per cent primary and upper primary schools is not completed. Additionally, 62 per cent of the newly formed primary schools did not open and most of the sanctioned teachers' posts were not filled. Lastly, post-matric and merit-cum-means scholarships were not given up to 12 per cent and 32 per cent respectively.

  The Ministry of Human Development through the Department of Social Education and Literacy spent Rs. 1.80 cr. on modernization of 45 Madarssas and Rs. 11.43 spent on infrastructural development for 58 minority institutions in the state.

  As many as 60 per cent Aanganwadi centers had not been completed by the Women and Child Department.

- **Welfare sector:** The Rural Development Department has not provided housing to 35 per cent of people under Indira Awas Yojna. Further, 63 per cent people were not provided housing in urban areas fom HUPA under JNNURM—Integrated Housing Slum Development Programme in urban India.

  Further, HUPA has not been able to provide basic infrastructural services for 82 per cent projects under JNNURM scheme.

- **Employment Sector:** The 15 point program also provides provisions for skill training, encouragement and support for micro entrepreneurs, the self-employed, etc. in in urban areas through Housing and Urban Poverty Alleviation Department (HUPA).

  At the superficial level, the achievements of HUPA have been better, but the implementation is not remarkable. The reason for saying this is the actual achievement in this field depends on good productive performance of trainees after their training, creation of good marketing avenues, proper credit facility and other support facilities. This was not provided to the trainees. Additionally, no follow-ups are done to check if the trainees have been able to sustain their enterprises. These follow ups should also be part of implementation process which is completely overlooked.

  The Ministry of Finance released on amount of Rs. 33.37 cr. for upgradation for 13 Industrial Training Institutes (ITIs), but 17 per cent of that amount had not spent by the State Department of Labour & Employment. Similarly, 52 per cent of Rs. 90187 cr. provided by the Ministry of Finance for priority sector lendings had not been spent by the state.

  In reference to particular schemes under the 15 point programme, the Aajivikayojna (earlier called Swarna Jayanti Gramin Swarojagar Yojana (SJGSY)) and Swarna Jayanti Shahari Swarojagar Yojana (SJSSY) are two other schemes which were meant for employment generation. Both the schemes performed poorly in the state.
- The Ministry of Water and Sanitation released Rs.1608 cr. for rural drinking water programme. Out of this amount, 6 per cent has also not been spent by the state.

Through an overview of all these schemes under the 15 point program, it can be seen that despite the provisions in some cases, the implementation has been very poor, with either the funds not being utilized or with the lack of appropriate follow-ups. The highlighting of a few of the schemes and sectors reveal the immense lacunae in implementation of schemes and the arbitrariness of their implementation. Further, it shows the lack of political and bureaucratic will to implement the schemes and work for the development of minority communities.

Multi-Sectoral Development Plan (MsDP)

The Multi-sectoral Development Programme (MsDP), was designed to address the development deficits identified by a baseline survey in the Minority Concentrated Districts (MCDs). This was launched for Buldhana, Jalna, Parbhani, and Washim, districts of Maharashtra in 2008-09. The programme aimed at improved provision of amenities so as to enhance the quality of life of the people and reduce the imbalances in the MCDs during the 11th Five Year Plan period. Accordingly identified "development deficits" were to be made up through a district specific plan for the provision of better infrastructure for schools and secondary education, sanitation, pucca housing, drinking water and electricity supply, besides implementing beneficiary oriented schemes so as to create income generating activities. The MsDP was expected to improve the socio-economic indicators of minorities and the basic amenities of the district as a whole to bring them on par with the national average or even higher.

Before going into a detailed analysis of the implementation of MsDP program, one would like to shed light on the districts selected for MsDP in Maharashtra, viz. Buldhana, Jalna, Parbhani, and Washim. These districts have seen a concentration of Muslims. As per the census 2001, the share of Muslim population was 13 per cent. This selection of districts, however excludes 92 per cent of the rural and urban Muslims who are completely deprived of the benefits of MsDP.

- There is lack of a standard index to evaluate the socio-economic status of selected districts and the criteria takes into account only the literacy rate and working population ratio as indicaters for socio-economic conditions and does not cover parameters such as per capita income or expenditure.
- Even if the lack of a comprehensive selection criterion is overlooked since these districts have been categorized

backward by the State Human Development Report of Maharashtra, 2000, it is important to note that the backwardness of these districts is not because of the minority concentration.

- *The Dandekar and Rath Committee Report* (1975) had concluded, on the basis of various indicators, that these four districts are backward. This Report brought out massive inequalities. After 1980, larger districts were reconstituted into smaller ones on the basis of their geography for effective implementation of development programmes in rural hinterlands. Consequently, Washim and Hingoli districts were carved out from Parbhani and Akola districts.
- In the last decade, essential infrastructure facilities in health and education as well as road construction grew at a very slow pace in these four districts. This was despite the fact that these districts have been covered under the TSP and CSSP. As a result, in these four districts all socio-economic indicators appear extremely low in the baseline survey done by the ICSSR in 2008 under the Ministry of Minority Affairs. The backwardness however can be attributed to the regional imbalance in the development rather than the presence of minority communities. Hence, the development of these four districts should not be taken under the ambit of minority schemes.

Performance of MsDp

Nevertheless, the MsDP was introduced in 2008-09. During the 11th Plan, Rs. 6,000 lakhs was earmarked for MsDP for Maharashtra. While the total approved amount was Rs. 5,993.93 lakhs, the actual released amount was Rs. 5,671.69 lakh. Of this released amount only Rs. 4,302.63 (75 per cent) was spent for the implementation of various projects. The completed components of MsDP programme included the construction of IndiraAwas houses, Anganwadi centres, and educational infrastructure such as school buildings, additional classrooms, provision of teaching aid, lab equipment and the construction of ITIs. The construction of girls' hostels was also started in

2010-11. A detailed scheme-wise and district-wise allocation of funds under MsDP are shown in Table 3.

Table 3: Detailed Scheme-wise and District-wise Allocation of Funds under MsDP

	Amount (Rs. in Lakhs)				*No. of Units – Work TARGET*			
District	*IAY*	*AWC*	*Total of Education*	*Grand Total*	*IAY*	*AWC*	*Total of Education*	*Grand Total*
Parbhani	577.50	645.00	267.48	1489.98	2200	215	2	2417
Buldhana	787.50	711.00	0.00	1498.50	3000	237	0	3237
Hingoli	1044.60	126.00	319.10	1489.70	3730	42	2	3774
Washim	551.25	396.00	332.00	1279.25	2740	132	2	2874
All Four Districts	2960.85	1878.00	918.58	5757.43	11670	626	6	12302

Source: http://minorityaffairs.gov.in/msdp

Despite the huge allocation to IAY contruction of Angaanwadi centres under the MsDP, only 77 per cent of the target under IAY 65 per cent of the target of Angaanwadi centres were achieved and work is under progress. Besides, contruction of polytechnics and ITIs has also not been completed.

Further, the IAY scheme benefited individuals, but did not provide or create public assets under the MsDP programme like drinking water facilities, road connectivity, health centres, sanitation, etc.

With regard to the economic activities, it has been observed that the focus of the plan was on creating physical infrastructure to improve linkages which would create economic opportunities. However these creations which are necessary for social and financial infrastructure were completely missing. The optimal utilization of physical infrastructure and human resources created through the MsDP will not be achieved unless programmes for improving the social and financial infrastructure of these selected four districts are included.

It is to be noted that people's participation in the MsDP programme was not ensured either by bureaucracy or by panchayat members. There was no periodic discussion of the programme related plans and problems with the members of the minority community. The public information system relating to this programme was inadequate and even the software requirements was not provided by the State Government.

Additionally, even the baseline survey of the minority concentrated 70 districts, which was conducted by the Ministry of Minority Affairs (MOMA) in 2008 where it was suggested that while there is a demand for creating livelihood resources for the Muslim community, no action was taken. The outlay for livelihood only provided training programmes.

Further analysis of programmes suggests that in the allocation for various schemes, the largest amount of funds are allocated for schemes which focus on community level facilities such as sanitation, burial grounds (*kabrastans*), constructions of Aanganwadis, classrooms, schools, hostels, buildings, health centers, etc. Although such schemes are a part of the larger support that the community needs, it is important to note that these facilities are necessary not only for the minority community, but to all people. It is thus the duty of the state to provide such facilities. Hence the utilization of funds for such minority schemes and the creation of such general facilities defeats the purpose of targeted schemes which was supposed to address the specific problems and the development lag faced by the minority community.

Further, the minority development schemes at the individual level include schemes such as scholarships, parent allowances, housing, etc. Even though all these schemes are important for individuals, such measures provide only temporary stability. Schemes like scholarships, parent allowances and housing are the supportive elements of welfare schemes, but almost no minority development scheme encourages sustainable development of individual assets and common property assets which will help the community in the long term.

It has been observed that even when there were general schemes which could help communities (whether minority or not) in asset generation, the Muslim community did not benefit proportionately from these schemes. For instance, several Muslims in urban and rural areas rear and sell sheep, goats, poultry birds, etc. These activities can be supported under agriculture and allied development schemes. However, there is no data available regarding Muslims benefiting from these schemes. Marginalized sections were beneficiaries of distribution of surplus land. However, marginalized sections of Muslims were never considered for distribution of surplus land.

These and many other instances can be seen as examples of disguised discrimination in the implementation of policy. Further the disguised discrimination is implicit as the administration and the bureaucratic system is dominated by the people from the elites of the majority community who are either biased and prejudiced or are unwilling to work towards the development of marginalized communities. This lack of the will to work towards the betterment of a marginalized community can be one of the reasons for the use of the word "minorities" whose usage came as late as the 8th Plan in policy documents.

Thus the analysis of the allocation of outlay sheds light on the basic flaws in the state's approach towards minority development which highlights, amongst other things, a non-holistic approach towards the question of minority development, the non-addressal of the demands of minorities and the implicit prejudices and biases in the process of implementation.

Conclusion

India is not a homogenous country. The complex web of social stratification in the country makes it one of the most complex societies in which there are many types of marginalities. Religious identity and marginalization based on that identity is one of the many facets of that marginalization.

After independence, the Constitution of India recognized these marginalities and created some provision for the development of the marginalized. But the lack of development of some marginalized groups, especially social religious groups, reveal the lack of social will towards the development of those communities.

It is to examine this apathy within the system that we have reviewed not only policy implementation as also the context in which these policies conceptualized, and finally implemented.

The first part the chapter looked at the provisions made for the religious minorities at the policy level and its trajectory throughout. It was observed that even though the Five Year Plans made an attempt to work towards equality and development of all communities, they failed to even mention the minorities till as late as the 1990s. Further, despite the mention of minorities in the policy documents, actual implementation of appropriate policies for the development of minority communities was invariably delayed. It was only during the 11th Plan that formal policies were implemented for minority groups.

Additionally, these policies and their implementation were far from perfect. To begin with, an understanding of the varying requirements of different minority communities is lacking in the minds of policy makers.

Further, the implementation of certain schemes meant for minority concentrated areas did not specify concentration of identified minority groups. Thus all could not benefit equally from them. For instance, the four districts chosen for MsDP in Maharashtra have a larger proportion of Buddhists than Muslims. Hence Buddists benefited more from the scheme. Muslims, on the other hand, are the most backward social religious group (as shown by the several reports including the *Sachar Commission Report*) and require more support.

This lack of understanding the needs of minority groups, especially Muslims in the policy process may be attributed to the fact that Muslims are underrepresented at all levels in the state machinery, including health and education sectors which leads to a lack of perspective in policy formulation. The implementation machinery too is dominated by majoritarian values, prejudices and biases against Muslims which results in lethargic implementation of schemes. It is important to note even when the responsibility of implementation of development schemes is given to Muslim officers, they are afflicted by a double disadvantage one of being from the minority community and the charge of being biased towards their community, and second, the job insecurity which stems from working in a majoritarian system.

Even if these flaws in factors are ignored and if we concentrate only on the process of implementation, there are huge gaps such as the lack of appropriate follow up, of the systematic discrimination that people from minority groups, especially Muslims face, their insecurities, lack of literacy, etc.

Thus in conclusion, it would be fair to say that although the Constitution makes provisions for affirmative action for the marginalized minorities, the state has been highly lackadaisical in working towards their development. A positive step is the form of formation of the MOMA and other structures, which will look at the specific minority issues. One can still be hopeful that with appropriate pressure from civil society along with proper policy formation and implementation, the development deficit faced by the minorities can soon be overcome.

Annexure I: Region and District-wise Minority Population in Maharashtra State 2001

Region	*State/ District*	*Muslim*	*Buddhist*	*Jain*	*Chris-tian*	*Sikh*	*Other religions & persu-asions*
	Maharashtra	54.0	30.7	6.8	5.6	1.1	0.5
Konkan	Raigarh	58.4	32.0	3.7	3.5	1.5	0.6
	Ratnagiri	57.5	39.5	1.4	0.9	0.2	0.4
	Thane	54.2	19.0	9.2	14.9	2.0	0.2
	Sindhudurg	35.7	36.7	2.2	24.1	0.4	0.8
	Osmanabad	80.1	15.0	2.7	0.4	0.4	1.2
	Latur	77.2	19.6	1.6	0.4	0.4	0.6
	Bid	76.8	19.5	2.6	0.4	0.2	0.4
Marathwada	Aurangabad	65.7	28.5	3.1	1.8	0.5	0.3
	Parbhani	60.0	37.7	1.4	0.3	0.2	0.3
	Jalna	59.1	33.8	2.5	3.5	0.4	0.6
	Nanded	53.9	42.3	0.7	0.5	1.8	0.6
	Hingoli	40.0	57.3	2.0	0.2	0.2	0.3
	Chandrapur	19.5	70.1	1.1	2.9	1.3	0.6
	Gondiya	13.8	75.3	0.9	0.8	1.1	0.4
	Bhandara	12.8	79.1	0.5	1.0	0.4	0.3
	Gadchiroli	11.4	51.5	0.2	2.3	0.4	4.6
North East	Dhule	80.8	7.9	7.1	2.6	0.8	0.5
	Nashik	76.5	12.2	5.1	3.3	1.3	1.2
	Jalgaon	71.9	19.9	4.3	0.9	0.4	1.3
	Ahmadnagar	70.2	9.5	10.2	6.9	1.6	1.3
	Nandurbar	62.9	4.6	5.3	15.9	0.5	4.7
Vidherbha	Akola	48.9	48.4	1.7	0.6	0.2	0.2
	Amravati	48.0	48.4	1.6	1.0	0.4	0.2
	Buldana	46.8	50.2	2.0	0.4	0.2	0.2
	Yavatmal	42.9	48.3	2.4	0.9	0.4	0.6
	Washim	40.9	55.1	3.1	0.4	0.2	0.2
	Nagpur	30.4	60.3	2.3	3.2	2.0	0.3
	Wardha	20.7	73.6	2.6	1.1	0.8	0.4
	Solapur	81.6	8.3	6.0	2.1	0.6	1.0
Western	Sangli	59.9	10.3	25.0	2.9	0.4	1.2
Maharashtra	Kolhapur	53.1	8.5	33.0	3.6	0.5	0.8
	Satara	45.6	46.6	4.4	1.4	0.4	1.1
	Pune	43.7	31.1	10.1	11.3	2.1	0.7
	Greater Mumbai (M Corp.)	56.9	16.0	12.2	11.4	1.8	0.1
Mumbai	Mumbai (Suburban)	55.4	17.3	11.9	12.7	2.0	0.1
	Navi Mumbai (M Corp.)	39.6	33.7	4.9	14.6	6.6	0.1

Annexure II: Grant-in-aid Outlay and Expenditure for Minority Schemes in Maharashtra: 2009-10 to 2012-13

Category & Sr. No	*Maharashtra Minority Scheme Name*	*Total outlay (Rs in Lakhs)*				*Total Expenditure(Rs in Lakhs)*			
		2009-10	*2010-11*	*2011-12*	*2012-13*	*2009-10*	*2010-11*	*2011-12*	*2012-13*
I	**Administration**								
1	Grant in aid to State Minority Commission	0	274	300	300	0	0	0	0
2	Grant- in-aid for Help Line.	0	25	25	25	0	0	10	10
3	Grant- in-aid for Research, Training & Publicity of Plans.	240	250	300	200	240	0	160	150
4	e-Governance Project in Minorities Development	0	0	10	10	0	0	0	0
5	TOTAL of 1 to 4	240	549	635	535	240	0	170	160
II	**Area, Sectoral and MsDP Schemes**								
6	Grant- in-aid for Area Development Schemes in Minority Concentrated Areas	1473.72	2000	2500	1800	1473.72	1468.76	2175.62	1440
7	Grant in aid for sectoral development of minority concentrated rural areas	0	0	0	1900	0	0	0	0
8	Multisectoral Development Programme : STATE	1521	2500	1500	200	1521	2500	1375.36	614
9	Multisectoral Development Programme : CENTRE	1600.5	4000	2500	1000	1338	3734.7	439.44	1000
10	Multisectoral Development Programme : Total S+C	3121.5	6500	4000	1200	2859	6234.7	1814.8	1614

11	TOTAL of 6 +7 + 10	7716.72	15000	10500	6100	7191.72	13938.16	5805.22	4668
III	**Education**								
12	Grant- in-aid for Uniforms for Students of Minority Community	2100	1800	1800	1800	2100	1620	1350	1440
13	Allowance as an Incentive to Parents for Attendance of Minority Students of Primary Schools	3085.28	1800	1800	1800	3085.28	1620	1530	1440
14	Grant- in-aid for Scholarship for Students of Minority Community pursuing Higher Education	1500	4000	7268	7300	1500	5472.41	7583	0
15	Grant -in-aid for Free Coaching & Allied Scheme.	0	10	10	10	0	0	0	0
16	Grant- in- aid for hostels for Girls from the minority communities in cities.	500	500	400	900	400	450	600	829
17	Grant in Aid to Industrial Training Institutes in Minority Concentrated Areas	0	1000	700	100	0	200	0	0
18	Grant in aid for starting of new polytechnics for minority students	0	450	150	150	0	0	588	453
19	Grant in aid for starting of second and third shift in existinf ITI for minority students	0	200	1800	1000	0	180	900.73	1211
20	Grant- in- aid for Short Term Trade base Courses	203	400	500	400	186.69	336.03	366.14	291
21	Grant in aid for modernisation of Madarsas	0	0	0	0	0	0	0	0
22	Starting of second shift in existing polytechnics for minority students	0	0	958	1000	0	0	134.85	453

Category & Sr. No	*Maharashtra Minority Scheme Name*	*Total outlay (Rs in Lakhs)*				*Total Expenditure(Rs in Lakhs)*			
		2009-10	*2010-11*	*2011-12*	*2012-13*	*2009-10*	*2010-11*	*2011-12*	*2012-13*
23	Assistance to Universities imparting education exclusively minorities	0	0	4700	0	0	0	0	0
24	Grant in Aid to provide bicycles to minority students	0	0	0	500	0	0	0	0
26	Grant -in-aid for Providing Basic Ifrastructure to schools for minorities.	1562	4000	4000	3000	1536.16	3775.27	4157.55	3732
27	**TOTAL of 12 to 26**	**8950.28**	**14160**	**24086**	**17960**	**8808.13**	**13653.71**	**17210.27**	**9849**
IV	**Finance for Institutions**								
27	Grant -in-aid to Maulana Azad Alpa-sankhyank Arthik Vikas Mahamandal. STATE	15	15	30	5	0	0	0	0
28	Grant -in-aid to Maulana Azad Alpa-sankhyank Arthik Vikas Mahamandal: CENTRE	0	67.5	18.12	40	0	0	0	0
29	Grant -in-aid to Maulana Azad Alpa-sankhyank Arthik Vikas Mahamandal.: Total S+C	15	82.5	48.12	45	0	0	0	0
30	Share Capital Contribution to Maluana Azad Alpasankhyank Arthik Vikas Mahamandal.	5899.5	1836.5	1000	3600	5899.5	1836.5	939.1	2880
31	Share Capital Contribution to National Minorities Development and Finance Corporation	30	30	886	100	30	30	664	80
32	**TOTAL of 30+31+32**	**5944.5**	**1949**	**1934.12**	**3745**	**5929.5**	**1866.5**	**1603.1**	**2960**

Category & Sr. No	*Maharashtra Minority Scheme Name*	*Total outlay (Rs in Lakhs)*				*Total Expenditure(Rs in Lakhs)*			
		2009-10	*2010-11*	*2011-12*	*2012-13*	*2009-10*	*2010-11*	*2011-12*	*2012-13*
V	**Welfare**								
33	Grant in aid to wakf Board	0	0	454	300	0	0	385.9	0
34	Grant- in -aid for Haj Committee.	900	700	500	100	900	0	0	0
35	Grant in aid to Urdu Ghar	0	0	222	100	0	0	0	0
36	Grant in aid for Communal Harmony Scheme	0	100	0	0	0	0	0	0
37	Grant in aid to women and other NGOs working for the welfare of minorities	0	100	0	0	0	0	0	0
38	Grant in aid to widows/ Abandoned/ Aggrieved women	0	0	100	0	0	0	0	0
39	**TOTAL of 34 to 39**	**900**	**900**	**1276**	**500**	**900**	**0**	**385.9**	**0**
VI	**Employment Oriented**								
40	Scheme for up gradation of power loom for Minority	0	0	100	100	0	0	0	0
41	Grant -in-aid for Self Help Groups.	0	5	105	100	0	0	0	0
42	TOTAL of 30+31+32	0	5	205	200	0	0	0	0
43	**Grand Total(I to VI)**	**23751.50**	**32563.00**	**38636.12**	**29040.00**	**23069.35**	**29458.37**	**25174.49**	**17637.00**

Source: mdd.maharashtra.gov.in

Annexure III: Schemes of Scholarships for Minority: 2006-07 to 2012-13

Minority	*Period 2006-07 to 2012-13*	*Pre Matric*		*Post Matric*		*Merit -Cum*		*All Scholarships*	
		Numbers	*Percentage Change*	*Numbers*	*Percentage Change*	*Numbers*	*Percentage Change*	*Numbers*	*Percentage Change*
Muslims	Target	607041	145.5	103909	36.1	7588	72.5	718538	128.9
	Achievement	1490083		141454		13090		1644627	
Christian	Target	52643	67.7	10737	-55.0	784	76.8	64164	47.3
	Achievement	88307		4832		1386		94525	
Sikh	Target	12880	79.4	2214	-35.4	161	96.9	15255	62.9
	Achievement	23105		1431		317		24853	
Buddhist	Target	344407	100.5	58814	-87.8	3319	-75.5	406540	71.9
	Achievement	690692		7204		813		698709	
Parsi	Target	1330	116.2	240	-79.6	28	10.7	1598	85.0
	Achievement	2876		49		31		2956	
All	Target	1039887	120.7	175914	-11.9	11880	31.6	1227681	100.8
	Achievement	2295063		154970		15637		2465670	
	Percentage of Girls Students	46.6	-	51.6	-	36.1	-	44.8	-
All Minority	Amount Sanctioned (Crore)	174.72	-	91.77	-	39.43	-	305.92	-
	Percentage share Amount	*57.1*	-	*30.0*	-	*12.9*	-	*100.0*	-

Source: mmd.maharashtra.gov.in

Annexure IV

Sr. No	Scheme/ Programme	Through Department	Unit	Target	Achivemnt	
1	Primary school Consructed	Department of School Education & Literacy, Sarve Shiksha Abhiyan (SSA)	Number	1369	1031	-24.7
2	New Primary Schools Opened	Department of School Education & Literacy, Sarve Shiksha Abhiyan (SSA)	Number	1032	392	-62.0
3	Upper Primary school Consructed	Department of School Education & Literacy, Sarve Shiksha Abhiyan (SSA)	Number	221	47	-78.7
4	New Upper Primary schools Opened	Department of School Education & Literacy, Sarve Shiksha Abhiyan (SSA)		83	25	-69.9
5	Additional Class rooms Constructed	Department of School Education & Literacy, Sarve Shiksha Abhiyan (SSA)	Number	10920	7727	-29.2
6	Kasturba Gandhi Vidyalay	Department of School Education & Literacy, Sarve Shiksha Abhiyan (SSA)	Number	3	3	0.0
7	Posts of Teachers Sanctioned	Department of School Education & Literacy, Sarve Shiksha Abhiyan (SSA)	Number	5397	2037	-62.3
8	Aaganwade Centers (AWCs) Operationalization of anganwadi centres under Integrated Child Development Services (ICDS)	Ministry of Women And Child Development	Number	7430	2951	-60.3
9	Swarnajayanti Gramin Swarojgar Yojna (SGSY- Aajivika)	Ministry of Rural Development	Number	136064	70504	-48.2
10	Indira Awas Yojna (IAY)	Ministry of Rural Development	Number	144414	93709	-35.1

No.	Scheme	Ministry / Department	Unit			
11	Swarna Jayanti Shahari Swarojgar Yojna (SJSRY)	Housing And Urban Povert Allivation(HUPA)	Rs in Crore	47.9528	32.6972	-31.8
12	Skill Training for Employment Promoted Urban Areas	Housing And Urban Povert y Allivation(HUPA)	Numbers	40255	74104	84.1
13	Micro Enterpriners Urban Self Employment(USEP)	Housing And Urban Povert Allivation(HUPA)	Numbers	14376	20759	44.4
14	Upgrations of Industrial training Institutes (ITIs) Total No of ITIs : 13	Department of Labour & Employment	Rs in Crore	33.37	27.52	-17.5
15	Priority Sector Lendings	Ministry of Finance	Rs in Crore	90187	43153	-52.2
16	Urban Infrastructure & Goverence(UIG)	Ministry of Urban Development	Rs in Crore	3285	3285	0.0
17	National Rural Drinking Water Programm(NRDWP)	Ministry of water and Sanitation	Rs in Crore	1608	1513	-5.9
				Total Cost	Sanctioned cost for minority area	
18	JNNURM- Basic Services to the Urban Poor(BSUP)	Housing And Urban Povert Allivation(HUPA)	26583	4758	-82.1	
19	JNNURM- Integrated Housing Slum Development Programme(HSDP)	Housing And Urban Povert Allivation(HUPA)	10079	3772	-62.6	
20	Modernization of Madarsas	Ministry of Human Development, Department of Social Edcation and Literacy	Rs. Crore	1.84	na	na
			No. of Madersas	45	na	na
			No. of Teachers	132	na	na
21	Infrastructural Development for Minority Institutions	Ministry of Human Development, Department of Social Edcation and Literacy	Rs. Crore	11.53	na	na
			No. of Institutions	58	na	na

REFERENCES

1. B.K. Bajpai, 'Impact of Multi Sector Development Plan on Muslims: A Case Study of Moradabad District' in *Uttar Pradesh Islam and Muslim Societies: A Social Science Journal*, Vol. 5, No. 2, 2012.
2. Reshmi P. Bhaskaran, 'Report on Baseline Survey in the Minority Concentrated Districts of Maharashtra—Hingoli District', Institute For Human Development, New Delhi, Sponsored by Ministry of Minority Affairs, Government of India, and Indian Council of Social Science Research, 2008.
3. Reshmi P. Bhaskaran, 'Report on Baseline Survey in the Minority Concentrated Districts of Maharashtra—Washim District', Institute For Human Development, New Delhi, Sponsored by Ministry of Minority Affairs, Government of India, and Indian Council of Social Science Research.
4. Reshmi P. Bhaskaran, 'Report on Baseline Survey in the Minority Concentrated Districts of Maharashtra—Buldhana District', Institute For Human Development, New Delhi, Sponsored by Ministry of Minority Affairs, Government of India, and Indian Council of Social Science Research, 2008.
5. Shashi Bhushan Singh and Falendra K. Sudan, 'Report on Baseline Survey in the Minority Concentrated Districts of Maharashtra—Parbhani District', Institute For Human Development, New Delhi, Sponsored by Ministry of Minority Affairs, Government of India, and Indian Council of Social Science Research, 2008.
6. Basant, Rakesh and Abusaleh Shariff (eds.), *Handbook of Muslims: Empirical and Policy*, 2010.
7. Asghar Ali Engineer, 'Indian Muslims and Education', *Secular Perspective*, July 1-15, 2011.
8. Government of India 'The All Five Year Plans', Planning Commssion, New Delhi, (1951-52 to 2007-08).
9. Government of India, Planning Commission (2008) *Eleventh Five Year Plan 2007-2012*, Vol. I, Planning Commission.
10. Government of India, *Census of India—Maharshtra State, 2001.*
11. Government of India, Programme and Guidelines for Preparation of Multi-sectoral District Development Plans for Minority Concentration Districts, Ministry of Minority Affairs, 2008.
12. Government of Maharashtra, ALL Annual Issues of *Economic Survey of Maharshtra*, Planning Department, Mantralay, Mumbai, 1999-2000 to 2011-2012.

13. Government of Maharashtra, (2008-09 to 2011-2012), All Issues of 'ijalha saamaaijak va Aaiqa-k phaNaI: baulaZaNaa ijalha' Directorate of Economics and Statistics, Planning Department Mantralay, Mumbai.
14. Government of Maharashtra, (2008-09 to 2011-2012), All Issues of 'ijalha saamaaijak va Aaiqa-k phaNaI: prBaNaI ijalha' Directorate of Economics and Statistics, Planning Department Mantralay, Mumbai.
15. Government of Maharashtra, (2008-09 to 2011-2012), All Issues of 'ijalha saamaaijak va Aaiqa-k phaNaI: vaiSama ijalha' Directorate of Economics and Statistics, Planning Department Mantralay, Mumbai.
16. Government of Maharashtra, (2008-09 to 2011-2012), All Issues of 'ijalha saamaaijak va Aaiqa-k phaNaI: ihMgaaolaI ijalha' Directorate of Economics and Statistics, Planning Department Mantralay, Mumbai,
17. S.R. Hashim, 'Evaluation of Baseline Survey Report', Government India, New Delhi, November, 2008.
18. Amitabh Kundu, 'Comments on Baseline Survey Reports for Nine Minority, Ministry of Minority Affairs', 2008.
19. Ministry of Minority Affairs, 'Proceedings of the National Conference of the State Ministers of Minority Welfare, New Delhi, 2012.
20. Ranganath Mishra Commission: Report, Prime Minister's High Level Committee, Cabinet Secretariat, Government of India, 2007.
21. R. Robinson, 'Indian Muslims: A Varied Dimension of Diversity', *Economic and Political Weekly*, 2007.
22. Rajinder Sachar, 'Social, Economic and Educational Status of Muslim Community of India', Prime Minister High Level Committee Report, 2006.
23. Ghanashyam Shah, 'The Condition of Muslims', *Economic and Political Weekly*, Vol. XLII, No. 10, March, 2007.
24. Syed Ahmed, 'Charges of Irregularity in the Implementation of MsDP in Assam', TwoCircles.net., 2011.
25. United Nations Development Programme, 'Marginalised Minorities in Development Programming' (2010), Democratic Governance Group, Bureau for Development Policy, New York, USA, 2010.

10

The Dilemmas of Muslim Women in India

Zeenat Shaukat Ali

Introduction

Investigating the life and politics of Muslims in contemporary India, two opposing opinions surface. The first is that Muslims are 'appeased' and are a cause of hindrance to the social and political advancement of India by refusing to be modern. One example cited for this encumbrance, besides others, is the imposition of restrictions on Muslim women limiting them to the private sphere.

The other opinion views Muslims as a beleaguered minority: they have to deal with multiple problems in India, that they are threatened with physical as well as cultural annihilation. The threat to life is seen in the frequent outbreak of communal violence. The baggage of terrorism "every Muslim is not a terrorist but every terrorist is a Muslim" similarly depreciates their sense of dignity. Besides they have little representation in the socio-political-economic development of India.

This chapter examines the first standpoint. It briefly touches upon the issue relating to the myth and reality of "Muslim appeasement", some predicaments encountered by women in India generally and extensively goes on to investigate whether the position of Muslim women in India is due to any intrinsic properties of Islam.

Muslim Appeasement: Myth or Reality?

On 26th November 1949, India adopted the new Constitution, framed by Dr. Babasaheb Ambedkar, enforced two months later on 26th January 1950 assuring all the citizens equality, justice and security irrespective of class, creed, gender, religion or social status. These of course included minorities and women.

Yet on 9th March, 2005, 58 years after India's Independence, the previous Prime Minister of India, Dr. Manmohan Singh, found it necessary to issue a Notification for the Constitution of a High Level Committee to prepare a report on the social, economic and educational status of the Muslim community of India. The seven-member High Level Committee, chaired by Justice Rajinder Sachar, submitted its final report to the Prime Minister on 17th November, 2006.[1]

The Report was brought to the table by Justice Ranganath Mishra. Both the *Sachar Committee Report and Ranganath Mishra Commission* established that Muslims in India are the most backward community despite their rich cultural heritage and strong numerical presence. It must be noted that there was no woman member appointed in the Committee even though the condition of women is very important for any survey of the social scenario among Muslims.

The Report stated that Muslims are now worse off in India than the Dalits, or those once called untouchables. Some 52 per cent of Muslim men are unemployed, compared with 47 per cent of Dalit men. Among Muslim women, 91 per cent are unemployed, compared with 77 per cent of Dalit women.[2]

Almost half of Muslims over the age of 46 cannot read or write. While making up nearly 14 per cent of the total population of the country, Muslims account for 40 per cent of India's prison population. They hold only 4.9 per cent of government jobs and only 3.2 per cent of the jobs in the country's security agencies, thus creating a new set of "untouchable Indians" in the modern, democratic republic of India.[3]

The Sachar Committee compiled data from a number of sources. The comprehensive report frames issues as related to identity, security and equity. Barring some generic observations about the causes for the "development deficit" among Muslims, there is no explicit or detailed discussion of the causes of such conditions.

The findings of the Sachar Committee are a testimony to six decades of institutional neglect and bias that has left the country's Muslims far behind other Socio-Religious Communities (SRCs) in the areas of education, employment, access to credit, access to social and physical infrastructure and political representation. The Report clearly illustrates the myth of "Muslim appeasement". Although the Report does not largely cover the concerns of Muslim women, the Sachar Committee observed that the low aggregate work participation ratios for Muslims are "essentially" due to the much lower participation in economic activity by the women of the community.[4]

The Committee pointed out that despite a high share of Muslim workers in self-employment activity, especially in urban areas, women operate mainly from home, rather than offices or factories. Whether this trend is due to compulsion or their non-expectation for jobs in the government or non-government formal sector, or due to their inclination for certain types of work that are done best under a self-employment scheme, would be an important subject for study.[5]

The figure of Muslim women who are engaged in work from their homes rather than offices or factories is 70 per cent compared to the general figure of 51 per cent.[6] Notwithstanding the fact that Muslim women are among the most backward sections of Indian society, they have not received adequate attention of the government, social workers and academicians. Lack of education, poverty, economic dependency and ignorance of their rights have made them more vulnerable to exploitation. There is, therefore, an acute need to undertake research in this area in order to identity problems specific to Muslim women and mark out the causes of their diffidence.

It is interesting to note that one of the recommendations that this Report puts forward is the need for Muslim women to reclaim their right to *religious knowledge*, and to participate in the contemporary debate on Islam and women's rights in order to achieve their goals. The question is: can the goal of improvement of their condition depend only on enhancing *religious knowledge*, or is a social, cultural and political environment conducive for Indian Muslim women to articulate and define their own needs a necessary condition to improve their condition? As this Report documents, such an environment does not currently exist.

The Muslim community as a whole still awaits the implementation of the recommendations of the Rajinder Sachar Committee Report and the promised affirmative action.

The General Predicament of Women in India

Short-changing girls is not only a matter of gender discrimination; it is bad economics and bad societal policy.

Experience has shown, over and over again, that investment in girls' education translates directly and quickly into better nutrition for the whole family, better health care, declining fertility, poverty reduction and better overall economic performance".

Despite India's constitutional guarantee of impartiality and egalitarianism for all its citizens, discrimination against women stubbornly persists. *The overall status of a woman is lower than men. Right from birth preference for a male child over a female child is clearly visible. While the birth of a male child is considered a blessing, a female child from birth is considered more of a burden.*

According to the 2001 Indian Census, overall child male-female ratio was 927 females per 1,000 males. However, the 2011 Indian census shows that there are 914 females per 1,000 males.[7]

In the older group, there were only 933 females per 1,000 males, while the 2011 sex ratio was 940 females to 1,000 males.[8]

These new figures point out that the use of new technology contributes to the gender composition. Furthermore, the availability of and access to new technologies provides new ways for parents to achieve such goals of sex determination before birth.[9]

Due to the widespread use of this technology, the Indian government banned the sex determination test. In spite of these bans imposed by the government, the law is not widely followed.[10] As pointed out by Amartya Sen, educational and health inequality are the indicators of a woman's status of welfare.[11]

Despite Muslim 'backwardness' Muslims have the best sex-ratio among all Indians. Over the decades, the Muslim population shows an increasingly better sex ratio compared with other Socio-Religious Communities (SRCs).

Similarly, Muslims have the highest child sex ratio of any social group in the country. For instance, the child sex ratio among Muslims was 986 girls per 1,000 boys in the age group 0-5 in 1998-99, significantly higher than the ratio of 931 among SCs/STs, 914 among other Hindus, and 859 among other groups. (pp. 33, 34). This is a very significant finding. The fact that the sex ratio among Muslims is improving while it is on a dangerous decline among some sections of the population shows that among Muslims there is far less bias against the girl child.[12]

The policy of male preference and female negligence has led to what is known as "disadvantage female". Studies reveal discrimination continues with regard to food, health, education, domestic work etc. Due to family pressure even mothers sometimes show preference for a male child.[13]

Recent statistics in India reveal a shocking increase in violence against women. The gang rape and consequent death of Nirbhaya in Delhi and the gang rape of a journalist at the Shakti Mills in Mumbai are horrifying examples.

Women in Indian society have been victims of ill treatment, humiliation, torture and exploitation. As per 1994 Records of the Crime Record Bureau of the Central Home Ministry there has been an increase in 1993-1994. Records of social organizations are available regarding the same.[14]

These records are replete with incidents of abduction, rape, murder and torture of women. Crimes against women include dowry harassment, wife battering, kidnapping female children and eve teasing to name a few.

But regretfully, female victims of violence have not been given much attention in the literature relating to social or criminal violence. As per the report (1994) in India, on an average:

(i) Every day in every 6 minutes one atrocity is committed against women;

(ii) in every 44 minutes a woman is kidnapped;
(iii) in every 47 minutes a woman is raped;
(iv) every day there are 17 dowry deaths.

The same Report goes on to show that crimes against women have doubled in the last 10 years; instances of rape has increased by 400 per cent in the last 2 decades; instances of kidnapping and blackmailing by 30 per cent between 1993-1994. In 1993 alone 82,818 instances of crimes against women were registered. Many cases are not registered. It is said only 10 per cent rapes are reported.[15]

The Problems and Concerns of Muslim Women in India

India's Muslims, officially estimated at almost 200 million, make up the world's largest population of Muslims after Indonesia. Although numerical figures cannot be given in absolute terms, they form only around 13.4 per cent of the total Indian population. Muslim women constitute a little less than half the population, the rest consisting of children.

Yet, relatively little has been written about India's Muslim women and their struggles for gender justice. While considerable literature exists about the myriad economic and social, educational problems of Indian Muslim women, there is inconsequential documentation about how the socio-cultural-economic context as well as patriarchy exercise constraint.

It must be noted that theological scholarship and practices differ widely according to the country, region, or sectarian beliefs where an Islamic community is geographically positioned. According to, Global Muslim Population Research, the largest groups of Muslim women are in: Indonesia (over 100 million), Bangladesh (over 75 million), Pakistan (over 85 million), India (over 80 million), Egypt (nearly 40 million), Nigeria (nearly 40 million), Turkey (over 35 million) and Iran (over 35 million). These countries total more than 60 per cent of the world's Muslims; there are more than 750 million Muslim women worldwide, including sizable minorities in several countries of Africa, Europe, and in China.[16]

The source of their repression is sought to be positioned by some in Islam itself, which is assumed as hostile to women's rights and gender-justice.

In such an overview, the socio-cultural context within which Muslim women live and function and which profoundly influences their life is overlooked. In the context of Islam, the Marxist writer, Valentine M. Moghadam, argues, that the influence of the factors of the extent of urbanization, industrialization, proletarization and political ploys of the state managers are generally disregarded.[17]

Hence, gender-associated issues of Indian Muslim women must be recounted by and large economic, political, and educational marginalization of the Indian Muslim community, or large sections of it. It cannot be seen as merely developing from patriarchal interpretations of Islam or only due to patriarchal customs, practices and laws specific to the Indian Muslim community.

Recognizing Metamorphosis and Change

"Verily God does not change the state of a people until they change the state of their own lives." (Q; 13: 11)

"Change" encompasses transformation towards enlightenment at the personal, community, national level and global levels. For such a makeover, a scientific temper, ability, capability, proficiency, along with wisdom and compassion are the necessary ingredients.

One of the prime factors that constitutes or generates change, it is argued, is that society is like a living organism and like all organisms undergoes the evolutionary process. Whether the basic factor constituting the requirement for such change is the need to channelize scientific anarchism resulting from natural phenomena or the process of the question relating to a sort of historical determinism or the influence of powerful personalities in creating a fresh vision, there is no dispute that the process of change is fundamental to the human experience.

In Islam, the persona of Prophet Mohammed constituted a fundamental as well as a pivotal role in effecting change. In comparing the Prophet of Islam to the Prophets of old and particularly since Abraham, a common distinct factor emerges: that all these great Prophets promulgated their mission in the form of a rebellion against existing powerful political systems. Such systems made grand claims but deliberately ignored and failed to account for reducing men and women to slavery and serfdom.

The rebellion of Prophet Abraham against the might of Nimrod or of Prophet Moses against the arrogance of the Pharaoh in or the struggle of Prophet Jesus against the powerful Jewish priesthood and Roman Imperialism or the struggle of Prophet Mohammed against the haughty, suppressive oligarchy and aristocracy points to the orientation and spirit of such movements to restore justice and equilibrium.

Placed under a "given" environment from the sociological and historical standpoint, Prophet Mohammed's thinking and personality were the compelling forces that conceptualized human destiny with a new vision. From a historian's perspective the event of Prophet Mohammed's birth in the 7th century of the Christian calendar, while absorbing the aura surrounding it, laid the groundwork for a new sociological pattern.

Challenging the imbalance of the old warring, patriarchal oligarchic civilization established over a span of time, he initiated the notion of stability, democratic governance, secular inventiveness, economic equilibrium, social equality, a high moral order and gender justice Within a short span of time racism, ethnicity, chauvinism and gender issues underwent a fundamental metamorphosis and saw the light of another day.

One of the primary concerns of the *Quran* was consequently to effect change. Change from the liberation of the dangers of subservience, indignity or any phenomena to subjugate the human spirit. As a result, it introduced the skill to question and an ingrained, established oligarchic system.

This process to bring about this change was the exercise of reason over established injustices. The term the *Quran* used for such a system was that of *ijtehad*. This was suggested as the key by several scholars such as Jamaluddin Afghani, Rashid Rida, Mohammad Iqbal and a host of modern scholars like Khalid ibn Abdul Fadhl but alas was rarely brought to use.

Women: Beyond Inherited Frameworks

Critics consistently allege that the reticent position of Muslim women is principally due to Islamic scriptural instructions that are inherently misogynist and patriarchal, while Muslim apologists indignantly contest this argument with a converse reasoning that Islam confers them with undeniable rights. Both these stances seem cliched and need to be examined in the broader context of history.

It must be noted that as a number of schools exist within the framework of Islamic jurisprudence, a variety of opinions have emerged, each asserting authenticity, offering diverse interpretations on gender relations on the status of Muslim women.

Undoubtedly, traditional strongholds have asserted themselves from time to time. What is lesser known is the fact that key features such as the aspiration of universal standards for a balanced society in Islam have likewise made a strong argument.

Today, In almost all Muslim countries and communities there has been a history of resistance to a uniform, identical, authoritarian vision of society. Scholars grounded in the study of Islam have consistently challenged the traditional patriarchal monopoly over the interpretation of the feminine in Islam. Both women and men scholars have, over a stretch of time have assiduously questioned why the rights granted to women by the *Quran* which is the epitome of gender justice, have been diluted and watered down.

In a bid to recapture the spirit of Quranic revelation, several serious attempts have been made for a historical search and studied alternative interpretations with regard to determining the status of women. The arguments are systematically and cogently developed and there has been a paradigm shift from inherited frameworks. Pertinent Quranic verses and authentic Hadith relating to multidimensional issues on the subject of gender are analyzed hermeneutically as well as linguistically by scholars. The implications of these findings have been both interesting and impactful. They dispel much of the misogynist understandings and stereotypes about womens' marginalization or exclusion. On the contrary, their findings show both recognition and acknowledgment of women's participation, contribution and inclusion in both public and private spheres.

Earlier there have been men scholars who have defended the rights of Muslim women. Some important names are Ahmed Faris al-Shidyaq (1855), Rifa'ah Rafi al-Tahtawi (1801–1871), Mohammed Abduh (1849–1905), a founder of the Salafiyah (Islamic reforms) movement; Qasim Amin (1899) initiated much discussion; Lutfi al-Sayyid, publisher of Al-Jaridah, Turkish counterparts included Namik Kernal and Ahmed Mithat, Maulana Mumtaz Ali. In recent times we have had Maullana Shoaib Koti, Asghar Ali Engineer, Khalid Abou El Fadl and several others.

In other words, there is a struggle for gender justice where scholars undertake and call into question the very legitimacy of pre-Islamic impositions and its patriarchal dominated leadership alienating women from political, social, legal activities confining their roles within a traditional framework.

In changing the paradigm of gender related issues, the contributions of scholars offering a fresh dimensional approach with reference to Islam, Muslim women and leadership are, in general invaluable.

Some contemporary names are Amina Muhsin Wudud, Fatima Mernissi, Amira Sonbo, Riffat Hasan, Shatifa Al-Khateeb, Hibba Abugideiri, Dunya Maumoon, the late Annemarie Schimmel, Sachiko Murato among others.[18]

The Strength and Power of Women in Islam

In discussing gender relations within the parameter of Islam, it is necessary to understand that the issues raised by the modern concern with the politics of gender cannot be addressed through simple legalistic, sociological, Western inspired objections. Such an approach is not sound since it speaks little of the deeper reasons for the Islamic gender-related world-view.

A careful reading of the *Quran* and the authentic *Hadith* demonstrates that Islam's basic view of masculine and feminine postulates a complementarity of functions. Neither can be complete without the other. In Islamic cosmological thinking, the universe is perceived as equilibrium built on harmonious relationships between the "pairs" (51: 49), (953: 45) that make up all things. The qualities of centrality, all comprehensiveness, and vicegerency are inherent in both masculine and feminine as well as other creations.

There is no established form of hierarchy. For instance, Adam was created without a father or mother and Jesus—the spirit and word of God and one of the Prophets and perfect human being was created from Mary without an intermediary. This goes on to show how we understand relationships between the masculine and feminine depends upon our perspectives and what we regard as our essence.[19]

In reality, human beings are only two sides of a mirror, therefore Islamic views on feminine can in no way be separated from Islamic views of the masculine. A well known Hadith speaks of women being "the twin halves of men".

Evidence regarding this is that the progeny of the Prophet primarily emanates from his only surviving child, his daughter *Hazrat Fatimah*. Among the believers *Harzat Khadija*, wife of the Prophet was the first to believe in his message. It is also interesting to note that no Haj or pilgrimage is complete without running between the hills of the *Saffa* and in commemoration of the lady *Hajrah*, wife of Prophet Abraham. As the *Hadith i Qudsi* says *"rahmati sabaqat ghadabi"* or "my Mercy precedes my Wrath".

It is a strange paradox that one has to distinguish between the Quranic world view in relation to women with its ideals and the problems that arise from breaking those ideals. It is thus the spiritual-intellectual approach within Islam that can re-establish its ideals of gender equality.

Hence there is no impediment in Islam with relation to participation of women both young and old in the political, social or economic development of a nation. A systematic, historical approach clarifies the change wrought by the *Quran* in a society where inferiority or superiority of gender was carefully replaced by ability and action rather than sex differentiation.

Conquering and Surmounting Stereotypes

Both Quranic verses and authentic Hadith dispel much misunderstandings and stereotypes about women marginalization or exclusion. On the contrary their findings show both recognition and acknowledgment of women's participation, contribution and inclusion in both public and private sphere not merely as a rubber stamp but officially practiced.

The examples quoted above provide ample evidence that there are no religious restrictions on women regarding political participation. Cultural restrictions experienced by Muslim women presently are another matter. They are a assertion of patriarchal control and have no base in the Quran or authentic tradition and practice of Islam.

Imposition of cultural restrictions are often confused with religious restrictions. A fine distinction needs to be made between the two. Culture is often restrictive and binds women to tradition whereas the religion of Islam entitles women to be part of political, intellectual, economic, participation and be part of state affairs, national development or public life.

In the *Quran*, there is no evaluative distinction between the creation of men or women. The *Quran* states *"O mankind reverence your Guardian Lord who created you from a single person and created his mate of like nature"* (H.Q. 4:1). Here a "single person" does not specify a gender. God's creation of woman from man's rib, her responsibility for man's expulsion from paradise, her creation for pleasure which makes her existence merely instrumental or secondary and not of fundamental importance, have no historical or factual antecedents in the *Holy Quran*".[20]

A number of verses substantiate that all human beings are created in pairs, thus one is not derivative of the other. *"Glory to God who created in pairs all things that the earth produces as their own humankind"* (H.Q. 36:36), verses 51:49; 50:57; 22:5; 78:8 and several other verses emphasize the same theme. No priority or superiority is accorded to either gender. On the other hand, the existence of one is complementary to the other.[21]

Secondly in regard to the "Fall" from paradise, all verses in the *Quran* use the dual form in Arabic, "they both forgot", "they both ate", "they both repented and were forgiven" (H.Q. 7:19-23). Women in Islamic theology alone were therefore not responsible for the Fall.

Submitting that biologically men and women are not the

same, yet these differences do not mean that they are not of equal value. In the eyes of Allah, women and men are equal participants in both spiritual and material aspects of life. In several verses the *Quran* says: "For Muslim men and women... For believing men and women, for men and women who are patient and constant, for men and women who humble themselves, for men and women who give in charity. For men and women who fast, for men and women who guard their chastity and for men and women who engage much in God's praise—for them God has prepared forgiveness and a great reward". (H.Q. 33:35).

A specific address to both men and women is further seen. "Never will I suffer to be lost the reward of any of you, be he male or female..." (H.Q.3:195). Again, "He that works evil will not be requited, but by the like thereof: and He that works a righteous deed—whether men or women....such will enter the garden of bliss" (H.Q. 40:40). Hence, they share equal roles and responsibilities in their spiritual existence having equal rewards and punishments for their actions.

Women's right to participate in social, economic, educational, cultural and political activities was on par with their male counterparts. Hence equal rights for men to acquire, administer, dispose and inherit property; equal freedom to choose or refuse a spouse; to consent or not to enter into marital status or to the dissolution of marriage; equal conditions in matter of education, financial dealings are all part of Islamic norms.[22]

For instance, from the financial perspective women can enjoy the same benefits as men and follow any respectable profession as men " To men is allotted what they earn and to women what they earn" (*Quran* 4: 32)

Further, the *Quran* extols the leadership of Queen Bilques as "a women ruling over them provided with every requisite" (H.Q. 27:23). Her qualities of leadership are not measured by her gender but by her capacity to fulfil the requirements of office, her political acumen, the purity of her faith and her independent judgment. Similarly the operating principle is all the rights and privileges is for the one best suited to fulfil the requirements for a good and effective leadership and there is no *Quranic* prohibition which prohibits her from doing the same because of gender.

The *Quran* does not uphold or assert conceptions of female inferiority, nor can women be judged as less rational, more emotional, or less competent than men on the basis of divine law. It is clear from many Sunnah that the Prophet consulted women and weighed their opinions seriously. According to Imam Hanbal, a woman, Umm Waraqah, was appointed as the imam of her household by the Prophet and also led the prayers.[23]

Historical evidence shows that women contributed significantly to the reading and writing of the *Quran* and were entrusted with vital secrets affecting the Muslim community. Women were the first to learn of the revelation, were aware of the repose of the Prophet during his migration to Medina. They were entrusted with the Prophet's secret plans during wars. Regarding succession, the distinguished women of the community were consulted in the matter on his death.

Harzat Khadija was the first to learn of the revelation; Hazrat Asma, daughter of Abku Bakr was known as *"zun nataquain"* (one with two belts, as she used one to tie a bag carrying food and documents for the Prophet during his migration); Hazrat Fatima played an active role on discussions relating to succession and Hazrat Ayesha was politically active. Umm Salamah was entrusted with vital state secrets and Hazrat Hafsa helped with her in the compilation of the *Quran*.

Canonical records demonstrate women's important and respected role in Muslim society, as reflected in the incident of a woman, Khawla bit Salibah, who corrected the authoritative ruling (fatwa) of Caliph Umar ibn al-Khattab on the dower (*mehr*). The fact that women prayed in mosques and were involved in the transmission of *Hadiths* (Ibn Sa'd, the famous early biographer, records 700 cases of women who performed this important function). Women were known to give sanctuary (*jiwar*) to men and their involvement and interaction in public matters are expressed in history and traditions. They owned and disposed of property and engaged in commercial transactions. Like their male counterparts they were encouraged to seek knowledge, which, they pursued in the Prophet's own home, and women were both instructors and pupils in the early Islamic period.

Examples of women's participation in various activities, as the early history of Islam and the traditions of Prophet Mohammed point out the following. Women took part in national activities, acted as advisors, joined in congregational prayers in the mosque (Bu. 10: 162, 164). They were in the battlefield before the red cross nurses. (Bu. 6: 57), carried provision therein (Bu. 56:66), helped carry the wounded and slain from the battlefields (Bu. 56: 62, 63, 65). The Prophet's wife, Bibi Zainab prepared hides, devoting the proceeds of the sales for charitable work. Women helped as laborers in the fields (Bu 67:108), served male guests at a feast (Bu. 67: 78) and carried on business(Bu. 11: 40) The great Lady Khadija had a well established business.

In the political arena, the *Quran* refers to women who, independently of their male relatives, pledged the oath of allegiance *(bayah)* to the Prophet "O Prophet whenever believing women come to thee to pledge their allegiance to thee....then accept their allegiance"(*Quran*. 60: 12). Well-known examples of women making such pledges to the Prophet occurred at *al-Aqabah, al-Ridwan and al-Shajarah.* "In essence bayah is the acknowledgement of a leader for without bayah has no legitimacy and thus cannot be head of state". Undouted they were natural parts of the political process in Islam.[24]

In a number of cases, distinguished women became Muslims before their men did, again contradicting the traditional patriarchal view that women were incapable of independent action. Hazrat Khadijah was the first person to embrace Islam. As regards public posts, Caliph Umar appointed a woman, Shaffah bin Abdullah, to serve as an official *(muhtasib)* in the market of Medina, and Hanbali jurisprudence upholds the qualifications of women to serve as judges.

In addition to all the previous biographies of distinguished women, especially in the Prophet's household, show that women behaved autonomously in early Islam. These are the very women whom contrary traditionalists exemplify as models to justify women's seclusion and confinement today. The women about whom most data are available are Hazrat Khadijah, the Prophet's first wife; Bibi A'ishah, also his wife; Fatimah, his youngest daughter; Zaynab, his granddaughter; Sukaynah, his great-grand daughter; and A'ishah bint Talhah, the niece Hazratklisha. Such ladies—artists, poets, cultural patrons, soldiers—often challenged the wisdom of men, insisted upon equality with their husbands, and took initiatives sometimes directly counter to patriarchal authority. Contemporary exhortations to restrict the activities of women on the public platform by reference to the examples of these women are unrealistic and therefore invalidated by the reality of their lives.

Muslim Women in the Public Sphere

History demonstrates that Islam neither limits women to the private sphere, nor does it give men supremacy in public or private space. A study of Greek and Roman cultures preceding Islamic civilization did not produce a single eminent woman philosopher and jurist. Likewise, until the 1700s, Europe failed to produce a single woman social, legal or political jurist. Islam did exactly the opposite in every respect.

The responsibilities relating to different fields of activities lies with both genders equally. As the *Quran* states: "And as for the believer, men and women—they are friends and protectors of one another: they enjoin the doing of what is right and forbid the doing of what is wrong, and are constant in prayer, and render the purifying dues, and pay heed unto God and His apostle......" (*Quran* 9: 7)

Therefore we find that early Islamic history is filled with women who undertook various forms of political-social-economic-educational activism. The first martyr in Islam was a woman, *Sumaya Zawgat Yasir*. *Sumaya* was tortured and killed in the early period of Islam because of her belief in Prophet Mohammed and the message he brought.

A woman who also received praise from the Prophet was a woman traveller named Asma bint Umais who traveled by sea and emigrated to Abyssinia when Muslims were being persecuted in Mecca. It is significant to note in that Asma bint Umais and her travels in search of religious freedom appeared to be common knowledge and was noteworthy enough to receive praise from the Prophet.[25]

Women like men fought in battles to defend Islam. Umm Amara defended the Prophet during the Battle of Uhud after Muslims suffered losses. Umar ibn al-Khattab said: "I heard the Prophet (PBUH) saying, On the day of Uhud, I never looked right or left without seeing Umm Imara fighting to defend me".[26]

Another famous warrior was Nasiba bint Kaab who fought with the Prophet in the battle of Uhud (625 A.D./3 A.H.) and later on with Caliph Abu Bakr in the *Ridda* war (632 A.D./10 A.H.). She was known as such a courageous and dedicated warrior that Abu Bakr himself attended her reception upon her return to Medina.[27]

Umm Salama, the wife of the Prophet was instrumental in advising the Prophet during the crisis at *Hudaybiya* in 628 A.D. (6 A.H.). Her advice prevented disunity amongst the Muslim after the Treaty of *Hudaybiya* and her opinion prevailed over that of many men, including Umar ibn al-Khattab.[28]

Umm Salama was also an inquisitive student of Islam. She asked the Prophet why men were more mentioned in the *Quran* and in response God revealed *Surah* 33 verse 35.[29]

Umm Hani offered refuge to two non-Muslim men who sought protection after the opening of Mecca. After she offered them refuge she went to the Prophet and told him what she had done. He said to her, "We offer refuge to whomever you offered and we guarantee their safety". Thus, in essence, Umm Hani bint Abi Talib performed a significant political function, one often reserved only for the ruler, when she granted political asylum to these men.[30]

Hazrat Aisha, was also politically active and influential leader. In the year 658 A.D. (36 A.H.) Hazrat Aisha was the only woman on the battlefield, led thousands of men into the Battle of the Camel or Jaml.[31]

Khalid Abou El Fadl gives the example of Imam Zuhri, a famous scholar of the Sunnah when he indicated to Qasim Ibn Mohammed (a scholar of the *Quran*), a desire to seek knowledge,

Qasim advised him to join the assembly of a well-known woman jurist of the day, Amara bin al Rahman. Imam Zuhri took his advice and attended her assembly and later described her as a "boundless ocean of knowledge". In fact, Amara instructed a number of famed scholars such as Abu Bakr Mohammed ibn Hazama and Yahya ibn Said.[32]

Fatimah bit Qais tenaciously argued with Hazrat Umar and Hazrat Ayesha over a legal point and refused to change her opinion. And there was Umm Yaqab, who on hearing Abdullah ibn Masud explain a legal point, then confidently told him "I have read the entire *Quran,* but have not found your explanation anywhere in it".[33]

Arwa bint Ahmad served as the governor of Yemen in the late 5th and early 6th centuries. Zubaidah bint Ja'fr al-Mansur, a wealthy benefactress, funded the construction of Mecca's water supply system and the establishment of a pilgrimage route from Baghdad to Mecca in the late 8th and early 9th centuries.[34]

They played a vital role in education, scientific discovery, medicine and several other fields throughout the history of Islam.[35]

One could go on and enumerate the women who played important roles both in the history and mystical thought and practice of Islam as is evident from several biographies. Most of the spiritual leaders received their first religious inspiration from their pious mothers for did not the Prophet state that "Paradise lies at the feet of the mother". The question to be asked is why the feminine side to Islamic life is usually overlooked.

Islam did exactly the opposite in every respect. Hazrat Umar bin al Khattab appointed Shaffa bin Abdullah as an inspector over the market in Medina. Moreover, Islam is replete with exmples of femal professors tutoring male jurists. From the Traditions of the Prophet it is clearly seen that Hazrat Ayesha, Umm Salameh, Hazrat Hafsa, Laila bint Qasim, Khaula bint Abu Darda, Asma bint Abu Bakr were entrusted with preserving and teaching one fourth of the religion.[36]

Among some other well known names are Fatimah bit Asad, Umm Salima bint Malhan, Asma bint Yazeed, Ommayma bint Khalf, Umm Qais bin Mohsin, Habiba bint Khail, Arwa bint

Karib, Umme Asiya, Rabbi bint Muawaz, Fatimah bin Qais, Atiqa bin Zaid, Laila bint Abi Hashma and many others.[37]

According to the Hadith attributed to Prophet Mohammed, he praised the women of Medina because of their desire for knowledge "How splendid were the women of the ansar; fear did not prevent them from becoming learned in the faith."

The Hanbali jurist Ibn Taymiyah of Syria lists two women among his teachers and some women descendents of the Prophet such as his grand-daughter Zaynab and in a later generation Nafisah.

The examples quoted above provide ample evidence that cultural restrictions on education and other matters experienced by some Muslim women presently, have no base in the Quran or authentic tradition and practice of Islam. Cultural restrictions are often confused with religious restrictions and distinctions must be made that under the religion of Islam, women are entitled to intellectual, physical and emotional fulfilment, and they have the right to participate actively in the affairs of the state and society.

Muslim Women in Public Life: Some Examples

Famous Muslim female leaders include Razia Sultana who ruled the Sultanate of Delhi from 1236 to 1239. In the former kingdom of Touggourt (now part of Algeria) there was one Sultana: Aïsha.

In Aceh, Indonesia, there were five Sultanas who ruled:

- Sultana Seri Ratu Nihrasyiah Rawangsa Khadiyu of Pase (1400-1427)
- Sultana Seri Ratu Ta'jul Alam Syafiatuddin Syah of Aceh (1641-1675)—daughter of Sultan Iskandar Muda the Great, and wife of Sultan Iskandar Tani. She spoke languages, Acehnese, Malay, Spanish, Dutch, Arabic, and Persian.
- Sultana Seri Ratu Nurul Alam Naqiatuddin Syah of Aceh (1675-1678)—goddaughter of Sultana Safiatudin.
- Sultana Seri Ratu Zakiatuddin Inayat Syah (1678-1688)—goddaughter of Sultana Safiatuddin.
- Sultana Seri Ratu Kamalat Syah (1688-1699)—goddaughter of Sultana Safiatuddin.[38]

In medieval Egypt, Shajar al-Durr, a former slave of Turkish origin, ascended the throne in 1250, thereby becoming the only Muslim woman to rule a country in North Africa and Western Asia.[39]

Recent Muslim Women Leaders in Politics

Although a comprehensive list of Muslim women in political life is beyond the range of the present thesis, an attempt is made to present some names of Muslim women leaders in various countries.

Afghanistan: Governor – Habiba Sarabi– 2005; Fawziya Koofi (present) Military Commander, Shukriya Brekzai, (present) Shinkhai Zahine Karokhail Parlimentarian (present)

Bahrain: Member of the Council of Representatives–Lateefa Al Gaood – 2006 (first female MP in the Gulf region).

Bangladesh: Prime Minister – Khaleda Zia– 1991; Prime Minister Shaikh Haseena – 1996 and currently Prime Minister; Foreign minister –Dipu Moni – 2009;

Indonesia: President – Megawati Sukarnoputri – 2001; Governor – Ratu Atut Chosiyah – 2007;

Iran: Member of Parliament – Maryam Rezaee – 1963; Member of the Senate – Arezo Sediqi – 1964, Empress – Farah Diba – 1967; Minister of Education – Farrokhroo Parsa – 1968; Mayor—Dabir Azam Hosna – 1970; Minister of Women's Affairs – Mahnaz Afkhami – 1976; Advisor of President for Women's Affairs – Shahla Habibi– 1995; Vice President – Massoumeh Ebtekar – 1997; Chancellor of Alzahra University – Zahra Rahnavard – 1998; Deputy Speaker of Parliament – Soheila Jolowzadeh – 2000; Minister of Health – Marzieh Vahid Dastjerdi – 2009; Advisor of President – Nasrin Soltankhah – 2009;

Kazakhstan: Foreign minister – Akmaral Arystanbekova – 1989;

Kyrgyzstan: Foreign Minister – Roza Otunbayeva –1992; President – Roza Otunbayeva – 2010;

Kuwait: Minister – Massouma al-Mubarak – 2005; Member of the National Assembly – Aseel al-Awadhi, Rola Dashti, Massouma al-Mubarak and Salwa al-Jassar – 2009.

Malaysia: Governor of the Bank of Malaysia – Zeti Akhtar Aziz – 2000.

Pakistan: Benazir Bhutto – 1988 and again 1993; Deputy Speaker – Begum Jahanara Shahnawaz – 1947; Member of Parliament – Begum Shaista Suhrawady Ikramullah – 1947; Minister of Education – Begum Mahmooda Salim Khan – 1962; Ambassador, Governor, Woman Chancellor of a University– Begum Rana Liaquat Ali Khan – 1962 First Muslim woman ambassador and Doyen of the Diplomatic Corps (while in the Netherlands), First Muslim woman Governor (of Sindh province in the mid–1970s), First Muslim woman Chancellor of a university (all the universities in Sindh) First Muslim woman delegate to the UN, and First Muslim woman to win the United Nations Human Rights Award, First Muslim woman to receive the Woman of Achievement Medal, (1950); Shahida Malik—Pakistan's first woman who holds a two Star Rank of Major General, and the first woman Surgeon General of the Army, 2002; Haleena Iqbal—Pakistan's first traffic lieutenant and, Superintendent Traffic; Nusrat Bhutto – Chair of Major Political Party (Pakistan Peoples Party) – Nusrat Bhutto – 1979, Deputy Prime Minister – 1980; Dr. Attiya Inayatullah – Minister of Population, National Assembly 1985; Syeda Abida Hussain – Minister of Information, Education, Science and Technology 1996; Shahida Jamil – Minister of Law and Parliamentary Affairs, 2000; Tasleem Aslam – Foreign Ministry Spokesperson 2006; Fahmida Mirza – Speaker of the National Assembly of Pakistan – 2008;

Syria: Minister of Culture – Najah al-Attar – 1976–2000; Vice President – Najah al-Attar – 2006

Senegal: Mame Madior Boye was Prime Minister from 2001 to 2002.

Uzbekistan: Chairman of the Presidium of the Supreme Soviet – Yagdar Nasriddinova – 1959; Foreign Minister – Shakhlo Makhmudova – 1991.

The leaders mentioned belong to different groups, belong to all age groups both young and old.[40] The examples quoted above provide ample evidence that there are no religious restrictions on women regarding their political participation. Cultural restrictions experienced by Muslim women presently, have no base in the *Quran* or authentic tradition and practice of

Islam. These are often confused with religious restrictions and distinctions must be made that under the religion of Islam, women are entitled to political, intellectual, economic, participation and they have the right to contribute actively in the affairs of the state and society.

Conclusion

Unfortunately, the predicament in which Muslim women in India themselves can be thus summed up: the comparatively backward position in which she may find herself is the result of a want of culture among the community generally, rather than any special feature in the laws of her religion. As eminent jurist A.A.A. Faizee aptly puts it "the unfortunate position of women of India is due to the fact that women, being illiterate are ignorant of their rights, and men, being callous, choose to keep them ignorant".[41]

Leading scholars of Islamic Fiqh (jurisprudence), Tariq (history) and the Ulema need to put their heads together and effectively rejuvenate the spirit of Islam with its ideals, consciously eliminating existing misconceptions with relation to the status women in Islam. There must be a shift in focus of Muslims from identity based issues (and vote bank politics) to their manifold social, economic, and educational problems and concerns.

Again, on the national front, unless India's leading scholars propel a course of action, concentrating on Constitutional ideals of religious non-discrimination, equity before the law and the equality of all Indian citizens being upheld, the confidence of Indian Muslim women and the wider community will continue to be muted.

Furthermore, there is an urgent need to remove social prejudice against women, to disseminate and circulate information on existing government schemes beneficial to women on all fronts, including the socio-economic-educational fronts and to design and implement policies to ensure the participation of Indian women—including Muslim women – in political and in social and economic development.

It should be noted that Indian Muslim women are routinely

depicted in the media as feeble, dependant mortals, as completely lacking organization, and as cruelly subjugated by their patriarchal male counterparts. If they conscientiously mobilize themselves and join hands to demand their political-socio-economic-educational rights as citizens of India and demand a 33 per cent representation of seats in Parliament, their collective power would be a force to reckon with. If only they exercise the right to vote, their numbers are sufficient to influence and cause a shift to a government of their choice!

REFERENCES

1. *Social, Educational and Economic Status of the Muslim Community in India; A Report*; Prime Minister's High Level Committee, Cabinet Secretariat, Government of India, November 2006.

   The Rajinder Sachar Committee, appointed in 2005 by the Indian Prime Minister Manmohan Singh, was commissioned to prepare a report on the latest social, economic and educational condition of the Muslim community of India. The committee was headed by the former Chief Justice of Delhi High Court Rajinder Sachar, and included other six members. The committee prepared a report of 403 pages, and presented in the lower house (Lok Sabha) of the Indian Parliament on 30 November 2006 (20 months after obtaining the terms of reference from the PMO).
2. *The Express Tribune, with the International Tribune,* August 16, 2013.
3. Ibid.
4. *Mainstream*, Vol. LI, No. 37, August 31, 2013.
5. Ibid.
6. Ibid.
7. See the *Census of India, 2001.* The much-awaited provisional results of Census 2011 bring the news that the child sex ratio (0-6 years) has declined further from 927 to 914 girls for every 1,000 boys, due to a widening of the circle of daughter aversion, especially across western and central India. But in all the monitoring to correct this "imbalance" what place is there for a genuine engagement with the life chances of girls in diverse contexts?
8. *Census: 2001, India.* Sex Ratio 933 females to 1,000 males; 2011 Sex Ratio 940 females to 1,000 males.
9. *A Study on "Discrimination of The Girl Child in Uttar Pradesh"* Conducted by Social Action Forum for Manav Adhikar, New Delhi, July 31, 2011.
10. Ibid.

11. Amartya Sen, 'Many Faces of Gender Inequality', in *Frontline,* Vol. 18, Issue 22, October 27-November 9, 2001.
12. *The Rajinder Sachar Committee Report*. The Committee was appointed in 2005 by the Indian Prime Minister Manmohan Singh, pp. 34-35.
13. T.V. Sekher and Neelambar Hatti, 'Discrimination of Female Children in Modern India: from Conception through Childhood', in *International Union for Scientific Study of Population XXV Study of Population Conference Tours,* France, July 2005.

    Neelambar Hatti, T.V. Sekher and Mattias Larsen, 'Lives at Risk: Discrimination of Female Children in Modern India', in *Economic History,* No. 93, 2004, Lund University, Sweden.
14. The Crime Record Bureau of the Central Home Ministry says that there has been an increase in violence against women in 1993-94. Records of social organizations and family life are available regarding the same.
15. Anjana Mazumdar, *Essay on Problems of Women in Modern India,* Anjana Mazumdar, website 'Share Your Essays' October 2012.
16. *Mapping the Global Muslim Population (2009).* The Pew Research Center. Retrieved September 9, 2011.
17. M. Valentine Moghadam, *Modernizing Women: Gender and Social Change in the Middle East* (Lynne Rienner Publishers, 1993) p. 5. Unni Wikan, Review of Modernizing Women: Gender and Social Change in the Middle East, *American Ethnologist,* Vol. 22, No. 4 (November, 1995), pp. 1078-1079.
18. Zeenat Shaukat Ali (ed.), *Winning The Peace: A Quest* (Mumbai: Wisdom Foundation, 2010), p. 245.
19. Ibid., p. 245.
20. Ibid.
21. Ibid., p. 32.
22. Ibid., Maulana Wali Allah Sahab, *Sahabayate ke Shab-o-Roz* (Uttar Pradesh, 2003).
23. Ibid.
24. M.F. Osman, *Human Rights. Between Islamic Sharia and Western Legal Thought* (Dar ul Shuruq, 1982), pp. 110-111; (citing Abdel Wahab's Khallaf's Political Sharia).
25. Ibid.
26. Abu Shaqa Abdelhalim, *Emancipation of Women at the Time of the Prophet,* 1990, Vol. 2, p. 37 (citing Bukhari 13:245 and Muslim, The book of Pilgimage, 4:101.
27. M.H. Sherif, *The Muslim Women between the Truth of Sharia and the Fallacy of Falsification* (Dar al-Marifa al-Jamiyiya, 1987), p. 78

(citing Ibn Sad, Tabakat 4: 302-304).

28. Al-Ghazali Mohammed, *Fiqh al-Sira, Alim al-Marifa*, p. 363.
29. Memissi Fatima, *The Veil and the Male Elite* (Addison-Wesley Publishing Co., 1987), p. 118 (citing al-Tabari, Tafsir, Vol. 22, p. 10).
30. M.H. Sherif, *The Muslim Women Between the Truth of Sharia and the Fallacy of Falsification*, pp. 71-72 (citing Sirat Ibn Hisham, 4: 39-40).
31. Memissi Fatima, *The Forgotten Queens of Islam* (University of Minnesota Press, 1993), p. 66.
32. Khalid Abou El Fadl, *In Recognition of Women*, Vol. 1, No. 2, 1992.
33. Ibid.
34. James E. Lindsay, *Daily Life in the Medieval Islamic World* (Greenwood Publishing Group, 2005), p. 197.
35. Priscilla Offenhue, Alice Buchalter, *Women In Islamic Societies: A Selected Review of Social Scientific Literature.* A Report prepared by the Federal Research Division, Library of Congress under the Interagency Agreement with the Office of Director of National Intelligence/National Intelligence Council and Central Intelligence Agency/Directorate of Science and technology, 2005: Federal Research Division. Library of Congress, Washington DC. Introduction.
36. Khalid Abou El Fadl, *In Recognition of Women*, Vol. 1, No. 2, 1992.
37. Ibid Maulana Wali Allah Sahab, *Sahabayate ke Shab-o-Roz* (Uttar Pradesh 2003). http://en.wikipedia.org/wiki/Sultana_(title).
39. Philip Khuri Hitti, (2004) *Chapter XLVII: Ayybids and Mamlks. History of Syria: including Lebanon and Palestine (2nd ed.). Chapter XLVII: Ayybids and Mamlks,* (Piscataway, NJ: Gorgias Press), p. 629.
41. A.A.A. Fyzee, *The Bombay Law Reporter; Journal* 15-11-36, p. 123.

11

Muslim Women and Social Justice

Shamsuddin Tamboli

From the times of yore, liberal and reformist scholars were trying their best to bring reform in Indian Muslim law to end the pathetic plight of Muslim women. The efforts were concentrated to modify Muslim Personal Law in order to to provide social justice and equal status to women. Among these reformists, Hamid Dalwai's efforts can be described as really constructive and revolutionary. Before the establishment of Muslim Satyashodhak Mandal, he led a procession of seven Muslim divorcees to the Maharashtra Legislative Assembly and submitted a memorandum to the Chief Minister in 1966. He demanded the abolition of the one-sided oral triple talaq and the provision of polygamy. He also forcefully demanded a uniform civil code. For this purpose, he formed an organization *Sada-e-Niswan* (Voice of Muslim Women). He was perhaps the first reformist in India who was continuously insisting for gender equality and secular family laws. Secularism was the soul of his ideology. To achieve this goal he founded Indian Secular Society along with the well known secular thinker Prof. A.B. Shah. He wrote many articles in the magazines like *The Secularist* and *The Quest*. He had debates and discussions with masses, leaders and the scholars. He established Muslim Satyashodhak Mandal on 22nd March 1970. One of the main objectives of this organization was to eradicate outdated, discriminatory traditions and rituals related to Muslim women and to provide legal and social justice based on humanitarian values.

The Muslim Satyashodhak movement organized a conference in Pune on 27th-28th December 1971. Apart from Maharashtra, Muslim women came from Ahmedabad, Delhi, Kolkata and other cities. Sharifa Tayyabaji presided over the conference and a resolution was passed for equal rights and to prohibit polygamy and oral triple divorce. It was the first conference of its kind in the history of Indian Muslims. Later, similar conferences were organized and activists started Muslim Mahila Madad Kendra in different cities of Maharashtra. To protest and to oppose these efforts the orthodox sections of the community formed the Muslim Law Protection Committee. The committee organized a conference to oppose changes in Muslim Personal Law. More than ten thousand Muslims participated in the conference. Hamid Dalwai along with his activists protested against this conference. Under the leadership of Hamid Dalwai, the Muslim Satyashodhak Mandal organized a couple of conferences like Forward Looking Muslim Conference in Delhi, Maharashtra Muslim Social Conference in Mumbai, Muslim Education Conference in Kolhapur, Muslim Women's Conference in Pune and many Jihad-e-Talaq conferences. Hamid Dalwai devoted his time and energy to bring in modernization, secularism, education and equal status for women. Unfortunately he could not continue his efforts for long. Due to ill health he passed away on 3rd May 1977. In the one decade of struggle he has contributed a lot to bring in progressive and reformist ideas in the community

After the unfortunate demise of Hamid Dalwai, Sayyedbhai, (Pune), Meherunnisa Dalwai, (Mumbai), Babumiya Bandwale, (Ahmednagar), Hussain Jamadar (Kolhapur) and other activists of the organization continued forward the task of Hamid Dalwai. In 1985, the well known Shah Bano episode came on Board. The Supreme Court justice Chandrachud gave the judgement in favour of Shah Bano. According to the verdict Muslim divorcee was entitled to get maintenance as per IPC Section 125. The Jamate-Ulema-e-Hind, Muslim Personal Law Board and other fundamentalist organizations opposed the judgement. They came out on the streets and created communal tensions. During this period, Muslim Satyashodhak Mandal supported Shah Bano and met the Prime Minister, the President, Law Minister and many MPs and made an appeal to enforce the provision of maintenance according to IPC Section 125. The secular activists organized many programmes at the national level to support the judgement of the Supreme Court. Nevertheless, the Parliament surrendered before the communal forces and passed a new bill: Muslim Women's Protection Bill, in 1986.

The Muslim Satyashodhak Mandal organized a Talaq Mukti Morcha from Kolhapur to Nagpur from 3rd November to 18th November 1985 to create awareness among the community. It was a historical event. In Parabhani, Aurangabad and Ahmednagar the fundamentalists not only opposed the procession, but also attacked the activists. The activists got associated with many like-minded people and formed a platform named the All India Progressive Muslim Conference. The first conference was held on 26th-27th September 1987 in Kolahpur. About 400 representatives attended the conference. Justice S.M. Daud, Abdul Latif Azami, Dr. Durrani. Rashida Mujawar, Sara Abubakar, Dr. C.R. Dalawi, Seema Kazi,Yasin Dalal and many other representatives came from all over India. Similar conferences were organized in Ahmedabad, Bangalore, Madurai, Hyderabad and other major cities. There was wonderful response in favour of uniform civil code and to abolish oral divorce and polygamy. There was a demand for invocation of IPC Section 125 to protect the rights of Muslim divorcees and for the establishment of rehabilitation centers for them. Many like-minded women's organizations came together and decided to form a network of organizations working on the issue of Muslim women. Through the network, different programmes were organized in which Naya Nikahnama was prepared. Presently individual organizations are working at their respective levels to provide justice and protect human rights of Muslim women. Some organizations are of the opinion that the work done should be within the framework of liberal Islamic preaching and some of them are willing to continue the work by bringing changes in Muslim Personal Law, with the help of the Indian Constitution.

The issues related to Muslim women are multi-dimensional, and there are different approaches to solve their problems.

Patriarchal society and orthodox religious authority misunderstood, misinterpreted and misrepresented the original thought of Islam and made Muslim women's condition pathetic. There is a need for appropriate efforts to highlight the progressive and liberal elements of Islam.

The Muslim Personal Law is the source of inequality and injustice. Therefore, whatever is against the spirit of Islam in it should be removed or reformed. It should not go against constitutional values. There is a need of spreading democratic and secular values among the Muslims. Constructive efforts are needed to improve social, educational and economic conditions of Muslim women. Muslim woman becomes the victim of communal riots, terrorism and orthodox attitude. Necessary provisions should be made to stop honour killings and violence against women.

Muslim women and social justice is the most discussed and important issue from the point of view of gender equality and social justice. There are different areas where Muslim women are discriminated and insulted in secular and democratic India, which is against the spirit of constitutional values. Problems, particularly oral *Talaq*, polygamy, maintenance of the divorcees, and pathetic educational and economic status have restricted the development of Muslim women.

If the word *Talaq* is uttered even in one sitting, it is construed as an irrevocable divorce. It may be uttered in the presence of the wife or it may be uttered in the presence of a person who knows the wife. *Talaq* may be expressed on telephone, internet or cell phone, that too in anger, sleep or intoxication. As soon as it is made known to the wife, the divorce is supposed to be complete and irrevocable. The erstwhile husband and wife are free to marry again—not to each other till Halala process is completed. Halala refers to an obligation on the woman to get married to another man and her husband should give divorce to her on his own.

Talaq is an Arabic word derived from *Turr* which means to free or undo the knot. In legal terminology, it means *Khula* when resorted to by the wife. The right of women to seek divorce (*Khula*) was not available in pre-Islamic society. Before Islam, a man could divorce at the drop of the hat. The Prophet legitimized divorce but also made it plain, that it was a disliked act by Allah.

It has been mentioned that "In Islam, marriage is a civil contract." *Nikah* means marriage and *Nama* means a contract. It sounds very good but in practice the second party i.e. the woman is forced by the patriarchal community to obey the diktats of the first party i.e. man.

On divorce, the *Quran* is clear that triple talaq in the same sitting is not permissible. "If you fear a breach between them, appoint two arbiters. One from his family and other from hers. If they wish for peace, God will cause their reconciliation." *Talaq* given in one sitting by uttering *Talaq* three times is contrary to *Quran* because it is irrevocable. That is why in many Islamic countries like Pakistan and Tunisia, the *Talaq* cases are referred to the Board of Conciliation (Arbiters). This is compulsory and the permission of this board is necessary before divorce become effective.

The All India Muslim Women's Law Board's chairperson Shaista Amber, Zeenat Shaukat Ali, Awaz-a-Niswan, All India Progressive Muslim Forum, have prepared a new Nikahnama which explicitly bans men from pronouncing triple talaq in one sitting or in anger, intoxication, sleep or on phone.

Asghar Ali Engineer, an eminent Islamic scholar has pointed out that in many Islamic countries, arbitration is compulsory. He says, "This is completely in line with Quranic instructions." It will also prevent oppression of Muslim women by men. According to Zeenat Shaukat Ali, the practice of triple talaq in India is based upon the practice or custom and not on the *Quran*. Ali says, "There should be a debate with the Muslim community on whether they want the laws based on *Quran* or laws created on the basis of certain customs and rituals."

The All India Muslim Personal Law Board is entirely dominated by men. They pretend to represent the entire Muslim community. The board has rejected the new Nikahnama saying "it is a 'publicity stunt' ", irrelevant and impractical. The Board agrees that the triple talaq in one sitting is contrary to the injunctions of the *Quran* but refuses to take any step in the right direction.

According to Asaf A.A. Faizee "The Muslim Personal Law of India cannot be considered as Shariyat because Islam is not the state religion, the judges are not Muslims, and there is no Khalifa to enforce Shariyat. Indian jurisprudence does not recognize that Islamic law and its philosophy should be the predominant source of Indian law. India is a secular democracy where all citizens are declared to be equal and no one system of law is found to be unjust. It can be changed by legislation to conform to our present day notions of what is justice or equality." He has given example that the Islamic law of Evidence or the Islamic Criminal Law have been completely abolished and we, therefore, have a new system of law governing the subjects. He has also given in the booklet a number of rules drawn ostensibly from the *Quran* but which are no longer a part of Mohammedan law in India. It is, therefore, quite possible for Muslims to urge the government to alter some of their laws in consonance with their ideas of natural justice.

It is well known fact that after Shah Bano's court judgment and the allegations by the guided and misguided Muslims all over India, the decision was taken that IPC Section 125 would not be mandatory unless book the wife and husband mutually decide to file the case under IPC Section 125. This provision is also included in Muslim Women's Protection Bill of 1986. Even after Shah Bano, there are many Muslim women who are getting maintenance after divorce.

The judgement given by Justice Surdashan Reddy and Justice Deepak Varma in the Supreme Court on 4th December. 2009 in the case of Shah Bano vs. Imran Khan throws light on the cases tried by the family court. Earlier, the family court and high court had dismissed Shah Bano's petition saying that she could not claim maintenance from her husband as per IPC's Section 125.

According to the Supreme Court directive, the case was filed in the family court because the family court had provision of equal protection for all women and so had the jurisdiction to try the cases under IPC Section 125. Consequently, the Muslim divorcee is entitled to get maintenance till she remarries. It means: 1) With mutual understanding wife and husband can take benefit of IPC Section 125; 2) Except the family court Muslim women cannot take the benefit of IPC Section 125 if the husbands refuse to abide by it; 3) This shows there is no clarity and uniformity regarding the provision of maintenance. So there is a need of codification of Muslim Personal Laws.

Opinions of Scholars

"According to the principles of the *Quran,* Muslim divorcee should get maintenance till she gets remarried."

—*Justice Bahrul Islam, Retired Supreme Court Judge*

"The *Quran* has clearly ordered that Muslim divorcee must get maintenance."

—*Justice Fazal Ali, Retired Supreme Court Judge*

"If Muslim divorcee is unable to maintain herself, you cannot bring her on the road along with her children."

—*Justice Abdul Rashid. Ex. Chief Justice of Pakistan*

"According to the *Quran,* it is mandatory for the husband to make the arrangement of maintenance for his divorced wife."

—*Justice Yeshwant Chandrachud, Retired Chief Justice*

"The judgement given by the Supreme Court in the case of Shah Bano is entirely based on the principles of the *Quran.* Whether this judgement is based on the Indian constitution or humanitarian ground, this discussion is wrong. It is also wrong to consider that the Shariyat and Muslim Personal Law is divine or made by Allah."

—*Dr. Moin Shakir, Scholar*

Modification in Muslim Law in Muslim Countries

Many Muslim countries have modified Muslim laws. Some of them are listed below:

Yemen: Prohibited and imposed ban on child marriage and oral divorce system.

Jordan: For polygamy, a petition in the court and the permission of first wife is a must.

Morroco: Oral triple divorce is prohibited.

Indonesia: Oral triple divorce is banned. Petition and permission from the court is mandatory.

Sri Lanka: Oral triple divorce is not allowed.

Egypt: After divorce, providing maintenance to the divorcee is compulsory.

Pakistan: Oral triple divorce is prohibited and for second marriage, a petition in the court is compulsory.

Iran: Ban on child marriage, restrictions on polygamy, right to get maintenance.

Turkestan: Registration of marriage is compulsory, ban on child marriage and oral triple divorce is prohibited.

It is only in secular and democratic India that a Muslim Personal Law, with all its discriminatory provisions, is in existence. In spite of consistent demands by womens' organizations and progressive forces, no attempts have been made to ban oral divorce and to restrict the provision of polygamy.

Many Muslim young girls and women are forced by males of the community to wear burkhas. Male dominated ideology has successfully cultivated the mindset of women that wearing burkha is their religious duty. It has also become a religious identity. In many families, parents and grandparents insist young girls to wear burkhas while going out of their homes. There are different opinions about the system. It is related more to semi-feudal culture than Islam. The practice of wearing burkha is prohibited in some countries like Tunisia. Muslim women all over the world dress just like other women without feeling the necessity of wearing any special dress to make known their Muslim identity. Muslims in some countries do wear naquab, hejab or burkha out of habit or compulsion. Nobody has shown any authentic provision in the *Quran* in support of burkha. It is in existence due to a wrong interpretation of the *Quran*. In Indonesia, a predominantly Islamic country, all women do not wear burkha. The ex-Prime Ministers of Pakistan, Bangladesh and an ex-Foreign Minister of Pakistan do not wear burkha. Muslim women work in offices, hospitals, schools, colleges, banks, radio and television stations and some of them are politicians, as do not wear burkha. The Chief Justice of Peshawar High Court told a woman lawyer, "You are a professional and should be dressed as required of lawyers."

It is only in Saudi Arabia that all Muslim women are forced to wear burkhas. It is probably due to the influence of the Wahabis that patriarchied norms are thrusts on Muslim women. Egypt's highest religious authority said that he woud issue a religious edict against the growing trend of women's full veils or naquabs. Shaikh Mohammad Tontawy, the Dean of Egypt's largest university, called full face veiling a custom that has nothing to do with Islamic faith. Seeing a girl in a school wearing naquab, the grand Imam ordered her to remove the veil from her face. The Minister of Higher Education decided to ban women wearing naquab from entering the university precincts. Now, Muslims are realizing that wearing of burkha has no religious mandate.

Islam is always blamed for violence against women. The cases of honour killings are mostly reported from Jordan, Saudi Arabia, Yemen, Morocco, Egypt, Uganda, Palestine, Pakistan, India and Bangladesh. Women are killed in different ways in the name of family prestige. It is usually done by a father, a husband, brothers and other close relatives in the name of bringing disgrace, shame to the family. According to Zaheer Ali, "In India, transgressions against women are usually explained in terms of caste or communal violence. While in the Islamic world, they are called honour killings, the real motives that prompt men to commit such reprehensible crimes against women have nothing to do with family honour. Most of the crimes against women are committed for economic reasons."

Many scholars are of the opinion that this inhuman system existed in pre–Islamic times and such practices are completely contrary to the spirit of Islam that considers life as a sacred gift of God. According to Islam, "Killing of an innocent is a massacre of humanity." How can the *Quran* support such cruel practice? Honour killing is the product of tribal, patriarchal and misogynic culture of a violent society. It has nothing to do with

Islam. Honour killing is a crime against humanity and Muslim women are victims of this system. We must make strong efforts to stop such barbaric actions.

Justice Rajender Sachar Report reveals the pathetic condition of Muslim women in the field of education. Though attempts are made by some individuals and some organizations to improve educational plight of women, the condition of Muslim women is far from satisfactory. Many Muslim women have shown their talent in sports, politics, literature, science and in different professions but at the grass root level Muslim women want to learn to improve their *Hunnar, Hisab and Himmat* (skills, mathematics and courage). Socio-economic conditions, communal prejudices against Muslims, combined with patriarchal and orthodox views are the major obstacles in the educational development of Muslim women.

It has been also observed that orthodox men have deliberately deprived women of education as that would make women conscious of their rightful place in society. The demands of Muslim women are dismissed as contrary to the commands of God. The innocent Muslim women accept this because of the lack of education. Orthodox mullahs have kept them in the dark to preserve and promote their vested interests. This state of affairs will continue as long as Muslim women remain educationally backward. If they acquire education, they will give up superstitions, outdated customs and traditions and will fight for their rights.

The state, social activists and educated men and women should help motivate Muslim women to seek education. This alone will ensure the progress and development of the Muslim community. A community whose women are backward and occupy low status will remain backward. The community which gives full respect to its women and protect their equal rights can only prosper and progress.

Economical independence is an important pre-condition for women to enjoy in actual life the rights conferred on them by the Constitution of India. This is more important to Muslim women than the women of other communities. Progressive leaders should institute programmes for imparting productive skills to

Muslim women. Likewise, co-operative societies working in the field of cottage and small-scale industries can provide an important avenue for promoting the economic independence of Muslim women as well as make socially valuable use of their talents. The state and its development agencies like co-operative banks, social welfare department, small-scale industries, corporations and similar other organizations should design and provide suitable programmes for promoting co-operative economic activities among the Muslim women. This will help not only to improve the economic status of Muslim women, but also make them self-reliant and self-supportive, which are necessary prerequisites for self-respect.

The Justice Sachar Committee has highlighted the socio-economic and educational condition of Muslim women. His recommendations along with Justice Ranganath Mishra's recommendations will prove useful for the all-round development of the community including women.

Some Progressive Organizations and Publications in Muslim Countries

Following organizations and publications are fighting for justice to Muslim women.

1. Women's Action Forum of Pakistan.
2. CRY –Algeria
3. Center for Human Rights Legal Egypt.
4. Al-Taler –Tunisia
5. The Arab Organization for Human Rights –Sudan.
6. Asia Pacific Forum on Women-Malaysia
7. Aurat: Publication and Information service Foundation—Pakistan
8. Tunisian Association of Democratic Women – Tunisia.
9. Women's Health Research Network Nigeria
10. Al-Raida, Beirut, Lebanon.
11. Noon – A magazine by Arab Women's Solidarity
12. Subah – Pakistan.
13. Journal of Islamic and Comparative Law – Nigeria.
14. Periodical Islamica – Malaysia.
15. Resource Update – A magazine by Women's Development Collective – Malaysia.

And many other organizations are working in the Muslim world to bring equality and social justice to Muslim women.

Recommendations

1. Registration of marriage in Marriage Registration Office should be made compulsory.
2. After Nikah, marriage should be registered under the Special Marriages Act of 1954.
3. New Nikahnama should be popularized among the community.
4. Codification of Muslim Personal Law is a must.
5. Family courts should be established in each district place.
6. A Muslim Women Commission should be established at the state and national level.
7. Muslim girls should be encouraged to pursue education through mainstream and secular educational institutes.
8. Recommendations of Justice Rajender Sachar Committee and Ranganath Mishra Commission should be implemented.
9. A national level common platform of progressive forces should be created to create awareness about the rights of Muslim women. If possible, it should have links with the progressive organizations of all Muslim countries.

REFERENCES

1. Zaheer Ali, *Honour Killing and Islam, There is no 'Honour'* in *Killing in Islam*! (Pune: Masum Publication, 2008).
2. Asghar Ali Engineer, 'On Codification of Muslim Personal Law', in *Secular Perspective*, CSSS, Mumbai, August 16-31, 2010.
3. Asaf A.A. Faizee, *The Reform of Muslim Personal Law in India* (Mumbai: Nachiketa Publications Ltd., 1971).
4. R.A. Jahagirdar, *Rationalist Speaks* (Pune: Rationalist Foundation, 2010).
5. Indira Jaising (ed.), *Justice for Women* (Goa: The Other India Press, 1996).
6. Shamsuddin Tamboli, *Muslim Samaj Prabodhan Aani Vikas* (Pune: Navin Udyog, 2010)
7. Shamsuddin Tamboli, *Sahabano te Shahanabano* (Pune: Muslim Satyashodhak Mandal, 2010).

12

Backwardness Among Indian Muslims: A Need to Go Beyond Sachar

Shuja Shakir

Introduction

This chapter seeks to address two important issues pertaining to the problem of Muslims in India: backwardness among Indian Muslims and the need for a change in their attitude in the changing socio-political context of the country. After independence, even as the country embarked on a definite path of growth and its myriad communities joined the bandwagon to progress, the Muslims have tended to remain comparatively stagnant and underdeveloped. On all possible parameters—social, educational and economic—Sachar Commission found them lurching at the bottom with their condition being worse than that of Dalits. Sachar Commission did not, however, say anything new when it said that Muslims were seriously lagging behind in several areas. It only confirmed what Muslim scholars—M. Mujeeb, A.A Engineer, Moin Shakir, Rafiq Zakaria, Wahiduddin Khan, Mushirul Hasan and others—had been saying for long about Muslims who were increasingly being marginalized and ghettoized in independent India. What *Sachar Report* did was to put the extent of Muslim deprivation in a perspective in an organized way and thus opened the Pandora's box in the context of Muslim backwardness. Following this report, the community leaders as well as Muslim well-wishers from other communities started nailing the state for its failure to uplift the sagging community from the throes of marginalization. Most of them demanded that if the government of the day was serious about capacitating the Muslims, it needed to implement the recommendations of the *Sachar Report*. In short, the solution offered by the *Sachar Report* has been made out to be a panacea for all the ills that afflict Muslim society in contemporary India.

However, it is hard to agree with the claim that recommendations in the *Sachar Report* carry a ubiquitous solution to the Muslim problem. True, state support is indispensable to enabling a community. But it is difficult to accept that only a political solution is enough to effect the requisite change in the socio-economic conditions of as huge a section of population as Muslims. For a change to be genuine it must come from within. No community can tap its full potential without bringing about crucial changes in its outlook and attitude first. Having said that, however, it is equally necessary to underline that it would be preposterous to ask somebody to try out a remedy when one does not even know the nature of malaise. And that's a grave problem with Muslims: most of them do not fully comprehend the nature of their malaise. For them, the probable cause of their backwardness is a pervasive discrimination and lack of faith in their loyalty, which requires them to repeatedly prove that they are well-meaning and peace-loving citizens; they must show that they don't resist change and that, leaving aside their outmoded traditions, they are ready to accept modern way of life. By and large, they feel that no matter what they do, they would remain second-class citizens, segregated and discriminated against. If changing is going to yield similar consequences as not changing, then why take the trouble to change at all? To a Muslim mind, what is thus a redundant exercise to the Hindus, is orthodoxy and rigidity. An unending vicious cycle of recrimination thus continues to operate in the mass psyche across communities. In this context, it is imperative to understand the real facets of Muslim backwardness and attempt to dispel certain misunderstandings about it.

Whence Muslim Backwardness?

Viewed in the historical context, there is nothing unique about Muslim backwardness. India had always been a predominantly agrarian society and masses, both Hindus and Muslims, were more or less fated to live under economic hardships. What is, however, extraordinary about Muslim backwardness is it went from bad to worse while the other communities in India, notably Hindus, gradually came out of it or at least made efforts in that direction, which raises two important issues. One, the establishment, both foreign and indigenous, did not do anything substantial to prevent the downward slide of Muslims. Two, there were no significant efforts within the Muslim community, which, given its conservative outlook, failed to improve the lot of its members.

Role of Establishment

While there is a little evidence to show that Muslims masses were prospering earlier, Muslim backwardness is usually traced from the aftermath of 1857, when British suspected that the ill-planned uprising had a predominant Muslim character and chose to chastise the community for its anti-establishment stance. And so harsh was this chastisement that the renowned Urdu poet Mirza Ghalib, who was a witness to the macabre dance of British vengeance, wrote, "Here there is a vast ocean of blood before me, God alone knows what more I have to behold."[1] It may be noted that the British specifically targeted the Muslim elite, whom they deprived of all the luxuries these fortunate (now unfortunate) few had so far enjoyed. The British justified their action on the grounds of a humane and civilized administration. "The truth is that under Mohammedans the government was an engine for enriching a few...it never seems to have touched the hearts or moved the consciences of the rulers that a vast population was toiling bare-backed in the heat of summer and in the rain of autumn, so that a few families in each district might lead the life of luxurious ease."[2] After the Uprising, the British understood the significance of keeping Hindus and Muslims divided. An essential part of Muslim chastisement also consisted in promoting Hindus in the administration with the result that "all sorts of employments great and small are being gradually snatched away from Mohammedans and bestowed on men of other races particularly the Hindus."[3]

But does that mean that Muslims had no economic issues before 1857? It is usually assumed that since Muslims ruled India for 800 odd years, the situation for the ordinary Muslims was a bed of roses and that only Hindus bore the burnt. This is clearly a misperception. History does not bear out that the Muslim rulers ever Islamized their rule at any point of time. A few hardline names like Aurangzeb might crop up occasionally, but they remain more of an exception than the rule. Mostly, Muslim rulers ruled like any other power-hungry monarchs. Their administration remained oppressive for the commoners largely comprising small-time peasants and artisans, no matter what community these gullible masses belonged to. And this oppressive machinery of administration was kept well-oiled by the nawabs and zamindars who exploited Hindus as well as Muslims to sustain themselves in power. Muslim backwardness therefore definitely dates back to a period much earlier than 1857.

Partition and Beginning of Discrimination

Partition dealt a deathblow to Indian Muslims. Overnight, they became a minority in the land where they once were a majority. Partition caused their loyalty to India to be questioned. The majority community felt that since Muslims had got what they had wanted—Pakistan—they had no business staying in India. Rightist Hindus resented the Islamic makeover that Pakistan was gradually beginning to acquire immediately after its formation. India adopted a secular constitution with all her citizens enjoying equal rights; with Pakistan, however, the case was different. Despite Jinnah saying that "You will find that in the course of time Hindus would cease to be Hindus and Muslims would cease to be Muslims, as citizens of the state,"[4] Pakistan finally surrendered to the growing pressure, both from within and without, to Islamize. Very soon Jinnah's Savile Row suits were discarded in favour of traditional Sherwani and

Shalwar; and his favourite cigar yielded place to the "Jinnah Cap". Very soon the country's first Dalit Hindu Law Minister, Jogendra Nath Mandal, had to flee and take refuge in India because Pakistan's first Prime Minster was busy declaring Islam as the official religion of the country and Mandal's cabinet colleagues were already shunning him and denying him access to secret files.[5]

It is an open secret how minorities are treated in Pakistan.[6] In May 2007, Islamic militants threatened Christians to convert to Islam within a few days or face dire consequences.[7] The victims were wary of reporting the matter to the police for obvious reasons. The constitution of Pakistan segregates its citizens on the basis of religion, which can lead to serious issues of human rights.[8] The zealots amongst Hindus in India took a cue from these developments. So when Golwarkar said, "Right from its inception it (Pakistan) has been indulging in inhuman atrocities and religious domination of the worst type on its hapless minority..."[9], it is not hard to understand why it carried such penetrating appeal for an ordinary Hindu.

Partition compounded the problems of Muslims both at psychoneurotic as well as economic levels. Thanks to the violence and bitterness bred in its wake, it made the Muslims in India just 'Muslims' with nobody caring to differentiate between them based on their caste and occupational markers.[10] None cared for the fact that it was a matter of life and death for the Indian Muslims to make both ends meet; none cared, although it was out long before Sachar Report, that for instance 75% of Muslims in Ahmedabad were destitute[11]; and none cared that majority of Muslims were engaged in traditional production activities that hardly guaranteed them two square meals. In fact, in the eyes of a Hindu who was increasingly moving to a rightist position after partition, the entire Muslim community that stayed back were implicit supporters of Pakistan. It was even construed as a ploy on the part of the Muslim League to leave behind a section of Muslims in India as its agent that could report to it. The suspicious attitude about Muslims was not restricted to the rightist Hindu organizations as such. It was growing thick even amongst the so-called secular Congressmen.

"Every Indian Muslim should 'realize clearly' what loyalty to the nation would mean if Pakistan invaded India.... Every Muslim in India would be required to shed his blood fighting the Pakistani hordes, and each one should search his heart now, and decide whether he should migrate to Pakistan or not."[12] Consequently, Hindu suspicion of Muslims became the fountainhead of discrimination against Muslims, no matter what category they came from. The sad part of the story is it is very much alive as of now, needing just a small waft of air to set the entire embers aflame again. George Fernandes reported that during the Bangladesh War in 1971, the then Municipal Commissioner of Bombay transferred a large number of Muslim workers from Vaitarna water works to the city. When the workers' union insisted upon knowing the reason, the commissioner replied that he had special instructions from the Union Home Ministry that Muslims should not be kept in sensitive posts. Vaitrana Water Works supplied drinking water to then Bombay city and Mrs. Gandhi's government was not prepared to trust Muslims in such sensitive posts. During the same time, a young Muslim girl stenographer was removed from Bhaba Atomic Power Centre at Trombay on the same grounds.[13]

It is usually assumed that because of the discriminatory attitude of Hindus in general, Muslims have remained backward in India. They have been denied job opportunities as well as loan facilities. The result is Muslims have been irretrievably pushed to the periphery. Muslims employed in the government jobs is less than a third of their population share; even in West Bengal that saw uninterrupted rule of Leftists for a significant length of time, Muslim percentage in government jobs was a paltry 4.2.[14] More than half of the Muslim population reels below the poverty line. The rest is marginally or self-employed. Not a single Muslim figured among the 50 industrial houses up till 1985. Muslim industrialists owned only 4 units in a group of 2,832 industrial enterprises, each with sales of Rs. 50 million and above. In the smaller industrial sector, they owned about 14,000 units out of a total of 600,000 of which 2,000 belonged to the 'small' category with a limited capital outlay.[15] And the

Sachar Report came as the last nail in the coffin of Muslim backwardness. It established that unemployment rate among Muslim graduates is the highest among all socio-religious communities in India. Banks avoid disbursement of loans to Muslim entrepreneurs. In fact, the average amount of bank loans disbursed to Muslims is two-thirds of the amount disbursed to other minorities and in some cases it is half. Some banks that call themselves professional have marked out Muslim localities as "negative zones" where bank credit and other facilities are not generally given. The commission found substance in the charge that there appeared to be a methodical conspiracy to deny Indian Muslims any meaningful political participation. For example, in states like Bihar, UP, and West Bengal, "Muslim concentration assembly constituencies are declared as 'reserved' constituencies where only SC candidates can contest elections."[16]

There is no denying the fact that Hindu discrimination of Muslims, rooted in the cruel facts of history, constituted a crucial component of Muslim backwardness in India. But the question is whether precarious socio-economic condition of the Indian Muslims is solely due to the "discriminatory attitude of Hindus". Would it be appropriate to assume that if there were no discrimination, the situation of Muslims would have been totally reversed? It is hard to answer in the affirmative.

Muslim backwardness, like backwardness of any other community in India, needs to be understood in its historical context. Like their poor Hindu counterparts, a larger section of Muslims live in rural parts of the country. Locational differences, regional disparities and the nature of the state cannot be side-tracked while attempting to assess the economic conditions of a community. If so-called "Hindu discrimination" was the only cause of Muslim backwardness, Muslims in the nations where they are in majority and where there are no Hindus would have been well-off without any problems. Statistics clearly show that this is not the case.

Muslims are Not Homogenous

It is pertinent in this context to understand the composition of Muslim society in India. A myth sought to be perpetuated is that Muslims are a homogenous community and to prove this their so-called *"en bloc"* voting pattern is cited as evidence. This is a trashy argument. Islam forbids the caste system, but the class and status divide amongst Indian Muslims is often so glaring that it often leaves the advantage of not having caste system truncated. Muslims have different sect-based identities (Shia or Sunni for example). They may subscribe to different juridical lineage (Hanafi, Hanbali, Shafi or Maliki). Even ethnically, they are vastly different, for Bohras and Ahmediyas are also counted among Muslims though the orthodox within the community do not agree. Religiously, they may have different means of reaching God. Those following the Wahabi brand of Islam advocate strict adherence to the *Quran*, the Prophet and his Hadith, while the Sufis would have an additional divine intervention of the Walis (Saints). The orthodox would see bowing before the grave of a saint in a *Dargah* an unforgivable violation and a mark of blasphemy, but, to Sufis, the *Dargah* represents an eternal symbol of spiritual solace and divine pervasion.

The class divide also shows up and usually in surprising contexts. Muslims are *ashraf* (high class), *ajlaf* (low class) and *arzal* (lowest class akin to the Hindu Dalit). No less a person than Sir Syed Ahmed Khan, held that those of "low birth" were useless to the country and only the high born could be could be loyal to the nation and government. He and with him the Muslim nobility opposed the British proposal for democratically electing the members to the legislative council and insisted that only those from the nobility and those of "High birth" be made members. He opposed merit as a criterion saying even if a boy from an *Adna* (low) family is able to acquire a B.A. or even an M.A. degree, he cannot be allowed to sit in the Viceroy's Council. Sir Syed also opposed the holding of the Indian Civil Service exams in India. His argument was that if the "low born" will be able to sit for the exams and God forbid they could become officers, they would lord over those of so called "noble birth". Sir Syed had elsewhere argued that it was only the "low born" Muslims that had taken part in the 1857 revolt and that the Muslim nobility was always loyal to the British. He also stated fairly clearly that he had opened his college for the sons of the *shurafa* and not for the *arzal*, the sons of weavers and water carriers.[57] Then there is a regional dimension. Muslims of Kerala, for example, have no linguistic or cultural problems as faced by the Muslims of UP and Bihar. There cannot be any common language and common culture for all Muslims in the country.[18]

There is no dearth of divisions among Muslims and they keep surfacing from time to time. Recently, activists like Ali Anwar have been raising the issue of *Pasmanda* (low-caste/*Dalit*) Muslims whose class interests are immensely different from those of the better-offs within the community and who find themselves at the bottom of the socio-economic ladder. Demand for the betterment of *Pasmanda* Muslims might have been a recent phenomenon, but their presence had been recorded as early as in 1901 Census, which mentions about 133 low castes amongst Muslims, some of which are so low that with them "no other *Muhammedan* would associate, and who are forbidden to enter the mosque or to use the public burial ground."[19]

Is Islam Growth-Curbing?

Quite obviously, in matters other than religious, there is little to tell the Muslims from Hindus in India. Then why is it that, roughly after 100 years of the fall of Mughal Empire, even as Hindus made significant economic strides, Muslims started getting more and more marginalized? There are a few theories in this area, some of which sound plausible while others, though more popular, look implausible.

A theory that sounds somewhat plausible and has been advanced by Kuran and Singh, says that pre-modern commercial and wealth management practices delayed the Muslim economic modernization, thus contributing to Muslim underperformance. Muslim backwardness and Hindu forwardness did have something to do with the inheritance system of both communities. "In Islamic law, property rights reside in individuals; there is no such thing as collective ownership, except by contract, through a revocable partnership of actual individuals. Thus, an estate consists of assets owned by a deceased individual, and these assets are partitioned among individuals. By contrast, Hindu law recognizes individual ownership as well as collective ownership by a family whose membership changes through births and deaths. When a Hindu patriarch dies, he may leave behind, along with personal property, the assets of a business collectively owned by his survivors. The survivors may choose to keep the assets together under a new family patriarch."[20] It means that if on the one hand, Hindus, under their *'inegalitarian'* inheritance system (because it did not give women share in property) could consolidate the wealth, Muslims on the other hand lost it due to fragmentation (despite their inheritance system being egalitarian that gives share to daughters from father's property). Earlier despite mass conversions, there were little differences in cultural practices of Hindus and Muslims, but the British judicial system, that had begun to interpret property issues strictly according to scriptures, turned out to be a crucial factor in promoting Muslim economic backwardness. Sidestepping the class/clan/caste/cultural diversities among Indian Muslims and herding them all under one law, it proved to be the single most villainous factor in keeping Muslims backward.

For some it implies that the very nature of Islam is a causative factor in the backwardness of Muslims. The proponents of this standpoint cite the case of Islamic countries where despite oil wealth, the conditions of citizens remain pathetic following "high illiteracy rates, deterioration of education, the slow-down of scientific research and technological development, poor production bases and competitive capacity, rampant poverty and mounting unemployment rates."[21]

Is Islam then actually responsible for this sorry state of affairs amongst Muslims the world over?

Nothing of this sort has so far been conclusively established because there is a lack of scientific interest in investigating the link between Islam and development, the reason being "uncommonness of interdisciplinary contacts between religion and economics."[22] Yet there are theories that seek to establish a link between Islam and underdevelopment. For instance, Earnest Renan says that early Islam and its Arab propagators were hostile to science and philosophy. Knowledge advanced under Arab domination only under the Persian and Hellenic influences. Finding Islam a deterrent to growth, Arther Lewis contends that this can be proved by looking at the "Moslems in India" who constitute a lethargic minority.[23] These theories look implausible for the reason that none of them answers a simple question that if Islam is growth-inhibiting, how could Muslims (between 8th and 13th centuries) easily surpass the Europeans in scientific and technological innovations?

Maxime Rodinson, a reputed Islamic scholar, on the other hand, says that Muslim economic conditions have nothing to do with Islam per se; rather, material conditions and the response of resignation to them led to the economic descent of Islamic civilizations. Marxist scholars largely agree with this point of view. "Religion has a role but it's of secondary importance. Primary consideration is naked self-interest."[64] Again, it's not religion as such but the "coercive apparatus of the state and the 'robust authoritarianism' that is responsible for the conditions of poverty, backwardness, illiteracy and resistance to democracy in the Middle East and North Africa."[25]

From the analysis of various social, economic, political and religious factors impacting Muslim backwardness, we can broadly summarize that,

1. Muslim backwardness in India is an age-old phenomenon and cannot be traced from a specific period;
2. Hindu discrimination of Muslims constitutes a small link in the chain of Muslim backwardness;
3. Muslims being as heterogeneous as Hindus do not have a similar range of problems across the various regions of the country;
4. Faith in Islam is not responsible for keeping Muslims backward; rather, the material conditions and the kind of response that the community frames for them proves to be a determining factor in its economic condition; and,
5. State support can mitigate Muslim backwardness, but only to an extent. Major efforts in this direction need to come from the community itself.

Need for Change amongst Muslims

Muslims need to change their outlook on a number of issues so that they become a part of the mainstream and also retain their identity as Muslims. Muslims largely feel any talk of joining the mainstream implies abandoning religious identity, which is a mistaken thinking. The need of the hour for them is to focus on "(1) Education (2) Employment (3) Social adjustment with Hindus (4) Family Planning and (5) Political realism."[26]

The issue of education is crucial amongst Muslims today. It is ironical that pursuit of knowledge is the highest calling in Islam, yet one seldom sees Muslims winning intellectual prizes at national or international level. Sachar Commission notes that "25% of Muslim children in the 6-14 year age group have either never attended school or have dropped out. In premier colleges only one out of 25 under-graduate students and one out of 50 post-graduate students is a Muslim. The Commission also stresses that one reason why Muslims send their children to Madarssas is access to government schools is seriously limited. Affirmative action of the state is certainly called for in this area. But it has to be understood that in this era of globalisation when the state is increasingly withdrawing from sphere of public welfare, too much of reliance on affirmative action of the state would not be fruitful.

The Madarassa system is very useful for the community as these Madrassas house a number of children from destitute Muslim families that cannot feed and school them. However, Madrassa syllabi need to be reassessed. Generally, the syllabi include learning of the *Holy Quran* by heart, *tajweed* (correct pronunciation of Quranic verses), *tafseer* (interpretation of Holy Scriptures), *fiqah* (Islamic Jurisprudence), *shariah* (Islamic law), *ahadis* (life and decisions of the holy Prophet on various issues brought before him by the faithful), *mantiq* (philosophy), *riazi* (mathematics) and *falakiat* (astronomy), and *tabligh* (spreading the word of God).[27] If other subjects physical sciences along with computer education, and a few vocational courses are added, what is the harm? Islam certainly will not forbid imparting of latest knowledge. Muslims have to understand that the image of Madarassa has taken a beating in recent times. The Pakistani dictator, Zia ul Haq set up several Deeni Madarassas along the Pakistan-Afghanistan border to produce motivated jihadis to fight alongside the Mujahideens against Soviet forces in 1980s. The impression has ever since gained ground that Madrassas are nothing but a breeding-ground for jihadis. This is a vague generalization and the community needs to do something about dispelling this kind of impression.

Muslims need to understand the meaning of secularism properly. As the term has evolved in the Indian context, it does not mean opposition to any religion or any religious values. It is all about the idea of "citizenship" and how the Indian citizen can be free to follow his or her religion inside his house whilst being a citizen in public life. As societies across the globe are becoming multicultural, developing a truly secular mindset is mandatory for inter-community interactions. A general perception is Muslims would have sharia for themselves and want other communities to be secular, which is considered a double-standard. When Mustafa Kemal Pasha of Turkey abolished the caliphate and introduced secularism in Turkey, it had several fundamentalist Muslims across the world seething. But the great Muslim intellectual poet and philosopher, Allama Iqbal appreciated the idea and stressed that end of the caliphate was trigger for the emergence of a new Islamic Renaissance. "Modern Turk is inspired by realities of experience and not by scholastic reasoning of jurists who lived under different conditions of life. To my mind these arguments (Turkish Republicanism and secularism), if rightly appreciated, indicate the birth of an International ideal which, though forming the very essence of Islam, has been hitherto over-shadowed or rather displaced by Arabian Imperialism of the earlier centuries of Islam."[28] Certainly, a loud and clear message for Indian Muslims.

Finally, Muslims are perturbed about the spineless character of their leadership in the current times. Muslim leadership is seen taking up non-issues when the community is reeling under a variety of real problems. Some time back, the Shahi Imam exhorted Muslims not to join Anna Hazare's anti-corruption movement for a curious reason: they shout "vande maatram" and "Bharat mata ki jai", which is un-Islamic.[29] This kind of leadership gives the impression that it relishes not being a part of the mainstream. It hardly attaches any importance of democratic and secular rights of the people. Not a single Indian Muslim leader talked about supporting the people's democratic movement when the Jasmine revolution swept across the Arab World recently. Nor does it care that genuine problems of Muslims—poverty, unemployment, women's empowerment, and so on—are taking a back-seat even as the national attention gets diverted to emotional and cosmetic issues that community leaders usually dabble in. The situation is no different elsewhere. Muslims are disturbed about the fact that thousands of helpless Muslims continue to be killed and dislocated in Palestine, Iraq, Afghanistan, Libya, Syria, and so on and the so-called oil-rich Muslim countries despite their vast resources and effective networking with USA and Europe are just content with looking on. In India, Mullahs, representing a variety of rival Muslim sects, educated in traditionalist Madarassas, constitute the core of Muslim leadership. Many of them, particularly of the Deobandi variety, had been close allies of the Congress Party. Ruling parties patronize some of these groups (in some cases, providing ministerial berths and positions in Parliament to their members, as in the case of the Jamiat ul-Ulema-e Hind-Congress alliance), in return for which these groups seek to mobilize Muslim electoral support for these parties. The relationship thus works both ways, to the benefit of both.[30] Needless to say, it never works for the benefit of the masses. Unfortunately, educated and modern Muslim class that could have filled the leadership vacuum remains confined to its ivory towers. There is a little effort at plugging disconnect between the community's intellectual class and its masses.

REFERENCES

1. P. Hardy, *The Muslims of British India* (Foundation Books, 1998), p. 70.
2. W.W. Hunter, *The Indian Musalmaans* (London: Trubar and Company, 1876), p. 161.
3. Ibid, p. 142.

4. Cited in Gyanendra Pandey, 'Can a Muslim be Indian?' *Comparative Studies in Society and History*, Vol. 41, No. 4 (October, 1999), p. 612.
5. Tarik Fateh, *Chasing a Mirage: The Tragic Illusion of an Islamic State* (Canada: Wiley & Sons, 2008), p. 46.
6. Daaniyal Noorani, 'Jinnah, Minorities and Cake', *The Express Tribune*, August 25, 2011.
7. BosNewsLife News Centre, http://www.worthynews.com/1352-pakistan-militants-force-christians-to-convert-to-islam-and-shut-churches, as accessed on September 25, 2013.
8. Tarik Fateh, op. cit., p. 59.
9. M.S. Golwarkar, *Bunch of Thoughts* (Bangalore: Sahitya Sindhu Prakashana), p. 261.
10. Gyanendra Pandey, op. cit., p. 614.
11. A.A. Engineer, 'Communal Violence in Ahmedabad' in *Economic and Political Weekly*, January 23, 1982, p. 100.
12. Govind Ballabh Pant, Congress Chief Minister of Uttar Pradesh, cited in Gyanendra Pandey, op. cit., p. 617.
13. Moin Shakir, *Islam in Indian Politics* (New Delhi: Ajanta Publications, 1983), p. 5.
14. Seema Chisti, 'Even if Government is Employer, Muslims Fall off Job Map', *Indian Express*, Delhi Edition, October 30, 2006
15. Mushirul Hasan, *The Legacy of a Divided Nation*, (Delhi: Oxford University Press, 1997), http://www.rediff.co.in/freedom/03legacy.htm as accessed on April 14, 2013.
16. *Social, Economic and Educational Status of Muslim Community of India—A Report*, Government of India, November 2006, p. 25.
17. Sohel Hashmi, 'Myth of Muslim Vote Bank', Kafila.org, June 15, 2012.
18. Moin Shakir, op. cit., p. 14.
19. Tanweer Fazal, 'De-reserve these Myths', *Indian Express*, September 6, 2006.
20. Timur Kuran and Anant Deep Singh, *Economic Modernization in Late British India: Hindu Muslim Differences* (The University of Chicago, 2013), p. 510.
21. *Arab Human Development Report*, United Nations Publications, 2002, p. 8.
22. Timur Kuran, 'Islam and Underdevelopment: An Old Puzzle Revisited' in *Journal of Institutional and Theoretical Economics*, Vol. 153, 1997, p. 42.
23. Ibid, pp. 40-51.
24. Moin Shakir, op. cit., p. 6.

25. Eva Berlin, 'The Robustness of Authoritarianism in the Middle East: Exceptionalism in Comparative Perspective' in *Comparative Politics*, Vol. 36, No. 2 (January, 2004), p. 143.
26. Rafiq Zakaria, *Indian Muslims: Where Have They Gone Wrong?* (Popular Prakashan, 2004), p. 332.
27. Kamal Matinuddin, *Taliban Phenomenon, Afghanistan 1994-97*, (Diane Publishing Co., 1999), p. 16.
28. Mohammed Iqbal, *Reconstruction of Religious Thought in Islam* (Dodo Press, 2009), p. 67.
29. Zakia Soman, 'The Imam's Wrong Call', Tehelka.com, September 3, 2011, Issue 35, Vol. 8.
30. Yoginder Sikand, 'Accounting for Muslim Backwardness: Going beyond Sachar,' http://lifethelove.wordpress.com/2011/01/19/accounting-for-muslim-backwardness-in-india-going-beyond-sachar/, as accessed on Sept 27, 2013.

13

Gaps in Levels of Literacy, Education and Exposure to Media: A Comparative Study of Muslims and Others

Malika B. Mistry

Introduction

Education and exposure to media are very important in the modern world to empower individuals and communities. In achieving social mobility and success, the role of education and exposure to media is undeniable. We are interested in knowing how Muslim men and women fare with regard to the above variables. It is also worthwhile to find out where Muslim men and women stand in comparison with those from other religions groups.

Therefore in this chapter, a humble attempt is made to analyze the gaps in the levels of literacy, education and exposure to media among Muslims and other religious groups in India. The source used is National Family Health Survey–3 (NFHS-3). The objectives of this chapter are: (1) to ascertain the level of literacy, education, and exposure to media among the Muslims and other religious groups in India; (2) to make comparison in regard to above variables with those of men and women from other religious groups; (3) to try to find the causes for their current status: and (4) to make recommendations for improving their current status. Accordingly, in this chapter, we proceed from presenting exhaustive data on the above variables and comparing the same with those from other religious groups to pinpointing some causes for their current status and finally making some recommendations which will have some policy implications.

National Family Health Survey–3 (NFHS-3)

The NFHS program initiated in the early 1990s has emerged as an important source of data on population, health and nutrition for India and its states. The 2005-06 National Family Health Survey (NFHS–3), the third in the series of these national surveys, was designed to provide estimates of important indicators on family welfare, maternal and child health and nutrition. It also collected data on the levels of literacy, education and exposure to media among men and women, on the basis of classification of religious groups.

NFHS-3 covered all 29 states in India, which comprise more than 99 per cent of India's population. The survey used a uniform sample design, questionnaires (translated into 18 Indian languages), field procedures, and procedures for biomarker measurements throughout the country to facilitate comparison. A total of 515,507 individuals who stayed in the households the night before the interview were enumerated in the 109,041 NFHS-3 sample households.

Based on the religion of the household head, 82 per cent of the households are Hindu, 13 per cent are Muslim, 3 per cent are Christian, 2 per cent are Sikh and 1 per cent are Buddhist/ Neo-Buddhist (NB). All other religions together account for less than 1 per cent of households. Therefore, for our analysis, we have chosen the data from the NFHS-3.

Gaps in the levels of Education and Literacy

In the following section, an analysis of the gaps in the levels of education and literacy among Muslim men and women is undertaken.

Table 1: Respondent's Level of Education: Women

Per cent distribution of women age 15-49 by number of years of education completed, on the basis of classification of religous groups, India, 2005-06.

Respondent's Level of Education

Religion	*No education*	*<5 years completed*	*5-7 years completed*	*8-9 years completed*	*10-11 years completed*	*12 or more years completed*	*Total years completed*	*Number of women*
Hindu	40.5	7.9	15.0	14.1	10.3	12.2	100	100,151
Muslim	47.9	8.9	16.3	12.0	8.3	6.6	100	16,936
Christian	19.7	9.2	14.2	17.5	15.9	23.5	100	3,053
Sikh	24.7	3.5	17.2	14.7	20.0	19.8	100	2,222
Buddhist/ Neo-Buddhist	28.2	11.9	16.2	22.7	11.4	9.7	100	1,010
Jain	1.6	1.3	6.9	15.7	22.3	52.1	100	406
Others	65.9	7.6	9.5	9.0	3.4	4.6	100	484

The proportion of women who have never attended school is higher among Muslims (48 per cent) than among Hindus (41 per cent) and most of the other religions. Muslim women are also less likely than women of most other religions to have completed secondary education. Educational attainment is highest among Jain women, 52 per cent of whom have completed 12 or more years of schooling. Similar differentials are found among Muslim men and men of other religious groups (Table 2).

Table 2: Respondent's Level of Education: Men

Per cent distribution of men age 15-49 by number of years of education completed, India, 2005-06.

Respondent's level of education

Religion	*No education*	*<5 years completed*	*5-7 years completed*	*8-9 years completed*	*10-11 years completed*	*12 or more years completed*	*Total years completed*	*Number of men*
Hindu	17.1	9.8	16.1	21.1	15.1	20.7	100	57,112
Muslim	26.3	13.4	19.4	17.8	11.4	11.7	100	8,747
Christian	11.7	11.5	15.8	21.3	17.0	22.7	100	1,567
Sikh	14.0	3.6	18.6	19.6	24.0	20.3	100	1,270
Buddhist/ Neo-Buddhist	9.5	12.3	13.4	25.8	19.7	19.3	100	596
Jain	0.4	0.0	1.6	12.4	23.1	62.4	100	213
Other	36.4	14.2	19.2	15.6	5.2	9.3	100	232

Basic literacy, i.e., the ability to read and write, is a fundamental aspect of the ability of individuals to fully participate and take advantage of socio-economic development and health and nutritional advancements. In NFHS-1 and NFHS-2, the literacy measure was based on self-reported literacy. In NFHS-3, by contrast, respondents who had not completed at least standard six were given a literacy test. Each respondent who had not completed standard six was given a card with pre-printed sentences and asked to read a sentence. In most states, the card contained sentences in all the major languages in the state. According to their performance on this reading test, respondents were assigned to one of three categories: cannot read at all; able to read only parts of sentence; or able to read whole sentence. Persons who were visually impaired were excluded from the test. In a small number of cases, an individual could not be tested because there was no sentence in the required language. Accordingly, in this report, literate persons are those who have either completed six years of education or 'passed' the literacy test by being able to read all or part of the sentence on the card given to them in their language of choice. Tables 3 and 4 give the distribution of women and men, respectively, according to their performance on the literacy test by religion.

Differentials in literacy are similar for women and men to differentials in educational attainment. Muslim women and men, followed by Hindu women and men, are less likely to be literate than women and men of most other religions, although the differentials by religion are much greater for women than for men.

Table 5: Exposure to Mass Media: Women

Percentage of women age 15-49 who usually read a newspaper or magazine, watch television, or listen to the radio at least once a week, who usually visit the cinema or theatre at least once a month, and who are not regularly exposed to any of these media by religion, India, 2005-06.

In NFHS-3, respondents' media exposure was measured by asking women and men about the frequency (almost every day;

Table 3: Literacy: Women

Per cent distribution of women, age 15-49, by literacy, by religion, India, 2005-06.

No schooling or completed less than standard 6

Religion	*Completed standard 6 or higher*	*Can read a whole sentence*	*Can read part of a sentence*	*Cannot read at all*	*No card with required language*	*Blind/ visually impaired*	*Missing*	*Total*	*No. of women*	*Percentage literate*
Hindu	44.9	5.2	4.3	44.8	0.1	0.1	0.1	100	100,151	54.9
Muslim	36.4	7.4	5.7	49.3	0.9	0.1	0.2	100	16,936	49.5
Christian	66.0	5.5	4.4	23.1	0.9	0.0	0.1	100	3,053	75.9
Sikh	60.7	5.4	5.9	28.1	0.0	0.0	0.0	100	2,222	71.9
Buddhist/ Neo-Buddhist	56.1	2.5	5.3	35.6	0.3	0.0	0.2	100	1,010	63.9
Jain	94.1	2.2	0.8	2.5	0.0	0.4	0.0	100	406	97.1
Others	23.1	2.2	3.8	70.6	0.3	0.0	0.0	100	484	29.1

Table 4: Literacy: Men

Per cent distribution of men, age 15-49, by literacy, by religion, India, 2005-06.

No schooling or completed less than standard 6

Religion	*Completed standard 6 or higher*	*Can read a whole sentence*	*Can read part of a sentence*	*Cannot read at all*	*No card with required language*	*Blind/ visually impaired*	*Missing*	*Total*	*No. of men*	*Percentage literate*
Hindu	66.7	7.0	5.2	20.9	0.1	0.1	0.0	100	57,112	78.9
Muslim	52.3	10.7	7.2	29.2	0.4	0.0	0.1	100	8,747	70.2
Christian	72.4	6.5	5.6	15.2	0.2	0.0	0.1	100	1,567	84.6
Sikh	75.5	4.7	3.4	16.4	0.0	0.0	0.0	100	1,270	83.6
Buddhist/ Neo-Buddhist	73.3	6.5	7.5	12.4	0.1	0.0	0.2	100	596	87.3
Jain	99.6	0.0	0.0	0.4	0.0	0.0	0.0	100	213	99.6
Others	43.1	2.3	6.2	48.2	0.0	0.0	0.2	100	232	51.6

Table 5 : Exposure to Mass Media

Religion	*Reads a news-paper or magazine atleast once a week*	*Watches television at least once a week*	*Listens to theradio at least once a week*	*Visits the cinema/ theatre at leastonce a month*	*Not regularl exposed to any media*	*Number of women*
Hindu	22.7	55.6	29.1	6.0	34.4	100,151
Muslim	18.0	45.5	27.3	3.2	41.7	16,936
Christian	40.2	68.6	30.5	5.7	20.3	3,053
Sikh	33.0	80.4	20.2	4.6	16.0	2,222
Buddhist/ Neo-Buddhist	30.3	66.2	32.0	6.1	26.5	1,010
Jain	76.7	90.1	37.5	19.1	3.1	406
Others	9.0	22.2	16.7	4.8	68.0	484

at least once a week; less than once a week; or not at all) with which they read a newspaper or magazine, watch television, or listen to the radio. In addition, all respondents were asked whether they "usually go to a cinema hall or theatre to see a movie at least once a month". Individuals who do not read a newspaper or magazine, watch television, or listen to the radio at least once a week, or see a movie at least once a month are considered to not be regularly exposed to any media. Tables 4 and 5 give information on regular media exposure of women and men to each of the different types of media and the proportions not regularly exposed to any media by religion. Muslims are less likely than women and men of most other religions to be regularly exposed to any media. Jains have the highest exposure to all forms of media. After Jains, regular television viewing is most common among Sikhs and exposure to newspapers and magazines is most common among Christians. Variation by religion is least with regard to radio listening. Notably, however, no matter what the type of media or the religion, women have lower exposure than men.

What could be the Causes and Solutions?

From the above analysis, we can arrive at the causes and

solutions, which are discussed as follows: among many reasons for lower literacy and educational levels among Muslim men and women, the lower socio-economic status could be one of the reasons. If so, sincere efforts are needed to improve the socio-economic status of the Muslim community itself. The educational levels among Muslim women with regard to the categories of high school completed and above high school are very low. To improve this, drop-out rates among Muslim girls at lower levels of education need to be reduced substantially. When compared with Hindu women, the educational backwardness of Muslim women becomes more intense. In order to make Muslim women competitive in Indian society, they need to be given higher education by making concerted and long term efforts. For this special incentives should be provided and a change in the attitudes of Muslim parents in general and Muslim women in particular needs to be brought about.

Assuming that Muslim women would watch/listen to educational programmes on TV and radio, these media can be used to promote informal education among Muslim women.

Some specific suggestions are as follows:

1. We need to educate Muslim men and women in general and impart social work education in particular.
2. We need to increase their exposure to media.
3. Some activism needs to be imparted to Muslim men and women. Then only they would realize that good literacy, education and exposure to media are their rights, which would empower them to lead dignified lives.
4. Community leaders need to be involved in the development of Muslim community in general and the Muslim women in particular.
5. There is need for the government and the political parties to treat Muslims and Muslim women as equal citizens and not as vote-banks.
6. There is an urgent need for Muslims to organize themselves along with other communities and pressurize the government to implement the Sachar Committee recommendations.

Conclusion

To conclude, in order to make Muslim community a dynamic community which can face the challenges of modern society Muslim women and men have to become literate and their educational levels have to be improved substantially. Also exposure to media needs to be improved. To achieve this, it requires vision and hard work on the part of the Muslim community and its leadership.

REFERENCES

M.B. Mistry, *Fact-sheet on the levels of Education and Exposure to Media among Muslim Women in India* (Mumbai: Centre for Study of Society and Secularism, 1998).

National Family Health Survey-3 India 2005-06 (Mumbai: International Institute for Population Sciences, 2006).

14

Educational Problems of Muslims in India

Benazeer S. Tamboli

Education is the key to success of human beings which separates them from other species. It always leads to knowledge and its application for the betterment of one's own life. Education is pivot of any individual's socio-economic progress which enables him/her to enhance the competencies, skills as well as one's participation in the democratic process. Considering Indian social panorama, educational status of Muslims is a major concern in the progress of our country. If Muslims forming a considerable part of Indian population are lagging behind in education and other progressive aspects, it will surely affect the progress of the whole nation. The problem of education is not a Muslim problem but a national problem. Educational status of Muslims in India, existing conditions relating to the same problems and possible solutions to these problems should be the prime concern of researchers and academicians. This chapter tries to showcase the same, considering various dimensions of this conundrum.

The main objective of this chapter is to discuss some educational problems of Indian Muslims and to throw light upon possible solutions. Within certain limitations of time and study, this chapter tries to talk about these problems. Even after 65 years of independence, Muslim performance in the domain of education is astonishingly neglected. Demographically, Muslims in India are considered as a religious minority group, who have lower level education as compaired to other religious groups. Muslim children of 6 to14 age group are not enrolled in nearby schools to its full extent. Only 25 per cent of them are enrolled in schools and leave the schooling without completing their education. The ratio of dropouts is also very high. Only 17 per cent Muslim students complete their education till 10th standard and 50 per cent till 12th standard. Only 62.26 per cent of Muslims complete their higher education. Technically qualified Muslim students are only 0.4 per cent. If this is the present scenario of educational status of Indian Muslim, there is a serious need of implementing educational awareness programmes on the grass-root level.

Taking Muslims in mainstream education, improving their life standard through education is very important and much needed also. In all the stages of education, Muslim representation is far below their population percentage. The need of the day is to establish an effective and workable link between traditional education system of Muslims and mainstream education, so that Muslims can be brought to the level of other groups which is surely a hydra-headed task. The other side of the coin is a bit brighter with certain exceptions. Some Muslims in India are doing better than before in the field of education. A silent revolution is noticed but the speed and pace is very slow. We have to speed up this process. It is true that Muslims are taking to education which will surely open the doors of better employment and prosperity for them. Muslims need to develop right attitude and rise above their emotional impulses. It is possible only when the community gains education to understand the purpose of life and learns to live peacefully in a multicultural Indian society.

Muslim educational backwardness is a hard nut to crack and largely a byproduct of Muslim poverty and the neglect by the state along with political unwillingness. Muslim children become victims of acute poverty right from their birth. It should also be kept in mind that poverty is a deterrent to education. To eradicate poverty, the whole community needs to work together with the co-operation of the government. Small scale jobs also can help in this direction when marked with advanced and skillful manpower. Most of the common Muslims are uneducated or not much educated. They are busy in their small-scale businesses and expect the same from their children. Due to this, income levels are also inadequate. With these meager earnings, it is not possible for them to provide good and quality education to their children. To deal with this issue, political, religious and social leaders should work hand in hand with the government. The views of Muslims in this regard also need a change. Getting mainstream higher education and good jobs also can prove helpful in eradicating poverty amongst Muslim.

Changing the *social mindset* and so called *religious impact* is very important if Muslims really want to get the right kind of education. Islam is a religion which, from its core, supports its followers to take education. As a matter of fact, education has been prescribed as compulsory for every man and woman in Islam. The Prophet of Islam advised his followers to go as far as China to learn new things. The Almighty also commanded us to take proper education on a priority basis. His first commandment to His messenger Mohammed was *READ IN THE NAME OF YOUR LORD*. It is very important that the Almighty commanded us to read, which means to know, to learn and explore. Thus education is a top priority in Islam and hence to Muslims. If people would have obeyed this commandment, at least the last word of it *"READ"*, there had not been any want of peace, progress and honors for them.

Keeping girls away from education or co-education schools, sending girls to only Urdu medium schools, not spending money on a girl child's education, keeping children away from selecting some advanced technical courses which need mobilization from one place to another and other such problems keep Muslims away from progress. Muslim leadership should actively come forward in this regard and orient the masses. Unfortunately, this is rarely seen. Government schemes and scholarships are available, but Muslims are totally unaware of these facilities. Preparation and availability of the needed documents is one major problem. NGOs and community leaders should take the initiative in this regard. Another stumbling block in educational progress is *psychology of Indian Muslims*. It is the outcome of our politics and history which makes us think that we could survive even without education. Wrong notions and wrong psychology have adversely affected the average Muslim who equates graduation with government jobs. He would say that it is not an end-all and be-all in life to be a clerk in some office. He would argue why his child ought to struggle for twenty years to be a petty teacher or clerk in some distant place away from his family. Linking jobs with degrees and resulting inhibitions thereof has been a crucial problem, which needs serious and sincere attention.

When it comes to the *medium of instruction*, the problem of Muslims and their education becomes more intense. In spite of living in various regions of India, it has been propagated that the mother tongue of *all* Muslims is Urdu. A few areas in India are Urdu speaking areas. In such cases the mother tongue can be Urdu.

One more trend is observed that Muslims send their daughters to Urdu medium schools and sons to English medium schools. This is also very serious discrimination done to our own children. After getting education in Urdu medium, it is not an easy task for a person to get employment, where vernacular languages are used for daily communication. As a result they are engaged in lower level business with low quality skills leading again to the vicious circle of poverty and unemployment.

Internal conflicts amongst Muslims and the political implications is one of the serious problems in educational upliftment of Muslims. When we talk about problems amongst Muslims we consider only the Muslim urban middle class. We find total neglect to the condition of Muslim nomads. Even the Sachar Committee didn't mention anything about them. The Mandal Commission only talks about Muslims who come under the OBC category. Notified tribes are also considered under the same category by this commission, whereas their problems and issues are totally different. The national secretary of Tribal Research and Cultural Foundation Javed Rahi states that the Sachar Committee only talks of settled Muslims. Muslim nomadic tribes and their problems are neglected by political leaders as a sensitive issue. Non-Muslim leaders are reluctant to talk about this.

Muslims want to educate their children, and in many cases are educating their children, but finding it *extremely difficult to meet the demands of modern and expensive education*. Getting admission in medical or engineering courses is beyond the reach of a common Muslim as it is very expensive. Unless the child qualifies on merit or has sound financial background, one cannot even think of the Muslim masses getting good higher education. There are no support groups in the community to handle such problems and as a result, educational backwardness of the Muslims increase day by day.

To overcome such problems in the educational amelioration of Muslims, we have to work much harder and with commitment and dedication inspired by socialist ideals. Further mentioned points can be parts of possible solutions to the above discussed problems–

1) There is a great need to disseminate information about government scholarships and various schemes.
2) Support groups should be formed to help people to prepare essential documents availing of the benefits of such schemes.
3) Resources can be made available for children interested in seeking higher education such as good libraries, reference material, reading rooms and coaching classes.
4) Awareness campaigns should be conducted regarding girls' education, female employment, gender equality, etc.
5) Think-tanks should be formed in every state by non-political intellectuals in all communities for the educational upliftment of minorities.
6) To accommodate Madarssa educated children in mainstream education and the general job market, essential modifications in Madarssa curriculum and teaching methodology will also prove fruitful.
7) In the name of religious charity, well-to-do people from the Muslim community ought to adopt a child atleast for educational purposes.

These problems of Indian Muslims have persisted for a long

period. They cannot be solved overnight or in isolation from rest of the Indian population. For this, contribution should be taken by *all* Indians.

REFERENCES

1. A.B. Shah, *What Ails Our Muslims?* (Pune: Indian Secular Society, 1981).
2. S.M. Tamboli, *Muslim Samaj Prabodhan aani Vikas* (Pune: Navin Udyoga Prakashan, 2010).
3. Peer Mohammed, *Muslim Education in India: Problems and Prospects* (Baikampady: Karnataka Muslim Pragathi Parishat, 1991).
4. www.bie.org.in *Issues and problems of Muslim Education*–Prof. B. Shaikh –reviewed on September 20, 2013.
5. http://yuvadesh.in/179/*Indian—Muslims-Climb-The educational-ladder to success* reviewed on August 16, 2013.
6. http://www.slideshar.net/mdafsarali *Problems of Muslims community education in India and its remedies*- reviewed on September 4, 2013.
7. http://www.islamawareness.net/Aisa/India/indeucation.html: *Indian muslims and education* – Asghar Ali- reviewed on August 10, 2013.
8. Haji Mohammed Gaus Naik, *Bharatateel Muslim Samajyachya Aarthik, Shaikshanik va Samajik Sthiteecha Shodh* (Kolhapur: Muslim Samaj Prabodhan va Shikshan Sanstha, 2007).
9. Rafiq Zakaria, *Indian Muslims: Where They Gone Wrong?* (Mumbai: Popular Prakashan and Bharatiya Vidya Bhavan, 2004).

Contributors

Ali, Zaheer: Mumbai-based writer, academician, and social activist. President of Centre for Promotion of Democracy and Secularism.

Ali, Zeenat S.: Reputed Islamic scholar and Director of Wisdom Foundation, Mumbai.

Ansari, Khalid Anis: Writer, social activist, Assistant Professer, Glocal Law School, Glocal University, Saharanpur (UP).

Engineer, Asghar Ali (Late): Internationally recognised Islamic scholar.

Engineer, Irfan: Mumbai-based writer, social activist and Director of Centre for the Study of Society and Secularism.

Gatade, Subhash: New Delhi-based writer and social activist.

Hasan, Mushirul: Former Vice-Chancellor of Jamia Millia Islamia, former Director General of National Archives and an internationally acknowledged historian.

Jal, Murzban: Writer, Professor and Director of Centre for Educational Studies, Indian Institute of Education, Pune.

Mhatre, Sandhya: Social activist and Research Investigator in the Department of Economics, University of Mumbai.

Mistry, Malika B.: Social activist and Associate Professor, Department of Economics, Poona College, Pune.

Saif, Asad Bin: Social activist associated with BUILD, Mumbai.

Shakir, Shuja: Associate Professor, Department of Political Science, Dr. Babasaheb Ambedkar Marathwada University, Aurangabad.

Tamboli, Benazeer S.: Assistant Professor, Department of Education, Maharashtra Tilak Vidyapeeth, Pune

Tamboli, Shamsuddin: Professor, Marathwada College of Education, Pune.